CW00392916

HUSSERL: A GU[
THE PERPLEXED

CONTINUUM'S GUIDES FOR THE PERPLEXED

Benjamin Hutchens, *Levinas: A Guide for the Perplexed*
Alex Thomson, *Adorno: A Guide for the Perplexed*
Claire Colebrook, *Deleuze: A Guide for the Perplexed*
Chris Lawn, *Gadamer: A Guide for the Perplexed*
Mark Addis, *Wittgenstein: A Guide for the Perplexed*
Gary Kemp, *Quine: A Guide for the Perplexed*
Eric Matthews, *Merleau-Ponty: A Guide for the Perplexed*
Gary Cox, *Sartre: A Guide for the Perplexed*

HUSSERL: A GUIDE FOR THE PERPLEXED

MATHESON RUSSELL

continuum

Continuum International Publishing Group
The Tower Building   80 Maiden Lane
    11 York Road   Suite 704
London SE1 7NX   New York, NY 10038

First published 2006
Reprinted 2007, 2009

www.continuumbooks.com

© Matheson Russell 2006

All rights reserved. No part of this publication may be reproduced or
transmitted in any form or by any means, electronic or mechanical,
including photocopying, recording or any information storage or retrieval
system, without prior permission in writing from the publishers.

Matheson Russell has asserted his right under the Copyright,
Designs and Patents Act, 1988, to be identified as Author of this work.

British Library Cataloguing-in-Publication Data
A catalogue record for this book is available from the British Library.

ISBN 978 0 8264 8593 9 (hardback) 978 0 8264 8594 6 (paperback)

Library of Congress Cataloging-in-Publication Data
Russell, Matheson.
Husserl : a guide for the perplexed / Matheson Russell.
p. cm.—(Continuum's guides for the perplexed)
Includes bibliographical references and index.
ISBN 0–8264–8593–6 (hardback)—ISBN 0–8264–8594–4 (pbk.)
1. Husserl, Edmund, 1859–1938.   I. Title.   II. Guides for the perplexed.
B3279.H94R87 2006
193—dc22   2005037057

Typeset by RefineCatch Limited, Bungay, Suffolk
Printed and bound by the MPG Books Group

CONTENTS

Abbreviations   ix

Introduction: Approaching Husserl   1

**Part 1 The Idea of Phenomenology: Psychology, Logic and
Transcendental Philosophy**

1 The Critique of Psychologism   9
   Psychologism and its critics   9
   Husserl's arguments against psychologism   11
   Beyond psychologism: the 'mystery of cognition' and
      the project of phenomenology   17
2 Phenomenology and other 'Eidetic Sciences'   22
   Sciences of fact and sciences of essence   22
   Empirical and eidetic laws   24
   Overcoming naturalistic prejudices   27
   Kinds of eidetic science   30
   Phenomenology as eidetic science of the 'Ur-region'   34
3 Phenomenology and Transcendental Philosophy   39
   The mystery of cognition, scepticism and Husserl's
      transcendental turn   39
   Kant and the idea of transcendental philosophy   42
   Husserl and Kant   44
   Reforming Kant's transcendental method   50
   The Cartesian legacy in Husserl's transcendentalism:
      purified subjectivity, evidence and first philosophy   52
4 The Transcendental Reduction   57
   What is the transcendental reduction?   58
   The natural attitude and the natural world   59

The limits of naturalism and empiricism 62
The 'radical alteration' of the natural attitude 63
From psychological to transcendental consciousness 66
The annihilation of the world 69
Transcendental subjectivity as 'absolute substance' 71

Part 2 Phenomenological Topics

5 The Structure of Intentionality 79
The idea of intentionality 79
The critique of representationalism 80
Intentionality in the *Logical Investigations* 82
Noesis–noema terminology 84
Noematic and real objectivity 85
Husserl and the Kantian 'thing-in-itself' 89
Husserl's reinterpretation of thinghood 92
6 Intuition, Evidence and Truth 98
Intuition and evidence 98
Evidence as fulfilling intuition 100
The concept of truth 104
The principle of all principles 107
7 Categorial Intuition: Synthesis and Ideation 113
The problem of categorial intuition 113
The intuition of categorial forms (synthetic acts) 117
Ideative acts 121
8 Time-Consciousness 127
The horizonal structure of intentional experience 127
The constitution of temporal objects 130
The double intentionality of consciousness 134
Primary and secondary memory, and the constitution
of objective time 135
Absolute consciousness and the problem of
phenomenological reflection 137
9 The Ego and Selfhood 144
The transcendental or pure ego 144
The pure ego as subject pole 146
Habituality, conviction and self-conception 148
From the pure ego to the full human being 150
The psyche 151
The person 154

CONTENTS

The interrelation between the various conceptions of
the ego   157
10   Intersubjectivity   162
     The problem of objectivity and transcendental
intersubjectivity   163
     Transcendental intersubjectivity   167
     The problem of methodological solipsism and the
experience of the other   170
     The appresentation of the other   172
     Implications of the relation to others   176
11   The Crisis of the Sciences and the Idea of the 'Lifeworld'   180
     What is the crisis of the European sciences?   180
     The origins of the contemporary crisis in the
mathematization of nature   184
     The limits of the natural-scientific attitude   187
     The project of *The Crisis*   192
     The idea of the lifeworld   194

Conclusion and Further Reading   198

Index   201

ABBREVIATIONS

CES: *The Crisis of European Sciences and Transcendental Phenomenology*, trans. David Carr (Evanston, IL: Northwestern University Press, 1970).

CM: *Cartesian Meditations: An Introduction to Phenomenology*, trans. Dorian Cairns (The Hague: Martinus Nijhoff, 1960).

EJ: *Experience and Judgement: Investigations in a Genealogy of Logic*, ed. Ludwig Landgrebe, trans. James S. Churchill and Karl Ameriks (Evanston, IL: Northwestern University Press, 1973).

FTL: *Formal and Transcendental Logic*, trans. Dorian Cairns (The Hague: Martinus Nijhoff, 1969).

Ideas I: *Ideas Pertaining to a Pure Phenomenology and a Phenomenological Philosophy: General Introduction to a Pure Phenomenology* (First Book), trans. Fred Kersten (Dordrecht: Kluwer, 1982).

Ideas II: *Ideas Pertaining to a Pure Phenomenology and a Phenomenological Philosophy: Studies in the Phenomenology of Constitution* (Second Book), trans. Richard Rojcewicz and André Schuwer (Dordrecht: Kluwer, 1989).

IP: *The Idea of Phenomenology*, trans. William P. Alston and George Nakhnikian (The Hague: Martinus Nijhoff, 1964).

KITP: 'Kant and the idea of transcendental philosophy', trans. Ted. E. Klein, Jr and William E. Pohl. *The Southwestern Journal of Philosophy*, 5.3 (1974): 9–56.

LI I: *Logical Investigations*, Vol. 1., trans. J.N. Findlay (London: Routledge & Kegan Paul, 1970).

LI II: *Logical Investigations*, Vol. 2., trans. J.N. Findlay (London: Routledge & Kegan Paul, 1970).

PITC: *The Phenomenology of Internal Time-Consciousness*, trans. James S. Churchill (The Hague: Martinus Nijhoff, 1964).

And also:

CPR: Immanuel Kant, *Critique of Pure Reason*, trans. Norman Kemp Smith (London: Macmillan, 1929).

INTRODUCTION: APPROACHING HUSSERL

Perplexity is not an uncommon experience for those who have sat down to read the philosophy of Edmund Husserl. Indeed, even those who have studied Husserl for years struggle to piece together an entirely satisfactory understanding of his thought. There are various reasons for this. Chief among them is the sheer complexity and sophistication of Husserl's thought. Like all great philosophers, what makes Husserl worth reading is the wealth of original and insightful ideas he produced. But the original is also the foreign, and foreign ideas are often the hardest to comprehend – especially when they do not slot neatly into our own pre-established frameworks of understanding. A central aim of this book, therefore, is to assist the reader of Husserl to grasp the main ideas of his philosophy through a patient exposition.

A second obstacle the student of Husserl must overcome is the somewhat convoluted and laboured style of his prose. German philosophers are known for their often tedious and prolix expression, and to a certain extent Husserl lives up to this stereotype. However, his use of difficult terminology is always motivated by a desire for more clarity and precision, not less. At the same time, Husserl's 'phenomenological' philosophy is concerned to uncover and describe aspects of experience that we usually ignore, and for this purpose, as he himself remarks, we do not always possess adequate words. In such cases, language must either be invented or carefully reappropriated for the task; and this explains the appearance of some rather daunting terms in his writings (e.g. 'presentification', 'transcendental reduction', 'transverse intentionality'). It is not easy to render Husserl's philosophy in more lively prose, but in this book I aim at least to make some of his key terms intelligible.

A third difficulty stems from the remarkable fluidity of Husserl's own philosophical thought. He continually revisited, corrected and extended his analyses and positions – so much so, in fact, that by the time each of his major works reached the press he had often already found reason to be critical of them and had begun to think of the same matters differently. Intellectual honesty and tireless self-assessment were doubtlessly among Husserl's most notable and admirable traits. The downside to such constant revision, however, is that the reader is often hard-pressed to find a reliable way into the shifting world of Husserl's thought. Inevitably, one is forced to 'periodize' his output, and I do so in this book.

Before I give an overview of the contents of this book, it will be useful to provide a brief portrait of Husserl's life and work.

The name Edmund Husserl is synonymous with 'phenomenology', a distinctive approach to philosophy that has had an enormous influence on the philosophical world during the twentieth century. Husserl was born into a Jewish family in Prossnitz, Moravia (present-day Czech Republic) on 8 April 1959. His early university education was in the field of mathematics, first at the University of Leipzig and then at the University of Berlin. In Berlin he was instructed by Leopold Kronecker and Carl Weierstrass, two of the leading mathematicians of their day. Husserl later became a research assistant to Weierstrass after receiving his doctorate in Vienna in 1883. His fledgling career as a mathematician was interrupted, however, by a period of military service. It was during this time that Husserl's interest in religious and philosophical questions blossomed, and in 1884 he turned to the study of philosophy.

At this time Husserl came into contact with Franz Brentano whose lectures and writings were to have a profound influence on his philosophical development. Having decided to make philosophical research his life's work, Husserl relocated to Halle on Brentano's advice in 1886 to work with Carl Stumpf, a former student of Brentano's and an exponent of 'descriptive psychology'. Husserl married in 1887 and eventual had three children, one of whom was to fall in the Great War. He received his teaching qualification (*Habilitation*) in 1887 and taught at Halle until 1901. He was to spend the next 15 years at Göttingen, first as Extraordinarius (associate) professor and then as Ordinarius (full) professor from 1906.

In 1916 Husserl succeeded Heinrich Rickert to the chair of

philosophy at Freiburg University. There he met and worked with his most famous disciple, Martin Heidegger. The pair did not work together closely during their years at Freiburg. However, Husserl reportedly declared to Heidegger that 'you and I are phenomenology'.[1] However, about the time of Husserl's retirement in 1928, and after he had helped secure Heidegger's succession to the chair of philosophy at Freiburg, the pair experienced a falling out. Husserl had begun to realize the depth of their philosophical differences and simmering tensions in their personal relationship came to a head. Things became irreconcilable when Heidegger became a member of and spokesperson for the Nazi Party as Rector of the University of Freiburg in 1933. At the same time, Husserl was stripped of his university membership because of his Jewish heritage (notwithstanding that he had converted to what he described as a 'non-dogmatic Protestantism' early in life). During his exclusion from intellectual life in Germany, however, Husserl was invited to lecture abroad, notably in Vienna and Prague. He died on 27 April 1938.

Husserl's *Habilitation* dissertation 'On the Concept of Number: Psychological Analyses' formed the basis of his first major publication, *Philosophy of Arithmetic* (1891). His groundbreaking work, however, appeared in 1900 and 1901 in two volumes under the title *Logical Investigations*. On the strength of this work, he began to draw around him a number of philosophers who became known as the 'Göttingen School' of phenomenology, including Roman Ingarden and Alexandre Koyré. Husserl founded a *Yearbook for Philosophy and Phenomenological Research* in 1913 in collaboration with Adolf Reinach, Munich philosophers Moritz Geiger and Alexander Pfänder, and Max Scheler of Berlin University. Under its auspices Husserl published *Ideas Pertaining to a Pure Phenomenology and a Phenomenological Philosophy* which set forth his new 'transcendental' conception of phenomenology. Two further volumes of this project were announced for publication but never appeared. They have since been reconstructed and published from Husserl's notes (they are commonly known as '*Ideas II*' and '*Ideas III*').

Only a small number of other works appeared during Husserl's lifetime: *The Phenomenology of Internal Time-Consciousness*, edited by Edith Stein and Heidegger, in 1928; *Formal and Transcendental Logic* in 1929; *Cartesian Meditations* in 1931; and *The Crisis of European Sciences* in 1936. (Thanks to the editorial work of Ludwig Landgrebe, *Experience and Judgement* also appeared shortly after

Husserl's death in 1938.) Nevertheless, Husserl had taught continuously and had continued his own phenomenological researches relentlessly throughout his long career. Consequently, he left behind many bundles of manuscripts, amounting to some 40,000 pages (many written in shorthand). After his death, Husserl's extensive literary remains were smuggled out of Germany by the Franciscan Hermann Leo Van Breda to a monastery in Belgium, and an archive was established at the Institute of Philosophy in Louvain. To this day the archive remains an active centre of Husserl scholarship and is responsible (along with the Husserl-Archive at the University of Cologne) for the ongoing publication of a critical edition of Husserl's works, the *Husserliana*.[2] Most of Husserl's manuscripts will probably never see the light of day, but selections have and will continue to be published in the *Husserliana* series.

In a book this size, it is impossible to trace every line of thought developed by Husserl in his long and varied career. And so I have had to make choices. Broadly speaking, I have chosen to focus on those ideas for which Husserl is best known. This has inevitably meant majoring on the classic Husserlian texts and leaving to one side the very interesting lectures and manuscripts that have only more recently been published from archive material (much of which is yet to be translated into English). The upsides to this strategy are that the texts cited in this book should be easily accessible; and, philosophically, that from these discussions the student should be able to piece together a good understanding of what the name 'Husserl' represents within the world of twentieth-century continental philosophy. The downside is that certain emerging areas of interest and debate amongst contemporary Husserl scholars have, for the most part, had to be passed over without comment.

The chapters in Part 1 deal in different ways with the question 'What is phenomenology?' However, because phenomenology is, for Husserl, above all a *method* for doing philosophy, these opening chapters have a predominantly methodological flavour to them. The chapters in Part 2 tackle the main topics discussed in Husserl's major publications and roughly follow the chronology of his career. From the beginning to the end of the book, each chapter builds upon the one before and is intended to contribute to an overall portrait of Husserl's phenomenology. However, I have chosen to focus the discussion in each chapter on a selected text; and this means that each chapter can also be read alone as a mini-commentary on that text. The thought behind this strategy is to provide a book that functions both as a general introduction to Husserl's philosophy and also as a useful set of commentaries for anyone specifically studying the selected texts.

It should be clear to the reader which texts form the heart of each chapter. However, for the sake of easy reference, I shall list them here.

Part 1: The Idea of Phenomenology: Psychology, Logic and Transcendental Philosophy
    Chapter 1: 'Prolegomena' to the *Logical Investigations*
    Chapter 2: Part One of *Ideas I* (§§1–26)
    Chapter 3: 'Kant and the idea of transcendental philosophy'
    Chapter 4: Part Two of *Ideas I* (§§27–62)

Part 2: Phenomenological Topics
    Chapter 5: Part Three, Chapter Three of *Ideas I* (§§87–96)
    Chapter 6: Investigation VI of the *Logical Investigations*, esp. §§1–12 and §§36–39
    Chapter 7: Investigation VI of the *Logical Investigations*, esp. §§40–66
    Chapter 8: *The Phenomenology of Internal Time-Consciousness*
    Chapter 9: *Ideas II*
    Chapter 10: Fifth Meditation of the *Cartesian Meditations* (§§42–62)
    Chapter 11: *The Crisis of European Sciences and Transcendental Phenomenology*.

NOTES

1   Dorian Cairns, *Conversation with Husserl and Fink* (The Hague: Martinus Nijhoff, 1976), p. 106.
2   *Husserliana*, vols 1–26 (The Hague: Martinus Nijhoff, 1950–88); vols 27–37 (Dordrecht: Kluwer, 1988–2004).

PART I

THE IDEA OF PHENOMENOLOGY: PSYCHOLOGY, LOGIC AND TRANSCENDENTAL PHILOSOPHY

CHAPTER I

THE CRITIQUE OF PSYCHOLOGISM

Husserl made a name for himself as a philosopher thanks to his critique of 'psychologism'. Published as the first volume of his *Logical Investigations* in 1900 ('Prolegomena to Pure Logic'), this critique was intended to set the course for his own substantive studies in logic and epistemology. However, interest in the introductory volume quickly outstripped interest in the rest of the *Logical Investigations*, which was seen by many as containing little of value and perhaps even falling back into the clutches of psychologism.[1] In any case, the prolegomena were widely read and widely praised, and it is the critique of psychologism contained in them that is the theme of this chapter. The details of Husserl's critique of psychologism are rather technical, but studying it is nevertheless extremely helpful for coming to grips with three key distinctions that underpin Husserl's entire conception of phenomenology: pure/empirical, logical/psychological and ideal/real. I endeavour to highlight these distinctions in the course of the chapter.

PSYCHOLOGISM AND ITS CRITICS

'Psychologism' is a pejorative description for the view that psychology can account for the laws of logic. This view arose in the wake of a strong empiricist and naturalist upsurge in philosophy over the course of the nineteenth century. On a naturalistic worldview, there are no non-physical objects, and so, when it comes to the study of apparently non-physical phenomena such as numbers and thoughts, these can only be understood as features, properties or effects of some physical object. And what other physical object could step in to fulfil this role apart from the human mind? According to this line of reasoning, roughly speaking, the study of concepts and reasoning – i.e. logic – came to be seen as a province of psychology. The study of logic, it was argued, means the study of the psychical acts of judging, knowing, inferring, etc. 'Psychologism', then, amounts to the claim that thoughts and the laws governing them are reducible to the psychical acts in which they subsist and the lawfulness of those acts.

As it is understood by Husserl, there are two key components to the psychologistic standpoint. On one hand, it holds that logical objects (truths, propositions, meanings, relations, etc.) are reducible to psychological states of affairs. On the other hand, it holds that the laws of logic are norms governing the performance of mental acts of reasoning such that sound conclusions follow. In short, psychologism claims that, if one wants to study the foundations of mathematics or logic, one has to study the empirical processes that go on in the mind or psyche. Psychology is, on this view, 'the science from which logic in general, and the logic of the deductive sciences, . . . hope for philosophical clarification' (*LI* I 42). Ostensibly, then, all so-called 'pure sciences', which include not only mathematics, geometry and logic but also philosophy itself, find their ultimate explanation and ground in psychology. The place of philosophy as the queen of the sciences is usurped by psychology.

Under the influence of John Stuart Mill's *A System of Logic* (1843), and following the collapse of the idealist tradition, German logicians had increasingly tended towards such a 'psychologistic' conception of logic in the second half of the nineteenth century. And, by the end of the century, in Husserl's estimation, psychologism had become the dominant theory of logic. Leading this movement were Theodor Lipps, Benno Erdmann, Wilhelm Wundt and Christoff Sigwart.

Husserl was not the only philosopher, however, to see the collapse of logic into psychology as a disastrous turn of events. Bernard Bolzano, for example, had insisted on the 'non-actuality' of numbers in his *Theory of Science* (1837). Likewise, Hermann Lotze's *Logic* (1874) had presented a non-psychologistic interpretation of logical objects and the laws governing them. And Gottlob Frege, a student of Lotze, had also published several works arguing against psychologism.[2] In fact, Frege had published a review in 1894 of Husserl's own early work, *Philosophy of Arithmetic* (1891), in which he criticized Husserl's own psychologistic tendencies, and it has been suggested that it was this interaction that led Husserl to revise his stance.[3] In addition to Bolzano, Lotze and Frege, the neo-Kantian school had also developed a strong anti-psychologistic stance. Hermann Cohen and Paul Natorp of the Marburg School of neo-Kantians, as well as Heinrich Rickert and Wilhelm Windelband, had all written works on logic that attempted to assert and defend the independence of logic from psychology.

In the foreword to the *Logical Investigations*, Husserl admits that he himself had subscribed to a psychologistic standpoint in his early work, *Philosophy of Arithmetic*. Subsequently, under the influence of Bolzano, Lotze, Frege and the neo-Kantians, however, Husserl had become convinced that he was in error, and in the *Logical Investigations* he thoroughly repudiated his former psychologistic position. So thorough and incisive was his critique of psychologism that he quickly came to be regarded as a leading voice amongst the anti-psychologistic logicians of his day.

HUSSERL'S ARGUMENTS AGAINST PSYCHOLOGISM

In the 'Prolegomena to Pure Logic', Husserl argues that the stance of psychologism fundamentally misconstrues the nature of logic and brings in its wake catastrophic consequences, undermining the very idea of scientific theory and leaving not only the pure sciences but also the empirical sciences in tatters. But why, in Husserl's view, do such catastrophic consequences follow from the psychologistic standpoint? Stated briefly, psychologism deprives itself of the ability to explain the *validity* of logical laws and their '*a priori*' status, and it consequently deprives itself of the ability to explain the *logical unity* that belongs to any body of knowledge. Husserl's analysis of these errors can be broken down into three criticisms: (1) psychologism conflates psychological and logical lawfulness; (2) psychologism conflates the logical object with the logical act; and (3) psychologism fails to recognize logical objects in distinction to real objects.

(1) According to the psychologistic view (in its cruder forms at least), because logical reasoning is something that occurs *in the mind* of the logician, entailment is to be understood in terms of the laws that govern psychical events – in this case, governing judgements of entailment. More generally, all laws that govern the form and orderly interconnection of assertions in any coherent scientific theory are to be explained in *psychological* terms – that is, in terms of the way people actually think. Thus, to explain the laws of reasoning

(i.e. logic) means to give an account of the lawfulness of the psycho-logical processes of thinking. Logic, in this sense, is the study of 'laws of thought'.

But, according to Husserl's argument in Chapter 4 of the 'Proleg-omena', there is a fundamental distinction that this approach fails to respect: it conflates logical lawfulness with psychological (empirical) lawfulness. Contrary to the assertions of psychologism, the validity of the proposition 'A is not ~A' has a *universal* and *normative* character to it which cannot be deduced or grounded in the *fact* that, every time one thinks of 'A', one can deduce from it 'not ~A'. Generalizing from such psychological facts of reasoning gives an empirical description of mental acts, but does not give the 'pure' or 'formal' law of non-contradiction. Starting from facts, one can never arrive at anything other than empirical laws (*LI* I 98ff.). Logical laws, on the other hand, cannot be inferred from matters of fact. The same is true of mathematical and geometrical laws. The truths of such sciences are 'pure': they presuppose no factual being and are equally true apart from their being empirically instantiated. Think, for example, of the Pythagorean theorem. It remains true and can be shown to be true irrespective of whether a right-angled triangle ever exists in fact. If the theorem also applies to empirical realities, this is because it concerns the *idea* 'right-angled triangle' which *applies* to all real right-angled triangles, not because it is an *empirical* law. Truths of this kind display an exactness and certainty to which empirical truths can only ever approximate. Their truth is apodictic (i.e. indubitable) rather than assertoric (i.e. defeasible). Pure truths are derived from reason alone, whereas empirical laws are derived by generalization from matters of fact.

Husserl's argument then is that, strictly speaking, the laws of logic and the (psychological) laws concerning acts of thinking are respect-ively examples of these two distinct kinds of laws: the former are 'pure', the latter are 'empirical'. By rejecting the 'pure', non-psychological grounds for the validity of logical laws, and instead seeking to ground them in empirical facts, psychologism places logic on an 'empirical' rather than a 'pure' footing. But, in so doing, it trades away the apodictic certitude of logic.

Now, the fact that one can reason incorrectly is, for Husserl, a strong hint that we ought not to think of the laws of logic as empirical laws. A properly *empirical* law is one that applies to all known instances of a given phenomenon and is inductively assumed to apply to all others. The discovery of an anomalous case invalidates the law. Thus, for example, it is not an empirical law of nature that the gravitational attraction between two bodies is inversely proportional to the square of the distance if, in some cases, the attraction is inversely proportional to two times the distance. Likewise, it is not an *empirical* law of thinking that 'not ~A' follows from 'A' if, as a matter of fact, sometimes 'not ~A' *does not* follow from 'A'.

How then does the psychologistic logician justify regarding logical laws as empirically grounded? The psychologistic logicians were aware of this objection and typically recognized that logical laws do not describe *all* acts of thought; they describe and apply only to 'correct' (i.e. 'logical') acts of thought. Instead, they maintained that the laws of logic are the laws that can be inductively garnered from the observation of *correct* acts of reasoning. This move preserves the illusion that logical laws can be grounded empirically. But how are 'correct' acts of thought to be identified in the first place? Evidently, an idea of 'correctness' is *presupposed* and functions as a criterion of selection. But this exposes the fallacy: in order to achieve the desired result, the psychologist must presuppose what he aims to ground empirically. The laws of logic are not the *product* of his psychological study after all, but are surreptitiously smuggled in as *presuppositions*. This precisely illustrates the anti-psychologistic point: in order for logic and mathematics to be what they are, they must be the kinds of rules that are *normative* for our thinking. But to be so requires that they stand above and beyond factual being (i.e. mental life) rather than being discoverable within it. Hence, it is simply a category mistake to think that the validity of laws of logic can be grounded in the empirical study of psychic acts.

(2) In the paragraph above, I stated that, on Husserl's analysis, logical laws are normative rather than descriptive in the sphere of thinking. But, in fact, this it is not quite correct – and, in any event, the leading psychologistic logicians already acknowledged that the laws of logic must be regarded as normative for 'good' acts of reasoning. The decisive point, according to Husserl, is more precisely that the laws of logic *do not apply to the psychological sphere at all*. They are neither descriptive of nor normative for acts of reasoning. Rather the laws of logic apply to the *meanings* asserted in propositions; e.g. they apply to the content of a judgement, not to the act of judgement itself. In this strict sense, logical laws are 'theoretical': they govern the internal structure of theories themselves (*LI* I 186).

This is the point at which Husserl's argument departs from the standard neo-Kantian responses to psychologism. While the neo-Kantians recognized the conflation of the 'is' and the 'ought' prevalent in psychologism (i.e. argument (1)), they failed to see clearly that logical laws are, strictly speaking, not norms at all. A norm is a rule applicable in the sphere of free human activity, a sphere which includes acts of thinking. But a logical law is a rule that applies in the sphere of meanings. Logic relates solely to the *contents* of judgements as opposed to the *acts* of judgement. What 'is true' is not the thinking but the thought, not the judging but the judgement. The locus of truth, therefore, is not the act (e.g. the assertion that S is P), but the contents of the act (e.g. 'S is P') (*LI* I 142; also 189–92). In this, Husserl follows Lotze, who had argued that logic deals with the atemporal realm of 'validity' (*Geltung*) and with the laws that govern that realm. The logical and the psychological are, therefore, two separate domains. The 'purity' of 'pure logic' lies in its disconnectedness or indifference to the empirical domain of psychology. Husserl never renounced this fundamental insight into the distinction between reason and reasoning, thoughts and thinking, judgement and judging.

If there are also 'norms of thinking' that must be applied to acts of judgement in order to ensure sound reasoning, then these *derive from* the logical laws that pertain to the logical contents of such acts (*LI* I 168–71). This set of norms or rules belongs to 'applied' or 'practical logic' (*LI* I 75). But, strictly speaking, such norms apply only in the psychological sphere and are not to be confused with the logical laws from which they derive. Primarily, what makes a judgement sound is the fact that the meaningful elements asserted in the judgement are themselves logically related in the fashion asserted. The soundness of the judgement therefore has nothing to do with the process of thinking *as such* by which the asserted meaning is derived. Hence, whatever (empirical) laws psychologists discover to be operative in psychical acts of reasoning (i.e. acts of association, succession, and so forth), such laws are irrelevant to the study of logic *per se*. Likewise, a logical proof, on this view, is not a rehearsal of a sequential 'chain of reasoning' but an exhibition of the component meanings of a proposition and their interrelations such that the truth of each component and each relation can be seen.

In this regard, even the noble Kantian conception of pure logic – and, on Husserl's view, also its neo-Kantian descendants – failed to fully extricate itself from the anthropological domain (*LI* I, Proleg. §28 and §58). Rather than affirming the absolute universality of the *a priori* laws of logic, Kant and his followers ultimately limited their universality by referring them to the faculty of understanding – a component of *human* subjectivity. This comes dangerously close to what Husserl calls 'species relativism' (*ein spezifischer Relativismus*) (*LI* I, Proleg. §36). It is a 'relativism' because it risks limiting the universality of logical laws to the human species and leaves open the possibility that a proposition may be true for the species *homo* but false for another species (*LI* I 140). But, for Husserl, such a restriction of logical validity would misconstrue the character of *logical* validity: truth as such does not depend on any facts, including facts of human nature. The law of non-contradiction is not merely a law governing the species *Homo sapiens*. If there were no minds to think them the logical laws would still hold, though as ideal possibilities unfulfilled in actuality (*LI* I 149).

On what grounds, then, does Husserl assert the absolute validity of the laws of logic? Logic has its foundation, he argues, not in the contingent nature of human subjectivity but 'in the "sense", the "essence" or the "content" of the concepts of Truth, Proposition, Object, Property, Relation, Combination, Law, Fact, etc.' (*LI* I 144). In other words, logical laws have nothing at all to do with the constitution of human subjectivity; their validity is grounded in the logical structure of the domain of meaning itself, which is completely independent of the psychological domain. Thus, while it is possible to form a judgement in defiance of the laws of logic (e.g. 'A is ~A'), one cannot do so without falling into absurdity and logical contradiction.

(3) In his own struggle with psychologism, Husserl came to believe that one must recognize the *being* of logical objects such as meanings, relations, states of affairs, truths, laws and essences. Though these are not 'real' objects, they are genuine objects nonetheless. One reason for thinking of logical objects as genuine objects and not mere illusions is that we think and speak of them like any other objects: one can, for instance, think about logical objects and assert things of them truly or falsely (e.g. 'the number seven is prime'). In other words, linguistically and cognitively we already regard ideas as objects even though they are not physical things. But the more pressing reason for treating logical objects as genuine objects is that the idea of scientific knowledge requires it. For

instance, the very idea of science collapses without a conception of 'truths' that transcend the individual acts in which they are asserted. So, for example, when several people assert the Pythagorean theorem at different times and places, we take them to be asserting the self-same 'truth'. Even though multiple distinct acts take place, it will not do to speak of a multiplicity of Pythagorean theorems, each of which is individually true. This would be to deny the singularity and objectivity of the geometrical truth and would ultimately, according to Husserl, result in a vicious relativism (*LI* I, Proleg. §35). A body of scientific knowledge only 'exists' if it is constructed from a well-founded and coherent web of such mind-independent truths.

As a catch-all term for this class of non-real objects, Husserl uses the expressions 'irreal' or 'ideal'. Thus, the Husserl of the *Logical Investigations* could be said to be an 'idealist' in this sense: he affirms that there are *ideal objects* as well as *real objects*. He extends the concept of 'object' beyond that of 'something real'. And this extension of the concept is reaffirmed in *Ideas I*. There Husserl insists that the term 'object' (*Gegenstand*) must be understood in the most universal sense possible: namely, as 'anything at all', or 'the subject of a true (categorial, affirmative) statement'. He comments:

> I did not invent the universal concept of object; I only restored the concept required by all propositions of pure logic and pointed out that it is an essentially indispensable one and therefore that it also determines universal scientific language. And in this sense the tone-quality c, which is a numerically unique member of the tonal scale, the number two, in the series of cardinal numbers, the figure in the ideal world of geometrical constructs, and any propositions in the 'world' of propositions – in short, many different ideal affairs – *are* 'objects'. (*Ideas I* §22, 41)[4]

But what is the ontology underpinning this 'idealism'? What does 'there are' mean in the case of ideal objects? The 'being' that is attributed to ideal objects in the *Logical Investigations* is, in the first instance, a 'belong[ing] to the realm of the absolutely valid'. This does not mean that such an object 'hang[s] somewhere in the void', but rather that it is 'a case of validity [*Geltung*] in the timeless realm of Ideas' (*LI* I 149). In these formulations, Husserl more or less repeats the position of Lotze: ideal objects 'are valid [*gilt*]', real objects 'exist'.[5] It is disputable whether this constitutes a satisfactory answer to the ontological question regarding ideality. (Heidegger was perhaps the first to press this question.)[6] However, what is clear is that Husserl's positing of ideal objects is not equivalent to the claim that they 'exist' in the same sense as real objects, perhaps in some other world. Husserl repeatedly distances himself from such a position, which he calls 'Platonism'. Indeed, he criticizes Platonism precisely for its 'metaphysical hypostatization of the universal', i.e. for crudely regarding ideal objects as nothing more than a special class of real objects which exist in another sphere of reality (*LI* I 350f.; *Ideas I* §22). We should be very wary, therefore, about labelling Husserl a 'Platonist'. But, beyond this negative demarcation, it is difficult to nail down his position – not least because, at this time, his interpretation of the manner of the 'being' of ideal objects was in flux. I return to the question of Husserl's idealism in later chapters. At this stage, suffice it to say that Husserl takes ideas, meanings, logical objects, etc. seriously *as objects*; and he insists that, however they may ultimately be construed, they must not be interpreted away on the basis of some metaphysical presupposition (i.e. naturalism/ psychologism).

In summary, Husserl's anti-psychologistic arguments can be read as a restatement of Kantian logical transcendentalism: a 'pure logic' must be posited over against 'practical logic' (the so-called 'logical technology') and over against the empirical laws that govern the psychological sphere, because it is 'futile' to set out 'to use an empirical theory to ground something that is itself a presupposition of that theory' (*LI* I 115 fn. 1, quoting Windelband). By failing to respect this principle, psychologism inevitably finds itself caught in logical inconsistencies: it ends up either begging the question concerning the grounds of logical validity or becoming mired in a vicious relativism.

BEYOND PSYCHOLOGISM: THE 'MYSTERY OF COGNITION' AND THE PROJECT OF PHENOMENOLOGY

Strictly speaking, the arguments laid out in the 'Prolegomena to Pure Logic' are not themselves phenomenological analyses. Instead, for the most part, they have the character of traditional philosophical arguments. Nevertheless, they lay the foundations for Husserl's phenomenological analyses in the second volume of the *Logical Investigations*, allowing him to go on to examine logical objects and the acts in which they are given without being tied to psychologistic and naturalistic prejudices. The aim of the prolegomena, then, is not so much to construct a metaphysics (idealist or otherwise) but to *free* the subsequent investigations from metaphysical prejudices so that they might not be prevented from going 'back to the things themselves'. Here, as always for Husserl, the phenomena must be allowed to dictate the terms of their own explication.

More specifically, the critique of psychologism provides Husserl with a useful backdrop against which to clearly set in relief the distinctions between the *pure* and the *empirical*, the *logical* and the *psychological*, and the *ideal* and the *real*. These distinctions remain fundamental to the entirety of Husserl's mature work. Having drawn these distinctions, the task of phenomenological analysis becomes that of exploring the 'mystery of cognition' in which the pure, the logical and the ideal are 'given' to a consciousness which is itself empirical, psychological and real: what sort of thing is the act of thinking such that it can be thinking *of* idealities, of truths or of validities? 'One must clearly grasp what the ideal is, both intrinsically and in its relation to the real, how this ideal stands to the real, how it can be immanent in it and so come to knowledge' (*LI* I 193). In other words, Husserl wanted to explore how thinking can be thinking *of* thoughts – and, to extend this style of questioning, how perceiving can be perception *of* perceived objects, how imagination can be imagination *of* imagined objects, and so forth. As I explain in the following chapter, these are precisely the questions that drive phenomenological enquiry. In each case, the same 'mystery' announces itself: that consciousness is consciousness *of* something transcendent to itself.[7]

In the prolegomena to the *Logical Investigations*, no answers are given to these questions, but a prevalent explanation for this 'mystery' is forcefully ruled out: psychical acts do not *generate* logical objects (e.g. meanings) or 'have' them as intrinsic parts of themselves. Because logical objects are not the kind of things that come into being and pass out of being, the temporally unfolding *act* must be distinguished from the atemporal *object* made present in it. Logical acts make logical objects *manifest* – or, as Husserl will say, the acts bring the objects 'to intuitive givenness' – but they do not *create* them. The mystery of cognition, therefore, cannot be resolved by collapsing the object into the act in which it is 'given'.

On Husserl's interpretation, therefore, the study of logic must have two sides to it: one side that relates to the psychological acts in which logical objects are given, and another other side that relates to the interconnections between those objects themselves. These might be called the 'subjective' and the 'objective' faces of logic. The deficiency of the psychologistic approach, as we have seen, is that it seeks to make logic coextensive with the 'subjective' side. At the same time, it is important to see that Husserl does not simply reject the 'subjective' side in favour of the 'objective' side. He does not eschew the study of logical acts in preference for the study of logical objects. Both 'sides' are seen as necessary – with the proviso that they not be conflated. A broadly 'psychological' dimension would therefore have to be included in his 'logical' investigations if they were to investigate the mysterious *interface* or *correlation between* the psychological and the logical – and to do so in a way which does not collapse the two.[8] Indeed, even in a much later work Husserl is still able to write:

Logic, as the science of all the logical as such and – in its highest form, which embraces all other forms of the logical – as the science of all science as such, inquires *in two opposite directions.* Everywhere it is a matter of rational productions, in a double sense: on one side, as *productive activities and habitualities*; on the other side, as *results* produced by activities and habitualities and afterwards persisting. (*FTL* 33)

In so far as they include a 'subjective' side to them, Husserl could describe the six investigations that make up the rest of *Logical Investigations* as works of '*descriptive psychology*' (*LI* I 262f.).[9] However, the expression 'descriptive psychology' reinforced the impression for some that Husserl had relapsed into psychologism in the second volume of the *Logical Investigations*.[10] And, indeed, Husserl himself came to see that there was an element of truth to this charge and that further methodological clarifications were needed. As I discuss in Chapter 3, these clarifications led to a 'transcendental turn' in Husserl's conception of phenomenological philosophy during the first decade of the twentieth century. In this reinterpretation, the primary subject matter of phenomenology came to be located in neither the logical nor the psychological sphere but at the 'origin' of the two. As such, Husserl came to regret the choice of such an ambiguous expression as 'descriptive psychology' and expressly repudiated it as 'misleading' in the second edition of the *Logical Investigations* (published in 1913) (*LI* I 47, 261f.; cf. *Ideas I* §61). Notwithstanding these revisions, however, the 'transcendental phenomenology' that succeeded Husserl's 'descriptive psychology' was a continuation of the same project to conceptualize in ever more sophisticated ways the fundamental 'mystery of cognition': the relationship between 'the subjectivity of knowing and the objectivity of the content known' (*LI* I 42).

NOTES

1 Such was the assertion, for example, of Paul Natorp in his review of *Logical Investigations* in *Kantstudien* VI (1901): 270–83. A translation of this review can be found in J.N. Mohanty (ed.), *Readings on Husserl's Logical Investigations* (The Hague: Martinus Nijhoff, 1977), pp. 55–66.

2 See Gottlob Frege, *The Foundations of Arithmetic: A Logico-Mathematical Enquiry into the Concept of Number* (2nd edn), trans. J.L. Austin (Oxford: Blackwell, 1980) and *Basic Laws of Arithmetic: An Exposition of the System*, trans. Montgomery Furth (Berkeley, CA: University of California Press, 1964).

3 J.N. Mohanty, however, argues correctly in my view that Frege's criticisms were not as formative for Husserl as is usually thought, and, indeed, that Husserl's self-diagnosed 'psychologism' was never as thoroughgoing as the variety of psychologism he criticizes in the *Logical Investigations* ('Husserl, Frege and the overcoming of psychologism', in *The Possibility of Transcendental Philosophy* (Dordrecht/London/Lancaster: Martinus Nijhoff, 1985), pp. 1–11).

4 This is an oft-repeated point in Husserl's writings; for example, from lectures in 1925:

> Such irreal, or as one also says, ideal objects are, in their numerically identical singularity, substrates of true or false judgements just as real things are; conversely 'object' in the most universal logical sense means nothing else than anything at all concerning which statements can be made sensefully and in truth (*Phenomenological Psychology: Lectures, Summer Semester, 1925*, trans. John Scanlon [The Hague: Martinus Nijhoff, 1977], p. 15).

5 For an analysis of Lotze's influential idea of 'validity' (*Geltung*) and its relation to the critique of psychologism, see Daniel O. Dahlstrom, *Heidegger's Concept of Truth* (Cambridge: Cambridge University Press, 2001), pp. 29–47.

6 See Martin Heidegger, *Being and Time*, trans. John Macquarrie and Edward Robinson (Oxford: Blackwell, 1962), pp. 198f., 259ff., *et passim*.

7 According to Dallas Willard, it is precisely in addressing this question

that Husserl enters territory overlooked by most logicians in the 'analytic' tradition. See Dallas Willard, 'The Paradox of Logical Psychologism: Husserl's Way Out', in Mohanty (ed.), *Readings on Husserl's Logical Investigations*, pp. 43–54.

8 To avoid muddying the waters further at this point, I am passing over another possible rejoinder to Husserl's method which sees it as relapsing into psychologism on separate grounds to the ones mentioned above. These further objections, which concern the 'eidetic' status of the psychological analyses in the text, were clarified in the second edition (1913) of the *Logical Investigations*. I discuss these matters in Chapter 7.

9 The term 'descriptive psychology' derives from the work of his teachers Franz Brentano and Carl Stumpf.

10 See n. 1.

CHAPTER 2

PHENOMENOLOGY AND OTHER 'EIDETIC SCIENCES'

Fundamental to Husserl's idea of philosophy is the conviction that it *'lies in a wholly new dimension'* and 'needs an *entirely new point of departure* and an entirely new method of distinguishing it in principle from any "natural" science' (*IP* 19). He distinguishes philosophy from natural science along *two axes* – and these must not be confused. On one hand, Husserl's new science is distinguished from 'natural science' through its suspension of the 'natural attitude' in favour of the 'transcendental' or 'phenomenological attitude'. I discuss this axis of distinction in Chapters 3 and 4. On the other hand, phenomenology concern itself *not with matters of facts but with essences*; it is a 'science of essences' (*Ideas I* xx). Phenomenology is one of several 'sciences of essences'. But what is a science of essences and how does it differ from a science of facts? This is the question that occupies us in the present chapter. After I have distinguished these two kinds of science, I discuss the various kinds of eidetic science and the place of phenomenology among them.

SCIENCES OF FACT AND SCIENCES OF ESSENCE

Husserl's conception of scientific knowledge takes its start from a thoroughly Kantian observation: 'Natural cognition begins with experience and remains *within* experience' (*Ideas I* §1, 5). The idea of 'experience' (*Erfahrung*) is as central to Husserl as it is for Kant. Experience is prized by both thinkers as the touchstone of scientific truth: it is that which confirms or disconfirms our preconceptions and theories. What we discover in natural cognition is the 'world'; that is, the totality of individual objects that could possibly be experienced. The world that comprises the totality of such objects is what Husserl calls 'reality' (*Realität*). The sciences divided up the totality of real objects amongst themselves. To each science, then, belongs an 'object province' (*Sachgebeit*) which it seeks to describe and understand through direct experience of those objects themselves, i.e. through observation and experiments. Physics, chemistry, biology, psychology, sociology, anthropology, and so forth, each have their own discrete domain of objects into which they enquire, and they qualify as rigorous sciences to the extent that they confirm their results through direct experience. These sciences, whose objects are the various kinds of objects found in experience, are called the 'empirical' or 'natural sciences'. They are the sciences of 'matters of fact' (*Ideas I* §2, 7).

However, Husserl observes that, in addition to its describable physical properties, relations and so forth, every individual object has a 'concept', or more precisely, an 'essence' (*Wesen*). That is, every individual object that we come across in the world *is* something or other; e.g. this is a *Siamese cat*, that is a *carbon atom*, the other thing is a *volcanic rock*. Essences are what we name when we answer the question 'what is it?'; an 'essence' is simply defined as 'the What of an individuum' (*Ideas I* §3, 8). (An 'individuum' is an individual object, i.e. a singular, non-aggregated, object.) Moreover, the essence of some object X is the same for *any* X *whatsoever*. That is, the essence (as opposed to the object) is not individual but rather 'general' or 'universal'. Hence, essences can also be called 'universals'. Such 'universals' are indifferent to the number of instances or 'particulars' of them that actually exist. It does not matter where, when or how such instances come into being, it does not matter what state they are in, the essence they instantiate remains the same.

Whatever essences are, they are not made the subject of investigation by natural science. For example, the natural sciences may ask many questions about blue-tongue lizards, and add to our knowledge about that set of beings in the world; but the natural sciences do not ask what '*a priori* knowledge' we have about lizards, i.e. knowledge that holds true of lizards irrespective of their *factually contingent* biological make-up, geographical spread, social habits, and so forth. The natural sciences exclusively gather *empirical* or '*a posteriori*' knowledge about real beings; they pass over essential or '*a priori*' knowledge that may pertain to those entities. For knowledge of the latter variety we must look away from the experiential sciences to the 'pure' or 'eidetic' sciences. ('Eidetic' means 'relating to essences'.)

It may initially appear that turning away from empirical objects to the study of their essences could only lead to a dead end. After all, what value could come from contemplating the *idea* of a blue-tongue lizard? Surely we only *learn* something about lizards when we investigate actual lizards. Husserl, however, defends the value of eidetic sciences, and I shall try to give some sense of his arguments as we proceed. The important point here, however, is that essences can be contemplated and unpacked. If we look to the essential or 'eidetic' composition of objects, a certain set of *truths* can be established about them even before they are experientially investigated. This set of truths is called '*a priori* knowledge', or equally, 'eidetic knowledge'. Eidetic knowledge encompasses what can be known about any X purely by virtue of the fact that it is an X. Eidetic knowledge can be explicated and organized into a coherent science in its own right. Husserl calls this task the '*science of essences*' or '*eidetic science*'. In fact, he identifies several eidetic sciences, following more or less the traditional divisions. As I shall discuss below, these include formal ontology, formal logic, formal mathematical disciplines, regional or material ontology and material mathematical disciplines. Quite apart from the empirical sciences, then, there is another independent science or set of sciences that can be pursued. Apart from the 'sciences of fact', there are 'sciences of essence' that explore the sphere of essences independently of contingent matters of facts.

EMPIRICAL AND EIDETIC LAWS

There are, of course, limits to what eidetic sciences can tell us. In fact, Husserl observes that, strictly speaking, they tell us nothing at all about *actuality*; they only tell us about *possibility*. If we want to know about actuality, we need to consult experience. Only through experience can we learn about 'matters of fact'. That the world is the way it is, and that certain things exist and not others, is a contingent matter of fact. No science of essences can tell us what exists and how it came to be. Moreover, the way things stand in the actual world is continually in flux. 'Laws of nature' govern the flux of matter – physical, chemical and biological processes, for example. But these laws themselves are contingent, and thus can only be determined through empirical research. The lawfulness of matters of fact are '*de facto* rules which themselves could read quite otherwise' (*Ideas I* 7). The mere idea of a physical object will not yield the laws of physics.

So, again, what good is eidetic knowledge? It seems that all the genuinely useful knowledge is empirical. To answer this question properly, it is important to see that while *a priori* or 'eidetic' knowledge is knowledge about *possibility*, this does not remove it completely from the sphere of actuality. Though eidetic knowledge does not give us information about actuality *per se*, it does give us knowledge about actuality *in so far as* actuality is the realization of possibilities. This is so because the rules that govern the field of possibility also govern the field of actuality (the actual being a subset, as it were, of the possible). The traditional illustration in this connection is the geometrical figure. Real instances of the geometrical figures whose properties and lawfulness geometry investigates may or may not exist; but if and when they do exist, the science of geometry will be applicable to them. Actual shapes in the world are instances of the very same geometrical objects studied and understood by the geometer in an *a priori* fashion (at least ideally). In a like fashion, the other eidetic sciences explore possibilities that may or may not have actually existing exemplars; but the *a priori* truths belonging to essences will govern instantiations of those essences as a matter of necessity whenever they do exist. Every actuality conforms to the *a priori* 'conditions of possible experience' (*Ideas I* §6; *EJ* §90).

There are, then, two fundamentally distinct kinds of 'laws' or 'generalities' that make up the totality of scientific knowledge: the laws discovered by the empirical sciences ('empirical generalities') and the laws discovered by the eidetic sciences ('pure generalities') (*EJ* §86). Empirical generalities are conditional upon matters of fact and are grounded in the experience of factual existence. 'All polar bears are white' is an empirical generality. It just so happens that all polar bears are white. It is therefore also an empirically falsifiable generalization: perhaps one day we will discover a fuchsia polar bear. The laws yielded by the eidetic sciences, on the other hand, are unconditional; they are indifferent to the flux of actual existence. There is no possible change of circumstance that would render them void. This is because their universality stems from the structure of possibility itself and not from the contingent structure of the actual world.

Scientific rigour requires that these two kinds of lawfulness be kept distinct – a task complicated by the fact that their radically different epistemic grounds leave no mark on their propositional forms: the empirical generality that 'all bodies are heavy' is expressed in the same grammatical form as the pure generality that 'all material things are extended', and yet the former is empirically grounded whereas the latter is eidetically necessary. The first proposition generalizes from what is found to be true of individual bodies, whereas the second proposition is derived via a transformation of the eidetic law that the essence 'material thing' includes the category of 'extension'. (Propositions concerning particulars that are derived from eidetic laws in this way are termed 'necessities'; *Ideas I* 14.)

It follows, then, that any individual object can be taken up as a scientific object in one of two ways. It can be investigated with respect to the lawfulness governing its contingency, or it can be investigated with respect to the lawfulness of its essence. The individual object, therefore, is the point of intersection between the sciences of fact and the sciences of essence.

But there is an asymmetry between the two kinds of science. The eidetic sciences, for their part, do not rely on or incorporate any results from empirical science. The eidetic sciences do not presuppose anything contingent, whether empirical laws or existent entities:

> *Positing of* and, to begin with, intuitive seizing upon, *essences implies not the slightest positing of any individual factual existence; pure eidetic truths contain not the slightest assertion about matters of fact.* And thus not even the most insignificant matter-of-fact truth can be deduced from pure eidetic truths alone. (*Ideas I* 11)

However, the converse is not also true. The empirical sciences *must* presuppose and conform to eidetic laws. The investigation of actuality cannot proceed independently of the laws of possibility: 'There is *no science of matters of fact* which, *were it fully developed as a science*, could be pure of eidetic cognitions and therefore *could be independent of the formal or the material eidetic sciences*' (*Ideas I* 17). In short, then, the eidetic sciences enjoy a priority over the natural sciences, and certainly cannot be abandoned, denied or devalued.

OVERCOMING NATURALISTIC PREJUDICES

Conspicuous in Husserl's entire account of eidetic science is the assumption that it is legitimate to speak of essences and to subject them to scientific investigation. Husserl was well aware that this assumption flew in the face of the prevailing 'naturalistic' standpoint of the day. Naturalism is the doctrine that actuality is coextensive with 'nature considered as a unity of spatiotemporal being subject to exact laws of nature'.[1] The naturalistic tendencies of the late nineteenth century had led to a general 'hostility to ideas': 'what are "ideas", "essences" but Scholastic entities, metaphysical spectres?' (*Ideas I* 35). To ease the embarrassment, attempts were made to collapse the logical and philosophical disciplines into natural science. It was thought that in one way or another the so-called 'pure' or *a priori* sciences could be subsumed under the rubric of empirical science. As we saw in Chapter 1, one popular strategy was to bring logic under the rubric of psychology, i.e. the view Husserl dubs 'logical psychologism'. But psychologism was only one manifestation of the desire to explain all phenomena naturalistically, including 'ideas'. Therefore, Husserl set about justifying and defending the 'eidetic sciences' against what he saw as naturalistic prejudices.

It must be stressed at this juncture that Husserl was not unsympathetic to the positivistic dimension of empiricist thought. He writes, for example:

As we must acknowledge, empiricistic naturalism springs from the most praiseworthy motives. In contrast to all 'idols', to the powers of tradition and superstition, of crude and refined prejudices of every sort, it is a radicalism of cognitive practice that aims at enforcing the right of autonomous reason as the sole authority on questions of truth. (*Ideas I* §19, 35)

Where the empiricists err, however, is in taking this commitment to mean that all scientific judgement must confine itself to *experience alone*. 'The empiricist therefore takes genuine science and experiential science to be identical' (*Ideas I* 35). This is the 'naturalistic prejudice' that Husserl opposes. It dogmatically rules out the possibility of knowledge concerning essences – unless, of course, essences can be reduced to natural phenomena, e.g. states of mind. For the naturalist, then, the study of 'ideas' is possible – if it is possible –

within the province of psychology. But otherwise 'ideas' are to be regarded as mythical entities.

Husserl counters with the observation that in the normal course of events we seem to deal with many *objects* that are not 'things of Nature', and numerous *truths* that are not merely 'Natural matters of fact' (*Ideas I* 36). Consider, for example, the proposition that *three is a prime number*. Is this a meaningful proposition? Is this a true proposition? Does it count as knowledge? Most philosophers would answer all three questions in the affirmative. But is it empirically verifiable? It would appear not. Can it be grounded in psychology? Again, most philosophers would follow Husserl in saying no (see Chapter 1). What we appear to have, then, is an example of a meaningful proposition about a non-real object (i.e. the number three) whose truth is not empirically verifiable. That is, we appear to have an exception to the positivist's claim that all meaningful propositions find legitimation in experience. And yet, such mathematical truths form a class of truths which every empirical scientist already implicitly recognizes. The claim that the natural sciences have a monopoly on truth begins to look shaky at best, and downright prejudicial at worst.

Furthermore, mathematical knowledge is not the only 'eidetic science' whose validity the empiricists implicitly acknowledge. Husserl argues that the natural sciences also make use of geometry, logic, formal and material ontology (*Ideas I* §25). For the empiricist to deny the legitimacy of such eidetic sciences is to cut off the branches on which his own sciences sit. Moreover, warning other researchers off further study in eidetic disciplines means that the natural sciences prevent themselves from benefiting from whatever fruits such study might bring forth:

> [The] hostility to ideas [that] prevails eventually must endanger the progress of the experimental sciences themselves because, owing to this hostility, the still uncompleted eidetic founding of these sciences and the perhaps necessary constituting of new eidetic sciences indispensable to their progress have become inhibited. (*Ideas I* 34)

The awkward consequences of the naturalistic prejudice for empirical science do not stop there. Husserl also argues that the very conception of science espoused by the empiricist is itself a philosophical rather than empirical position (*Ideas I* §§19–20). That is to say, the claim that 'all knowledge is empirical' is not itself an *empirical* claim; it is not, for example, a result derived from a survey of all the pieces of knowledge that we actually possess. It is rather a claim about the *essence* of knowledge couched in terms of a generality; it is, in short, a properly philosophical claim. The empiricist's grounds for regarding philosophical knowledge as dubious, it would appear, are themselves philosophical. Therefore, if the empiricist were consistent, he would refrain not only from using the mathematical and logical sciences but also from asserting his own naturalistic principle – these all being 'eidetic' propositions of various sorts. Of course, the empiricist has the good sense not to actually refrain from making such eidetic judgements, but he thereby shows the contradiction between his professed 'positivism' and his scientific praxis (*Ideas I* 45).

Such arguments against a narrow empiricism or naturalism are now commonplace. This battle, it seems, has been won. But this apparently leaves the empiricist with a terrible dilemma: to abandon the principle of evidence or relinquish the service of eidetic sciences. Clearly neither path is acceptable. At this point, Husserl steps in with a bold proposal: rather than sacrificing either eidetic science or the principle of grounding scientific theories experientially (i.e. the principle of evidence), let us *extend that same principle to the eidetic sciences as well*. For, if the positivist's own principle of evidence is applied *universally*, then the investigation of essences too can be elevated to the level of a rigorous science. Let us therefore no longer restrict evidence to experience but 'substitute something more universal: "intuition" ' (*Ideas I* 37). In all matters, let us regard as *actual* only what is given in an evident intuition, and as *true* only what can be confirmed in repeatable and intersubjectively verifiable intuition. Husserl stridently proclaims:

> [W]e take our start from what lies *prior to* all standpoints: from the total realm of whatever is itself given intuitionally and prior to all theorizing, from everything that one can immediately see and seize upon – if only one does not let himself be blinded by prejudices and prevented from taking into consideration whole classes of genuine data. If *'positivism'* is tantamount to an absolutely unprejudiced grounding of all sciences on the 'positive', that is to say, on what can be seized originaliter, then *we* are the genuine positivists. (*Ideas I* 38f.)

The error of the so-called positivists (i.e. naturalists), then, is that they are not positivistic enough – theirs is a piecemeal positivism. The true positivist is the one who accepts *all* evidence, and not only that given in *experience*, i.e. in sensuous intuition. Once this restriction is lifted, the validity of both empirical and eidetic sciences can be seen. So long as the eidetic sciences also proceed according to the principle of evidence, then these too ought to be accepted as genuine sciences.

How the demand for evidence in questions of essence might be practically met is another matter. How exactly are essences to be made the object of an intuitive seeing? This is the juncture at which Husserl's famous doctrine of 'eidetic seeing' (*Wesenserschauung*) or 'ideation' steps in to fill the breach. Explicating this doctrine requires a conceptual foundation to be laid, and so I defer this until Chapter 7. The important point here, however, is that Husserl's doctrine of 'eidetic seeing' is *opposed* to all spurious claims of mystical insight into esoteric truths. It is intended to describe the event in which *legitimating evidence* is discovered for philosophical, logical or mathematical propositions – and this means, as we shall see, propositions grounded not in a '*feeling* of evidence' or a 'mystic *index veri*' but in evidential intuition (*Ideas I* 40).

KINDS OF EIDETIC SCIENCE

In this section, I would like to flesh out in more detail the kinds of eidetic sciences identified by Husserl, the eidetic sciences upon which the empirical sciences are essentially dependent. The eidetic sciences fall into three categories: (1) 'material' or 'regional ontology' (these terms are equivalent); (2) 'formal ontology' and 'formal logic'; and (3) 'eidetic disciplines' grounded in essences belonging to the first two categories (e.g. mathematics, geometry, set theory).[2]

(1) *'Material' or 'regional ontology'*: As I have mentioned, every individual object has a What or, to use the technical term, a 'material essence' (*ein sachhaltiges Wesen*). Such essences are never completely isolated. On the one hand, a number of other essences are always implied along with a material essence as equally applicable to the same object. These always follow a pattern of increasing levels of generality. For example, in identifying this thing as a Siamese cat, it is necessarily the case that it is equally a cat, an animal, a living thing and a physical thing. All of these increasingly general determinations

are said to belong to the 'essential composition' of the essence 'Siamese cat'. What we are noticing here is that essences belong to hierarchies of 'species' and 'genus'. The lowest, most determinate essences are called 'eidetic singularities'; higher, more general essences are called 'genera'; and the highest essences (e.g. 'any material thing whatsoever') are called 'universal species' (*Ideas I* §12).

Simultaneously, essences can also be explicated 'horizontally', as it were. With each genus is implied a set of essential predicates or 'categories' that necessarily characterize objects of that variety. For instance, if we know that an object is a physical thing, it is necessarily the case that it is an entity with temporal and spatial location, physical properties such as shape and colour, etc. Every possible description of a physical thing falls under one or other of the 'categories' belonging to its essential composition. Now, as Aristotle observed, categories are only ever present in connection with some 'substance' (*ousia*); that is, there is no being-coloured without something to be coloured. The substance has a primacy (of sorts) over its essential predicates; without it, they cannot be. Husserl similarly distinguishes 'abstract' objects (e.g. red) from the 'concrete' objects (e.g. car) on which they are dependent. The latter are also called 'primal objectivities' (*Urgegenständlichkeiten*) (*Ideas I* 20). Likewise, 'categories', by extension, are called 'abstract genera' (e.g. spatial shape) in distinction to the 'concrete genus' of the primal objectivity (e.g. physical thing) (*Ideas I* 29). In any case, any concrete genus bears within it a bundle of abstract genera.

According to Husserl, and contrary to what we might expect, it is *not* the case that the totality of individual objects fall under a single overarching genus. Depending on *which* individual object one chooses to start from, climbing the ladder of generality may lead to any one of several summits. At each of these summits, one finds a 'highest material genus' or, what Husserl calls a 'regional essence' (*Ideas I* 18). There are, in other words, multiple 'regions' (*Regionen*).[3] To each of these regions corresponds an eidetic science called a 'material-ontological discipline' or 'regional ontology' (*Ideas I* §9).

The regional ontology explicates the essential composition of the regional essence. In accordance with the laws described above, the regional ontology determines the hierarchies of genus and species that are ordered under a highest material genus or 'regional essence' down to the 'eidetic singularities', which are the most specific universals applicable to the individual objects in the region. It also determines the unique set of 'regional categories' that the regional essence bears within it, i.e. the categories that are universally and uniquely applicable to the concrete objects belonging to the region. (These 'categories' are also called the 'fundamental concepts' of that region.) According to Husserl, these categories yield the 'synthetic *a priori*' knowledge sought by Kant (*Ideas I* §16). Hence, the regional ontology determines what can be known *a priori* about that region of being, and so determines the concepts and laws that govern the empirical science(s) operative in that same region. For example, 'nature' is a regional essence and a regional ontology belongs to it. The eidetic science of nature, i.e. the ontology of nature, provides the 'rational' or 'pure' cognitions that ground the empirical sciences of that region. The regional ontology of nature explicates the categories 'physical property', 'physical relationship' and so forth that apply to the primal objectivity 'physical thing' (*Ideas I* 20).

(2) *'Formal ontology' and 'formal logic'*: As mentioned above, every individual object has a 'material essence' which places it in one region of being or another. But, in addition, every individual object also has a 'form' or 'formal essence'.[4] The form of every individual object is simply the idea 'object' or 'any object whatsoever' (*Ideas I* 26). The *formal essence* 'any object whatsoever' does not belong anywhere in the various hierarchies of *material essences*.[5] Formal essences transcend generality.[6] Thus, despite the fact that the essence 'any object whatsoever' appears to be a genus like 'any material object whatsoever', it is not in fact a material essence at all. The essence 'any object whatsoever', therefore, is not a highest genus which brings all the regions of being under one head. The plurality of regions remains irreducible.

'Formal ontology' is the science exploring the essential possibilities and laws related to 'any object whatsoever', i.e. anything in so far as it is an object, irrespective of its region. In contrast to the 'material essences' belonging to regional ontology, formal ontology consists exclusively of 'formal essences'. Every empirical science, says Husserl, is bound by the structures and laws of 'formal ontology', just as it is bound by the relevant 'regional ontology'. It is initially difficult to imagine what could meaningfully be said that would be applicable to any object whatsoever until one sees that it is under the formal category of 'object' that individual objects enter into logical relations, e.g. relations of 'genus and species', 'universal and particular', 'part and whole', etc. In other words, the 'formal essences' are nothing other than *logical forms*. Husserl therefore regards formal ontology and pure logic to be one and the same: 'formal ontology' means nothing other than 'pure logic in its full extent as *mathesis universalis*' (*Ideas I* 21).[7] The logical relations just mentioned, along with other logical forms such as 'object', 'number', 'property', 'state of affairs', make up the *logical forms* or *categories* studied under the heading of 'formal logic'.

Parenthetically, it should be noted that this definition of 'formal logic' does not correspond to the way the term is typically used today. 'Formal logic', in the contemporary sense, does appear in Husserl's analytic of eidetic sciences, but under a different name: 'apophantic logic'. This is a consequence of the fact that Husserl distinguishes the logical forms *per se* from the propositional forms by which they are linguistically expressed. So, for example, he differentiates the sentential form '*S* is *P*' from the logical form of the correlated object, i.e. the state of affairs that *S is P*. The eidetic science dedicated to the study of propositional forms in their own right is called 'apophantic logic', and *this* is what we usually mean today by the term 'formal logic'. In any case, Husserl recognizes that there is (ideally) a correspondence between the set of logical categories and the set of propositional forms or 'signification-categories'; the one 'mirrors' the other (*Ideas I* 22f.). And, because apophantic logic and formal logic share this intimate connection, Husserl places them together under the rubric of 'formal ontology in the fully comprehensive sense' (*Ideas I* 22).

(3) '*Eidetic disciplines*': Together material and formal ontology spawn a variety of subordinate 'mathematical' or 'exact' disciplines. To certain 'categories' belonging to certain material ontologies correspond '*material eidetic disciplines*' (*Ideas I* §72; cf. *LI* I, Proleg. §70). For instance, in relation to the regional essence 'physical thing', the category of 'spatial determinateness' provides the conceptual cornerstone for the eidetic science of geometry. Likewise, to certain 'categories' of the formal region correspond '*formal eidetic disciplines*'. For instance, the formal category of 'quantity' provides the fundamental concept for the eidetic science of arithmetic. The various eidetic disciplines derived from the 'formal essences' make up the extended fabric of the *mathesis universalis* (*Ideas I* 18).

Just as material ontology is governed by formal ontology, so the formal mathematical disciplines govern the material mathematical disciplines. Thus, the formal mathematical disciplines are universally applicable within the material mathematical disciplines, and the latter, in turn, are universally applicable within the field of particulars that fall under that region. In this way, all sciences are, in principle, grounded in the more fundamental eidetic sciences of formal and regional ontology. It is in these eidetic disciplines that eidetic science most obviously serves the ends of empirical science.

Despite the essential interrelations between the eidetic disciplines and ontology, various eidetic disciplines (including apophantic logic) have tended to separate out and become autonomous sciences. Husserl saw no need for philosophers to protest against this division of labour (*LI* I, Proleg. §71). Mathematicians, in any case, are more adept at the technical, constructive work required in the eidetic disciplines, he argues. It remains the job of philosophy, however, to investigate and secure the subject matter of the foundational eidetic sciences of formal and regional ontology. Hence:

> [Philosophy] does not seek to meddle in the work of the specialist, but to achieve insight in regard to the sense and essence of his achievements as regards method and manner. The philosopher is not content with the fact that we find our way about in the world, that we have legal formulae which enable us to predict the future course of things, or to reconstruct its past course; he wants to clarify the essence of a thing, an event, a cause, an effect, of space, of time, etc., as well as that wonderful affinity which this essence has with the essence of thought, which enables it to be thought, with the essence of knowledge, which makes it knowable, with meanings which make it capable of being meant, etc. (*LI* I 245)

Through radically pursuing research into regional and formal ontology, the philosopher thereby seeks to bring perspicuity, unity and scientific rigour to the foundations of scientific endeavour as a whole – including both *eidetic* and *empirical* disciplines – and to complete its achievements.

PHENOMENOLOGY AS EIDETIC SCIENCE OF THE 'UR-REGION'

Where then does phenomenology fit into this picture? For Husserl, philosophy and phenomenology are not strictly identical. Philosophy, as I have said, is concerned with formal and material ontology. Its concern is to secure the essences and axioms upon which the work of eidetic and empirical disciplines can be based. Superficially, this dictates a systematic project of 'ideational intuition', a project of 'eidetic seeing', by which the essences themselves are evidentially intuited (*LI* I 238). But, in a more radical and comprehensive sense, the essences of formal and material ontology can only be investigated in the context of a *phenomenology* which takes the entire domain of consciousness as its field of research (*Ideas I* 32). Only via phenomenological research can the basic concepts of formal and regional ontology be understood. The problem of ontology leads back to the phenomenological sphere – the domain of consciousness (*LI* I 237f).[8] Husserl writes:

> Genuine philosophy . . . is rooted in pure phenomenology; and rooted in it in a sense so important that the systematically strict grounding and working out of this first of all genuine philosophies is the incessant precondition for every metaphysics and other philosophy 'that will be able to make its appearance as a *science*'. (*Ideas I* xxii)

The internal quotation in this passage is to Kant's *Critique of Pure Reason*, which in an analogous fashion was to prepare the way for the substantive philosophical and empirical disciplines by offering a theory or 'critique' of reason. But Husserl now refers the task of 'critique' to the phenomenology of transcendental consciousness:

> . . . the science having the unique function of effecting the criticism of all others and, at the same time, of itself is none other than phenomenology . . . Thus, phenomenology includes all the eidetic (therefore unconditionally and universally valid) cognitions with which the radical problems of 'possibility' relating to any alleged cognitions and sciences become solved. As applied phenomenology, of essential necessity it produces the ultimately evaluative criticism of each specifically peculiar science; and thus, in particular, it determines the ultimate sense of the 'being' of its objects and the fundamental clarification of its methods. Accordingly, it is understandable that phenomenology is, so to speak, the secret nostalgia of all modern philosophy. (*Ideas I* 141f.)

I shall say more about the nature of this 'critical' dimension to phenomenology in the following chapter. In conclusion, however, I would like to return to the 'two axes' mentioned at the beginning of the chapter.

From the remarks above, it may appear that Husserl's idea of 'phenomenology' returns him to the psychologistic position he had so strenuously criticized: the attempt to ground philosophy, logic and mathematics in a science of consciousness. However, the science of consciousness proposed by Husserl is a fundamentally *new* science which has '*an entirely new point of departure*'. Thus, Husserl insists that phenomenology and psychology are *two entirely separate sciences*.[9] He differentiates phenomenology from the more familiar natural science of consciousness in *two respects*. First, psychology considers consciousness in so far as it is a *real* phenomenon. Phenomenology, on the other hand, considers consciousness in so far as it is a *transcendental* phenomenon, the origin of all objectivity. The separation of the latter from the former is the work of the 'phenomenological' or 'transcendental reduction' which I discuss in detail over the next two chapters. Second, phenomenology and psychology differ in the same way that geometry differs from physics: phenomenology deals with the *essential* structures of the domain of consciousness, while psychology deals with its *empirical* laws. Therefore, in addition to being a *transcendental* science, phenomenology is also itself an *eidetic* science (*Ideas I* xx–xxi): namely, the '*eidetic theory of mental processes* [*Erlebnisse*]' (*Ideas I* 161). As such, it concerns itself with the explication of ideas such as 'intentionality', 'intentional object', 'perception', 'reflection', 'intuition', 'evidence', 'reason', and so forth. Indeed, phenomenology might even be called the *regional ontology of* (*transcendental*) *consciousness*.[10]

However, from what has just been said, it is clear that for Husserl the (eidetic) science of (transcendental) consciousness cannot be just one regional ontology among others. In a remarkable way, the eidetic science of *this* region *grounds* the entire philosophical enterprise – i.e. formal and regional ontology. The realm of transcendental consciousness is 'the one in which all other regions of being are rooted' (*Ideas I* 171). The region of transcendental consciousness is consequently accorded the status of '*primal region*' (*Ur-region*) (*Ideas I* 171); and the eidetic science of this region is touted as *the most primordial science of all*, or simply: '*first philosophy*' (*Ideas I* 148).

NOTES

1 Edmund Husserl, 'Philosophy as rigorous science', in *Phenomenology and the Crisis of Philosophy*, trans. Quentin Lauer (New York: Harper & Row, 1965), p. 79.

2 The student determined to master these difficult conceptual distinctions will find a useful guide in Emmanuel Levinas, *The Theory of Intuition in Husserl's Phenomenology*, trans. André Orianne (Evanston, IL: Northwestern University Press, 1995), Chapter 6, 'The intuition of essences'.

3 How the number and identity of the regions is to be determined is a complex matter. For a detailed discussion of the problems involved, see *EJ* §§92–93. Regions mentioned include: Nature, Physical Thing, Consciousness, Psyche, Essence, Signification, Animal, Human, Cultural Formation (e.g. the state, the law, the family, the Church). However, to my knowledge, Husserl never offers a comprehensive list of regions, and certainly not one with competed tables of their respective categories. This was an outstanding task, and one actively taken up by Husserl's co-workers. It is further complicated by the way in which the various regions seem to be 'interwoven' with each other (*Ideas I* §152).

4 The distinction between forms and genera is discussed by Husserl in *Ideas I* §13. A material essence (e.g. 'red') is said to 'subsume' a particular/individual (a red patch), to be 'subordinate' to a genus ('colour', 'sensuous quality'), and to be a 'singularization' or 'materialization' of a form ('essence').

5 For this reason, it is strictly speaking improper to speak of 'the formal region'. Nevertheless, Husserl continues to use the expression: see *Ideas I* §10.

6 For a further discussion of this point, see Levinas, *The Theory of Intuition in Husserl's Phenomenology*, pp. 3–4 and 77–8.

7 Husserl refers the reader to *LI* I, Proleg. §§62–72 for an amplification of the idea of 'pure logic' (see especially §§65–69). Though he clearly stands by his earlier explication of the idea of 'pure logic', a quick comparison will show that in the intervening years (from 1900 to 1913) his categorization of the various sciences had become more sophisticated than that offered in *LI* I, Proleg. §64.

8 See also Edmund Husserl, *Ideas Pertaining to a Pure Phenomenology and a Phenomenological Philosophy: Phenomenology and the Foundation of the Sciences* (Third Book), trans. Ted E. Klein and William E. Pohl (The Hague: Martinus Nijhoff, 1980), pp. 65–79. Heidegger famously took up this same project under the title 'the question of the meaning of being', proclaiming that 'only as phenomenology, is ontology possible' (Martin Heidegger, *Being and Time*, trans. John Macquarrie and Edward Robinson [Oxford: Basil Blackwell, 1962], pp. 19 and 60).

9 Husserl addresses this question of the relationship between phenomenology and psychology at length in various places. However, in connection with the theme of the present chapter, I would suggest the interested

reader consult *Ideas Pertaining to a Pure Phenomenology* (Third Book), Chapter 2.

10 Though Husserl does not say that phenomenology is a regional ontology in so many words, we may assume as much from the fact that he describes transcendental consciousness as '*a new region of being never before delimited in its own peculiarity* – a region which, like any other genuine region, is a region of *individual* being' (*Ideas I* 63f.) and refers to phenomenology as its 'concrete-eidetic discipline' (*Ideas I* 164).

CHAPTER 3

PHENOMENOLOGY AND TRANSCENDENTAL PHILOSOPHY

Husserl's mature phenomenology operates in a 'transcendental' register. Grasping what Husserl means by this term is one of the most difficult tasks for the uninitiated, and yet it is central to the idea of phenomenology. The 'transcendental' character of Husserl's mature phenomenology can be explained by reference to Descartes, but it is equally fruitful to understand it through the Kantian tradition of transcendental idealism, and in the present chapter I favour the latter approach.[1] The chapter starts by reiterating the central problem of phenomenology that emerged in Chapter 1 i.e. the enigma of cognition – and then traces the crisis and eventual 'transcendental turn' that Husserl underwent. The transcendental turn itself is then analysed as having both Cartesian and Kantian dimensions. The Kantian dimension is explored at some length as a way of introducing the ideas of intentionality, constitution and the basic components of Husserl's phenomenological method: the principle of evidence, eidetic analysis and transcendental reduction. In the final section of the chapter, I explain how the resources of Cartesianism are employed to radicalize the project of Kantian philosophy. The stage is then set for a detailed analysis of the transcendental reduction in the following chapter.

THE MYSTERY OF COGNITION, SCEPTICISM AND HUSSERL'S TRANSCENDENTAL TURN

Husserlian phenomenology is best understood as being motivated by a desire to explain the 'enigma' of cognition: how does the human subject 'transcend' itself in order to know a world of entities that exists independently of it? How is it that we who are 'conscious' beings are able to experience the world and develop knowledge of it as it is in itself? And how is it that the truths we discover have 'objective validity'; that is, are true for everyone and not just for me? In short, how do we *achieve* objective knowledge? Such questions hold an intrinsic fascination for Husserl. But they receive added urgency when the spectre of scepticism is countenanced (Protagoras, Gorgias, Hume). The sceptic poses the same questions but as alternatives: 'Does the human subject "transcend" itself in order to know a world of entities that exists independently of it?'; 'Are we who are "conscious" beings able to experience the world and develop knowledge of it as it is in itself?'; 'Do the truths that I discover have objective validity?'; 'In short, do we *achieve* objective knowledge?'

According to the common-sense view, of course, such sceptical questions are not to be taken seriously. After all, surely our experience of those entities external to us can be confirmed by a scientific explanation of the causality of sensation. And is this not proof enough that we ourselves have genuine 'contact' with entities beyond us, and therefore knowledge of them? However, Husserl, like many philosophers, rejects what he sees as the futile attempt to answer scepticism in such a naturalistic manner. The natural sciences, he argues, *presuppose* that there is a trans-individual natural world, and therefore the answers they offer to the sceptic ultimately beg the question. In any case, what the natural sciences are able to describe is not a *cognitive* relation between subject and object (mind–world) but a *causal* relation between two entities in the world (person–thing) (*IP* 4). To be acted upon by something causally is not to have knowledge of it.

In his groundbreaking work, the *Logical Investigations* (1900/01), Husserl's curiosity about cognition found expression in a 'descriptive psychology'. Recognizing that the natural sciences lack the resources to explain the 'theoretical' nature of the work they themselves undertake, he attempted to account for the possibility of scientific theory by other means. Specifically, he investigated the 'acts of consciousness' through which knowledge is achieved and theories are developed. He studied, for example, the psychical phenomena of evidence, truth, entailment and reasoning – in short, all of the basic 'psychical acts' that make the construction of valid scientific theories possible. He sought to explain through observation and detailed description of such 'acts' how scientific theories can be built up out of deductions and inferences, and how these in turn are grounded in simple propositions derived from evident acts of perception. The results of these studies were the beginnings of what he called a 'pure logic', a theory *of* theory or theory *of* science (*Wissenschaftslehre*). (See *LI* I 235ff.)

However, in the year 1906 (or thereabouts) Husserl reached a point of crisis with respect to his philosophical position. Feeling the weight of sceptical arguments more intensely, he began to doubt whether his 'descriptive psychology' could truly serve as 'first philosophy'. Did it qualify as the radical and self-grounding science that philosophy aims to be? Did his 'pure logic' succeed in demonstrating its own possibility and redeeming all its presuppositions? As we have seen, Husserl's descriptive psychology was calculated to avoid the errors of 'psychologism', and yet he became convinced that even his more sophisticated 'phenomenological' philosophy was susceptible to sceptical attack. In particular, while Husserl had achieved a strict distinction between the psychical and the logical domains, he came to appreciate that he had not achieved the same clarity concerning the status of phenomenological philosophy itself *vis-à-vis* these domains: was phenomenology itself a form of psychological enquiry, a form of logical enquiry, or was it entirely independent of both? Despite various ambiguities, the overall impression given by the *Logical Investigations* was that phenomenology is a form of psychological enquiry. Not only did this leave a confused impression about the character of 'phenomenological' philosophy, it also left him open to the charge of psychologism, i.e. the charge that his philosophical analyses were not radically distinguished from the empirical science of psychology and thus that they did not possess the 'absolute' character of properly philosophical investigations. In other words, he had not won for phenomenological philosophy the same high (i.e. 'apodictic' and 'pure') status that he had attributed to logic.

The manuscripts from this period (roughly, from 1905 onward), as well as the lectures published as *The Idea of Phenomenology* (1907), show that Husserl's ruminations on these difficulties led him to a *'transcendental turn'*. What is needed, he concluded, is a more radical conception of philosophy, one that would circumvent the critical stance of the sceptic by achieving a radical purity from all naturalistic presuppositions. To do this would require a clear and absolute separation of phenomenology from psychology. After all, the subject matter of phenomenology is neither the psychological nor the logical but the *relation* between the two, and how could this relation be adequately investigated if it were forced onto either side of this divide? In short, then, Husserl came to hold that the study of empirical acts of thinking belongs to psychology; the study of the laws governing the logical interrelation of meanings belongs to logic; and, the study of the mysterious correlation between the two domains belongs to phenomenology. This is not to say, however, that phenomenology comes *after* psychology and logic in order to glue together two pre-existing disciplines. On the contrary, for Husserl, what phenomenology investigates is the original unity of consciousness from which psychology and logic *abstract* their respective subject matters. To investigate the 'mysterious correlation', therefore, is to trace logic and psychology to their source. Indeed, Husserl regards phenomenology as the science that explores the *a priori* grounds of all sciences, and to this extent it deserves the title '*philosophia prima*': first philosophy.

In the body of this chapter, then, I would like to discuss the difficult notion of 'transcendental' philosophy and to clarify what it means for Husserl's idea of phenomenology to have undergone a 'transcendental turn'.

KANT AND THE IDEA OF TRANSCENDENTAL PHILOSOPHY

The idea of 'transcendental philosophy' recalls the Scholastic notion of 'transcendentals' (*transcendentalia*). The 'transcendentals' are categories that applied to *any being whatsoever*; they 'transcend' all determinations of type and genus. In this sense, transcendental philosophy had to do with the most universal determinations of being, those that apply to the whole of existence. In current philosophical usage, however, the term 'transcendental' has two distinct and rather more specific senses. Both modern senses of the term stem from Kant's *Critique of Pure Reason*; however, they relate to rather different features of Kant's philosophy:

(1) The adjective 'transcendental' can refer to a *form of argumentation* which seeks to demonstrate that a sceptical position is meaningful only if it presupposes what it doubts; hence, if the sceptic's argument is meaningful then it is false, or else it is simply meaningless. Such an argument is found in Kant's refutation of idealism (*CPR* B 274ff.): we only have knowledge of inner (mental) states by first having knowledge of outer states; hence, any sceptical position

that restricts knowledge to knowledge of inner states alone also implies knowledge of outer states and is therefore self-refuting. The strategy of transcendental argumentation regained currency in the late 1950s and 1960s thanks to the work of P.F. Strawson. Consequently, this first sense of the term 'transcendental' is most frequently used by Anglo-American or 'analytic' philosophers.

(2) But 'transcendental' can also refer to the strategy of approaching philosophical questions by referring them to *structures of cognition*, i.e. to the (subjective) conditions that make knowledge possible. Indeed, Kant's stated definition of the term 'transcendental' correlates to this second sense: 'I entitle *transcendental* all knowledge which is occupied not so much with objects as with the mode of our knowledge of objects in so far as this mode of knowledge is to be possible *a priori*. A system of such concepts might be entitled transcendental philosophy.' (*CPR* A 11f., B 25). This conception of transcendental philosophy dovetails with what Kant famously describes in the preface to the second edition of the *Critique of Pure Reason* as his 'Copernican Revolution'.[2] Kant proposes there that the seemingly intractable disputes concerning the possibility of objective knowledge might be effectively resolved if the question is reframed: instead of assuming that our knowledge conforms to objects, what if we assume that objects conform to our knowledge of them (*CPR* B xvi)? This thought propelled Kant down a path that led him to consider the ways in which our experience of the world is determined in advance by the faculties belonging to the human subject ('the *mode* of our knowledge'). In the Copernican Revolution, therefore, the experience of objectivity is viewed as a function or *achievement* of the human subject, one that is made possible by various organizing structures or principles that the subject brings to the process of cognition. For instance, the possibility of objective knowledge concerning causal relations, Kant argues, is dependent upon the fact that experience conforms to the category of causality, a category the knowing subject brings to bear on all its experiences. Kant concludes that, because structures such as causality are brought to bear in all experiences of objects, we already possess a limited but essential knowledge of the world even before we experience anything in particular (i.e. in this example, that the world conforms to the law of causality). This kind of knowledge is '*a priori*' because it is not derived from experience but rather by reason alone, and it is 'synthetic' because it gives us substantive information about the world of

experience (in contrast to 'analytic' propositions which only explicate the meaning contained in concepts). Thus, the theme of Kant's
transcendental philosophy is the exploration of the 'sources and
limits' of 'synthetic *a priori*' knowledge. In short, then, transcendental philosophy – as opposed to transcendental argumentation – is
the attempt to elucidate the meaning and possibility of knowledge via
a consideration of *subjectivity* and the 'synthetic *a priori*' knowledge
that has its seat in subjectivity.

In this connection, also, one often reads about 'transcendental
subjectivity', by which is meant that aspect or essential structure of
subjectivity which makes experience of the world possible. The 'transcendental subject', in other words, is the human subject considered
as the 'I' who experiences the world and without whom the world
would not be knowable. It is usually contrasted with the 'empirical
subject', i.e. the human subject considered as an entity found in the
(natural) world. How these two notions of subjectivity are to be
reconciled is controversial (see Chapter 9). In any case, transcendental philosophy concerns itself exclusively with the study of transcendental subjectivity, i.e. with the essential structures of experience
– or, in a more Kantian turn of phrase, with the study of the conditions for the possibility of experience.

HUSSERL AND KANT

Husserl acknowledges the close relationship between his own 'transcendental phenomenology' and Kant's idea of transcendental
philosophy. For example, in reference to his post-turn conception of
phenomenology, he asserts:

> [T]here has emerged an obvious essential relationship between
> this phenomenology and the transcendental philosophy of Kant
> ... However essentially the phenomenological transcendental
> philosophy is distinguished from all historical philosophies,
> methodically and in the whole context of its basic results and
> theories, it is nonetheless out of inexorable inner necessity trans-
> cendental philosophy. (*KITP* 9, 13)

And, more concretely, Husserl acknowledges that he sees himself as
'in broad lines at one with Kant in the essential results of our work'
(*KITP* 13).

When Husserl describes his mature philosophy as 'transcendental', however, it is the second sense outlined above that is intended, not the first. His affinity is with the theories and methods of Kantian transcendental philosophy, not with its argument-strategies. More specifically, Husserl's debt to Kant is threefold: (1) his notion of 'intentional object' recalls the Kantian 'object of experience'; (2) his project of analysing the 'constitution' of objects has a precursor in the *Critique of Pure Reason*; and (3) his 'transcendental reduction' is anticipated by Kant's Copernican Revolution.

(1) The dominant theme in Kant's transcendental philosophy is the *synthesizing* function of subjectivity. Crudely put, according to Kant, sensibility and understanding together play the role of synthesizing the raw material of intuition (sensations) into objects of experience. Were it not for our receptive and spontaneous structuring, synthesizing and rationalizing of the world, we would not be able to experience the world in the way that we do. But thanks to our structuring and synthesizing powers, which operate already at the level of perception, we experience the world in such a way that we are subsequently able to make observations about it and draw inferences from it. In other words, we have a 'conditioned' experience of the world. This is not something to be lamented; on the contrary, a 'conditioned' experience is what *enables* us to get a handle on the world. For Kant, then, it is naïve and counterproductive to think that our experience of nature is simply 'receptive', as though perception were like peeking through a window and seeing the world as it is in itself. Rather, what we see is what *we* see.

In this way, Kant arrives at a fundamental distinction between the world as it is experienced and the world as it is in itself. This distinction implies at the same time that a correlative distinction is to be made between the conditioned object and the unconditioned object. Kant calls the former 'the object of experience' or 'phenomenon', and the latter 'the thing-in-itself' (*das Ding-an-sich*) or 'noumenon'.[3] The idea of 'objectivity' now has two distinct senses: (1) objectivity as 'the synthesis imposed upon the manifold of sensibility by apperception through the categories'[4] – empirical objectivity as intellectually structured representations; and (2) objectivity as the 'in-itself' – that which really exists beyond our sphere of representations, and which is posited by us without being strictly 'known'. How are these two senses of objectivity to be reconciled? This is a question that interpreters of Kant continue to debate. Broadly speaking, however, it is important to stress that, for Kant, the two concepts refer to one and the same entity: they refer to the selfsame thing *as* it is experienced and *as* it is in itself – or, equally, in so far as it is intuitable and in so far as it is not intuitable by finite human subjects. In other words, the phenomenal object is a genuine manifestation *of* the entity itself – but not an *exhaustive* manifestation of it; on the other hand, the thing-in-itself is the entity known only in the creative intuition of God (*intuitus originarius*) (*CPR* B 72). It makes sense, therefore, to speak of experience as the appearance *of* entities even though it does not reach to the things as they are in themselves.

As I discuss in a later chapter, for his part, Husserl rejects the positing of the thing-in-itself as existing beyond the domain of possible experience. Nevertheless, he finds Kant's notion of the phenomenal object indispensable. Indeed, the Kantian 'phenomenon' or 'object of experience' anticipates the Husserlian concept of the '*intentional object*': the object that is given to consciousness in the act of consciousness (as opposed to the transcendent real object). For Husserl, as for Kant, objects such as rhinoceroses, numbers and fairies are not themselves literally there *in* the stream of consciousness; nevertheless, they are there *for* consciousness, or – perhaps better – they are *given to* consciousness. As Husserl observes: 'What is objective can appear, can have a certain kind of givenness in appearance, even though it is at the same time neither genuinely (*reell*) within the cognitive phenomenon, nor does it exist in any other way as a *cogitatio*.' (*IP* 43). For example, both the mental processes of hearing and *also* that which is heard (e.g. the tone) are given in the sphere of conscious experience. (Phenomenology rests on one reflecting and 'seeing for oneself' whether such observations are so.) This illustrates that, even within the sphere of subjectivity alone, objects are given in – or better, *as the correlates of* – conscious acts. The perceived object is given in an act of perceiving, the judged object in an act of judging, the desired object in desiring, the hoped-for in hoping, etc. This 'correlatedness' of consciousness is what Husserl calls '*intentionality*'. Similarly, acts of consciousness are called '*intentional acts*', and their correlates, i.e. objects as they are given in conscious acts, are called '*intentional objects*'. Thus, without leaving the sphere of consciousness, we find two sides to the phenomena that make up immanent conscious life: the conscious act and the object given in it (the intentional object). Husserl describes these as 'two absolute data, the givenness of the appearing and the givenness of the object' (*IP* 9).

I deal with the concept of intentionality in detail in Chapter 5. The crucial point here, however, is this: quite apart from the world of actual beings, i.e. the totality of existent things, there is '*objectivity*' (*Gegenständlichkeit*): that is, objects as they stand over against (*gegen-stunden*) consciousness *for* consciousness itself. For Husserl, this already goes a long way towards explaining the marvellous ability of consciousness to transcend itself in order to experience the world. In 'having' an 'intentional object', the immanent sphere of subjectivity already, as it were, transcends itself. This objectivity-within-subjectivity is what makes it possible for consciousness to be consciousness *of* the world. It begins to appear to Husserl as though the 'mystery of cognition' might be fully explained once the 'intentional' structure of consciousness is properly understood. Thus, the central problem of phenomenological philosophy becomes to analyse the intentional acts of consciousness, i.e. to analyse the correlations of act and object that are found within the sphere of subjectivity itself.

(2) So then, how does the subjective process lead to the appearance of an object and to knowledge of it? Husserl discovered (albeit well after his own investigations were underway, it seems) that Kant's *Critique of Pure Reason* already contains some substantive contributions to this area of research. Kant's contributions in this direction, however, are obscured somewhat by his preoccupation with epistemology. For the most part, Kant speaks of objective knowledge as though it were made possible by the fact that we already pre-possess a set of synthetic *a priori* truths; these truths purportedly function as the epistemological bridge that allows us to have ordinary empirical knowledge about contingent states of affairs. In this respect, his philosophy is scarcely phenomenological in style. At other times, however, Kant's investigations take on a rather different character: he occasionally ventures into giving analyses of certain fundamental operations of mind (*Gemüt*) that bring about the appearing of an object. At these points, he moves from a discussion of concepts and judgements to a description of the unfolding of cognitive acts themselves.

In the 'Analytic of Principles', for instance, Kant provides what amounts to an analysis of how a physical thing is constituted in the course of a subjective experience of it. He describes the way in which an object appears as a unified object, synthesized under the categories of permanence, causality and reciprocity. Also, in the famous (and infamously difficult) chapter on 'The Schematism of the Pure Concepts of Understanding', we find a richly condensed analysis of the event in which any object whatsoever is brought together through 'the synthetic power of the imagination' (*CPR* B 233). And, in the section on 'The Postulates of Empirical Thought in General', the idea of existence is explicated by reference to perceptibility. At each of these points in the First Critique, Kant finds himself explicating certain universal experiences by considering the way in which they are constructed in the course of subjective experience.

Each of these analyses anticipates themes in Husserlian phenomenology. Generally speaking, Husserl considers the appearance of any object to be an *achievement* of the mental process (i.e. of the conscious act; 'the appearing'). In and through the flux of consciousness, an enduring object is somehow brought to givenness. For this reason, Husserl interprets objectivity as something *'constituted'* (*konstituiert*) by consciousness:

> *different types* of objectivity . . . are displayed in something like 'appearances'. These appearances neither are nor genuinely contain the objects themselves. Rather in their shifting and remarkable structure they create objects in a certain way for the ego, insofar as appearances of just such a sort and just such a construction belong to that in which what we call 'givenness' has been lying all along. (*IP* 56)

And again:

> . . . the things come to be *constituted* in these mental processes, although in reality they are not at all to be found in them. For 'things to be given' is for them to be *exhibited* (represented) as so and so in such phenomena. And this is not to say that the things once more exist in themselves and 'send their representatives into consciousness'. This sort of thing cannot occur to us within the sphere of phenomenological reduction [i.e. in the absolutely given sphere of subjectivity]. Instead, the things are and are given in appearance and in virtue of the appearance itself . . . Thus this marvellous correlation between the *phenomenon of cognition* and the *object of cognition* reveals itself everywhere. (*IP* 9–10)

Phenomenology, therefore, has the job of describing and analysing how objects come to be 'constituted' within the sphere of pure consciousness: 'And the task is just this: within the framework of pure evidence or self-givenness *to trace all forms of givenness and all correlations* and to conduct an elucidatory analysis' (*IP* 10). Transcendental phenomenology can thus be described as a 'science of "origins" ' – the origins of our experience *of* the world (*Ideas I* §56, 131).

In the light of this idea of 'constitution', it is not surprising that Husserl regards Kant as 'the first who, in gigantic sketches, embarked on the attempt, which must be made again and again until there is full success, of making nature . . . theoretically understandable, as a formation *constituting itself in the internality of transcendental subjectivity*' (*KITP* 52, my emphasis). Paul Ricoeur, apparently working without any knowledge of these remarks, also observes an 'implicit phenomenology behind the Kantian epistemology . . . that was frustrated in Kantianism and which remained there in an embryonic state, even though necessary to its general economy'.[5] Ricoeur goes on to argue that Husserl, for his part, merely frees this embryonic phenomenology and allows it to mature. This, it seems to me, is a useful way to understand Husserlian phenomenology. Husserl's research can be quite aptly characterized as a continuation of Kant's nascent investigations into the constitution of objectivity in the phenomenal sense. His phenomenology echoes and extends the Kantian conception of subjectivity as a *synthesizing* activity and investigates the specific kinds of synthetic acts that occur in perception, judgement, imagination, remembrance, inference, encountering other people, and so forth. What Husserl preserves from Kantianism, then, is not so much the interest in the putative 'knowledge' that the subject is said to possess in advance concerning nature – i.e. the epistemological element in Kant's philosophy – as the interest in the acts of objective experience that Kant began to thematize.

(3) The third aspect of the Kantian tradition to which Husserl is indebted is the Copernican Revolution itself, which shifts attention from the world of experience to the experiencing of that world, i.e. to the structures of experience that allow the world to be experienced in the way that it is. The Copernican Revolution is understood by Husserl as the demand for a 'change of attitude': a revaluation of the world as an *achievement* of subjectivity. For Husserl, the emergence of this methodological strategy, which he would retitle 'transcendental

reduction' or 'phenomenological reduction', is the basis of all rigorous philosophical research. However, according to Husserl, and contrary to what Kant himself claims, Kant was not the first to have developed this most fundamental component of transcendental philosophy. Descartes, Berkeley and even Hume had already managed to articulate the idea of transcendental philosophy and bring the transcendental path into view.[6] Nonetheless, Kant's greatness lay in the fact that he had taken the first steps down the path itself:[7]

> Kant's revolutionizing in philosophy is for us not merely a historical fact, but historically the first (and still imperfect) actualization of a turn . . . from the naïve positive stage of world-cognition to a world cognition through the ultimate self-consciousness of cognition – but not in empty generalities – concerning its active accomplishments, under the titles of reason, truth, science . . . With its appearance there was revealed to philosophy itself the methodological form essentially necessary to it as scientifically true philosophy, that is to say, the genuinely teleological idea which all further developments must strive to realize in consciously purposeful activity. (*KITP* 55, 54; see also *CES* 99)

There are already hints in the above quotation, however, that Husserl is not uncritical of Kant's actualization of the transcendental turn. He, like many others, seems to be suspicious of how Kant arrived at his detailed descriptions of transcendental subjectivity. How, for example, did he gain his apparent familiarity with the faculties and functions of the transcendental subject? The legitimacy of these descriptions is not clearly demonstrated. Husserl suspects that Kant had, in part at least, gathered up bits and pieces from the history of philosophy (especially from the Wolffian school) and cobbled them together in order to fill out his portrait of transcendental subjectivity (*KITP* 51).

REFORMING KANT'S TRANSCENDENTAL METHOD

Husserl attributes Kant's arbitrariness to an insufficiently clarified and naïve transcendental method. There are three points of vagueness in Kant's transcendental method that, according to Husserl, need to be rectified in order to put transcendental philosophy on the path of rigorous science: (1) Kant fails expressly to ground his theories in intuitive evidence; (2) his analysis of subjectivity does not remain at a purely 'eidetic' level; and (3) he neglects to secure the proper sense of transcendental subjectivity. These three points, incidentally, correlate to the three main components of Husserl's phenomenological method. (1) the principle of evidence (i.e. the so-called 'principle of all principles'); (2) eidetic analysis; and (3) transcendental reduction.

(1) Husserl willingly grants that 'Kant's thinking and research moves *de facto* in the framework of the phenomenological attitude' and that 'the force of these genuinely transcendental theories do in fact rest on pure intuitions which in their essential lines are drawn from original sources' (*KITP* 14). However, in his judgement, Kant had not clarified to himself what it is that truly legitimated his results: namely, that they were *intuited with evidence*. Consequently, he lacks a criterion or guide to prevent him from straying into spurious constructions. Kant's own critique of metaphysics has to be applied consistently – even to the detriment of his own system:

> Naturally, we must from the outset go beyond all of the, in the worst sense of the word, 'metaphysical' stock elements of the critique of reason (like the doctrine of the thing-in-itself, the doctrine of *intellectus archetypus*, the mythology of the transcendental apperception or of the 'consciousness in general', etc.), that oppose the phenomenological transcendentalism and with it the deepest sense and legitimacy of the Kantian position. (*KITP* 13; see also *CES* §30)

Only by investigating the acts of object-constitution firsthand, as it were, would it be possible to make good on the promising start Kant had made. Hence, Husserlian phenomenology attempts to go '*back to the things themselves*' by sticking solely to what can be demonstrated with evidence. And this means vigilantly avoiding all metaphysical speculation and positing of concepts and faculties. This demand for evidence is what Husserl calls 'the principle of phenomenology' or 'the principle of all principles'. He never fails to emphasize its centrality to phenomenology. Adherence to this principle would ensure that philosophical research attains the status of a 'rigorous science'. I discuss this fundamental principle of phenomenological research in Chapter 6.

(2) Husserl insists that 'constitutive' analysis, to be strictly

philosophical, must be 'eidetic' in character. That is, it must deal only with what belongs *essentially* to acts of consciousness. So, for instance, in investigating the essential structure of the act of perception, Husserlian phenomenology does not make any statements about whether such acts ever occur as matters of fact (in human beings or any other kind of being). It remains oriented strictly to the 'essence' or 'essential structure' of such acts. It therefore cannot proceed empirically; nor can it presuppose the existence of human subjects or limit the possible actualization of perception to human beings. As mentioned in Chapter 1, however, Husserl finds in Kant's philosophy a tendency to cloud this distinction by positing the existence of *human beings* as the precondition for empirical knowledge. Of course, Husserl does not deny that it is empirically true that a knowing subject must exist for an act of knowing to factually occur. But, in his view, philosophy is not concerned with *these* kinds of 'preconditions'. One must separate or 'purify' the *essential* conditions that philosophy investigates from the *empirical* conditions that the natural sciences investigate. As it happens, Husserl was not entirely sure that he had completely escaped this error himself in his *Logical Investigations*. In any case, after his so-called 'crisis' in the mid- 1900s, he came to see more clearly the importance of following a strictly 'eidetic' method. I discuss this method further in Chapter 7.

(3) Kant's third methodological deficiency is that, while the Copernican Revolution genuinely succeeds in bringing the domain of transcendental subjectivity into view, it does not do so with precision and clarity. To truly be faithful to Kant's insights, Husserl argues, requires that we strive 'to understand the ultimate sense of his revolution – and to understand him better than he himself, the trailblazer, but not the perfecter, was capable of doing' (*KITP* 55). Therefore, we must ask how the transcendental turn might be more rigorously formulated. In this way, the substantive advances of Kantian philosophy can be redeemed and purified. In the final section of this chapter, I explore this point further.

THE CARTESIAN LEGACY IN HUSSERL'S TRANSCENDENTALISM: PURIFIED SUBJECTIVITY, EVIDENCE AND FIRST PHILOSOPHY

For Husserl, the way towards a more precise understanding of transcendental subjectivity had already been discovered, in principle, by Descartes, whose '*ego cogito*' he regards as 'the source-point of all modern philosophy' and as containing the idea of transcendental philosophy 'in germinal form' (*KITP* 15, 53). I conclude this chapter, then, with a brief discussion of how Husserl completes his broadly Kantian 'transcendental turn' by adopting the Cartesian idea of absolute consciousness.

Husserl leaves no doubt that his phenomenological philosophy is intended to fulfil the traditional role of 'first philosophy'. 'Phenomenology', he writes:

> by virtue of its essence, must claim to be 'first' philosophy and to offer the means for carrying out every possible critique of reason; therefore it demands the most perfect freedom from presuppositions and, concerning itself, an absolute reflective insight. It is of its own essence to realize the most perfect clarity concerning its own essence and therefore also concerning the principles of its method. (*Ideas I* 148)

The idea of 'first philosophy' (*philosophia prima*) goes back to Aristotle, and it means to be the most fundamental of all sciences – the science that grounds all sciences, including itself. The empirical sciences may presuppose and utilize other sciences (e.g. logic and mathematics), but philosophy cannot defer to any other science – it must be self-grounding. This is what Husserl calls 'absolute reflective insight' in the above quotation. Whatever evidential grounds philosophy claims for itself, then, these must be 'absolutely ultimate'.

In his earlier critique of psychologism, Husserl had criticized the attempts to install psychology as 'first philosophy' by showing that psychology is incapable of furnishing absolutely ultimate grounds. But this still left the positive question unanswered: how is philosophy properly to reassert its birthright and be the first among the sciences?

It is Descartes who helps Husserl see that, in order to find an absolute foundation on which to build its autonomous science, philosophy must 'purify' itself of every assumption concerning the transcendent world, even those purportedly confirmed by scientific investigation. To this end, Descartes ingeniously uses sceptical doubt as a tool. He concedes to the sceptic that everything beyond the subjective sphere is doubtful. But even after the sceptic has done his worst, Descartes observes, a remnant is left over: the solipsistic ego who is thinking, the *ego cogito*. Though I can doubt the existence of all things, I cannot doubt that I am doubting; therefore, there is at least one thing that exists: the 'I' who thinks (*res cogitans*; the thinking thing). In this way, philosophy meets the demands of the sceptic and in the process wins for itself an 'absolute' ground from which to reconstruct the edifice of knowledge. From this humble and yet robust *residuum*, the philosopher must then redeem the possibility of knowledge and science. For Descartes himself, this means securing the existence of the world via the proof of the existence of God. In this way, the solipsistic starting-point could expand to reclaim all entities whose existence had been placed in question by the sceptic.

Husserl never tires of extolling Descartes' genius in embracing the sceptical path in order to overcome scepticism. And he accepts Descartes' conclusion that the first-person experience of the solipsistic ego is the irrefutable and secure starting-point for philosophy. Nothing is more certain, Husserl claims, than the events of conscious life: 'The *cogitationes* are the first absolute data' (*IP* 2). The sceptic has no foothold against the absolutely self-given contents of consciousness, for where there is no transcendence, i.e. no 'reaching beyond itself', there is no room for sceptical doubt. In short, then, the Cartesian idea of the *ego cogito* precisely marks out the domain of absolute evidence from which a science of consciousness might derive its results without fear of error. It yields an 'absolutely self-contained realm of purely subjective being' to be the proper object of transcendental philosophy (*KITP* 29). Herein lies the rigorous circumscription of the domain of subjectivity which was lacking in Kant's transcendental philosophy.

Nevertheless, Descartes had, in Husserl's view, misunderstood the value of his discovery of the *cogito*. Descartes believed that he had arrived at one certainty from which others would follow (i.e. *cogito, ergo sum*: I think, therefore I am). What he failed to recognize is that not only this singular proposition but also *the full experiential contents of consciousness* is given with 'clarity and distinctness' and is therefore admissible as absolutely (i.e. indubitably) given data. Thus, while Descartes believed that he had secured a singular verity, he had in fact discovered an infinite field of certitude: the stream of consciousness. 'Cognition itself is a name for a *manifold sphere of being* which can be given to us absolutely' (*IP* 23; my emphasis). For this reason, Husserl feels no need to follow Descartes' deductivist method of reconstituting the plenum of reality from the singular irrefutable truth concerning the ego's existence. Rather, the development of first philosophy (i.e. phenomenology) would be a descriptive, observational affair. It would roam throughout the vast field of absolutely given data found in conscious experience and develop a body of scientific knowledge based on these reflections. Specifically, phenomenology would seek to investigate how the achievement of consciousness (*Bewusstseinsleistung*), i.e. transcendence, might be explained from within the realm of immanence and without appeal to anything beyond it. But, by staying within the sphere of pure evidence (*Evidenz*) in this way, he would retain the immunity from scepticism enjoyed by the Cartesian *ego cogito*:

> Thus the field is now characterized. It is a field of absolute cognitions, within which the ego and the world and God and the mathematical manifolds and whatever else may be a scientifically objective matter are held in abeyance, cognitions which are, therefore, also not dependent on these matters, which are valid in their own right, whether we are sceptics with regard to the others or not. (*IP* 7)

Throughout the later part of his career, Husserl continually stressed the necessity of rigorously demarcating this 'field' of transcendental subjectivity in distinction to 'the psyche' (the object of psychology). For this purpose, he progressively developed and refined the method of 'transcendental reduction'. This aspect of Husserl's method is the topic of the following chapter. In any case, I have already said enough to clarify that Husserl's transcendental philosophy, though it resembles Kantian transcendentalism, has even grander ambitions. Kant had discovered in transcendental subjectivity the *a priori form* of the world; but Husserl locates in it *the origins of the world in its fullest sense*. Each and every transcendent object, therefore, would have to be analysed as an object 'constituted' in the sphere of pure subjectivity: inanimate objects, animate objects, persons, social entities, imaginary objects, ideas, numbers, the empirical self, and so forth. Not just the form of experience but also the matter of experience would have to be accounted for within the phenomenological attitude in terms of its essential structures. Manifestly, this would be an 'infinite task' occupying researchers for generations. Phenomenology was never intended to begin and end with one man.

NOTES

1 Whether Husserl had himself been directly influenced through the reading of Kant's work is another question. As far as we can tell, Husserl did not in fact seriously study Kant's writings until after his 'transcendental turn'. On this point, see Joseph J. Kockelmans, 'Husserl and Kant on the pure ego', in Frederick A. Elliston and Peter McCormick (eds), *Husserl: Expositions and Appraisals* (Notre Dame, IN: University of Notre Dame Press, 1977), pp. 269–85.

2 Despite the fact that the Copernican Revolution appears to be at the heart of what Kant himself calls 'transcendental' philosophy, in Anglo-American circles it is more common to refer to this same 'revolution' as Kant's 'idealism'. Perhaps this is motivated by a desire to avoid confusion with the first sense of the term 'transcendental'. Nevertheless, referring to Kant's transcendental philosophy as an 'idealism' brings confusions of its own – not least because 'idealism' today usually denotes the denial of the existence of the external world; but this is the very brand of 'idealism' for which Kant offers a refutation, as mentioned above.

3 The terminological equivalences asserted here are not, however, strictly correct. In particular, Kant's 'things-in-themselves' are only one sort of 'noumenal object'.

4 Paul Ricoeur, *Husserl: An Analysis of his Phenomenology*, trans. Edward G. Ballard and Lester E. Embree (Evanston, IL: Northwestern University Press, 1967), p. 189.

5 Ibid., p. 175.

6 A more extensive retelling of the prehistory of phenomenology by Husserl at the end of his career can be found in *CES* §§16–27.

7 Elsewhere, Husserl names David Hume as the first to discover and practise constitutional analysis, and hence as the first to implement the idea of transcendental philosophy (see, for example, *FTL* §100 and *CES* §24).

CHAPTER 4

THE TRANSCENDENTAL REDUCTION

Out of the 'crisis' that beset Husserl after the publication of his *Logical Investigations* emerged a conviction that phenomenology must follow the way of transcendental philosophy – the way of Descartes, Hume and Kant. Only in this way could it set itself on the path of rigorous science and reclaim the mantle of 'first philosophy'. To ensure that his researches truly attained the status of genuine science, Husserl expended much energy in clarifying the method of his transcendental phenomenology.[1] Its decisive element is the 'transcendental reduction'. Through it Husserl attempts to delineate precisely and isolate the field of transcendental subjectivity, which is to be the object of his primordial science. In this chapter, I discuss this most basic element of Husserl's phenomenological method.

It is worth stating that Husserl variously refers to this operation as 'the transcendental reduction', 'the transcendental *epoché*', 'the phenomenological reduction' and 'the phenomenological *epoché*'.[2] Strictly speaking, we are told, when the term 'transcendental' is used in preference to the term 'phenomenological', this implies a particular reference to the problematic of modern epistemology (Kant, Descartes); and '*epoché*' refers to the state reached by way of the 'reduction(s)' (*Ideas I* 66). However, Husserl does not consistently use the terms in this fashion, and, for all intents and purposes, the four terms are synonymous. Having said that, it is very important that the transcendental reduction be not confused with 'the eidetic reduction', which is the name Husserl sometimes gives to eidetic analysis (*Ideas I* xx, *et passim*). Likewise, the transcendental reduction is not to be confused with 'the philosophical *epoché*', which refers specifically to the 'bracketing' of all existing philosophical theories (*Ideas I* 33f.). All three reductions – transcendental, eidetic and philosophical – contribute to Husserl's phenomenological method. But, generally speaking, when reference is made to Husserl's 'reduction' or '*epoché*', it is the transcendental reduction that is being referred to, i.e. the reduction under discussion in this chapter.

WHAT IS THE TRANSCENDENTAL REDUCTION?

The transcendental reduction is the operation that *brings into view* the fundamental subject matter of Husserlian phenomenology – i.e. pure intentional consciousness – and *isolates* it as a sphere of being for investigation. Before Husserl developed the method of transcendental reduction, certain features of intentional consciousness had already announced themselves to philosophers and psychologists, but had done so in a relatively haphazard and *ad hoc* fashion. Until a clear methodological way of access to transcendental subjectivity is secured, Husserl thought, these initial insights into intentionality would remain partial and unscientific. Phenomenology cannot hope to attain the status of a fully-fledged science so long as it catches only occasional and fleeting glimpses of intentional being. The phenomenon of intentionality needs to be brought into captivity and studied under the microscope. 'Transcendental reduction' is Husserl's tool to do just that.

The transcendental reduction itself is comprised of a series of methodological preparations aimed at establishing the 'phenomenological attitude', which is the frame of reference that the phenomenologist must transpose him- or herself into in order to carry out phenomenological research. The methodological preparations that make up the 'reduction' play a dual role. On one hand, they train the phenomenologist to 'see' the subject matter of phenomenology; or, put the other way around, they bring that subject matter into vivid relief. This is not at all a straightforward matter because, for the most part, the subject matter of phenomenology lies hidden. As we shall see, this concealment is a consequence of the 'natural attitude' in which we ordinarily live. On the other hand, the reduction establishes the ontological sense of transcendental consciousness itself. Even before the substantive analysis of intentional consciousness is carried through, these preliminary methodological considerations determine the fundamental ontological characteristics of the field of transcendental being. I shall return to these ontological matters at the end of the chapter.

Over the duration of his mature philosophical career, Husserl offered several different (and perhaps contradictory) descriptions of just how one 'reduces' the natural attitude and 'proceeds' to the phenomenological attitude. It is described variously as the 'suspension of the natural attitude', the 'turning of regard (or gaze)', the 'exclusion of transcendencies', the 'bracketing of existence', the 'refraining from positing' and the 'placing of objects in inverted commas', to name but a few.[3] It is not possible to provide a comprehensive survey of all these metaphors here. In what follows, I endeavour to sketch out the main lines of thought that Husserl invokes to establish the reduction. The reconstruction here is based primarily on *Ideas I*, which was the first major exposition of the phenomenological reduction to appear. Husserl continued to modify and radicalize the method, but I reserve comment on these developments until the final chapters of this book.

THE NATURAL ATTITUDE AND THE NATURAL WORLD

Central to the idea of transcendental reduction is an account of 'the natural attitude' (*die natürliche Einstellung*). Now, by 'attitude' here is meant an overall manner of being or stance which *orients* our lived experience. In the 'arithmetical attitude', for example, we are oriented towards the world of arithmetical objects. But our normal waking experience takes place in 'the natural attitude'. This is our default 'attitude', the one to which we always revert. In it we are oriented towards the world of actually existing things – the real world – and our attention is given over to it. This is the pre-philosophical attitude that will be 'altered' in a specific way to bring about 'the phenomenological attitude'. Before discussing the phenomenological attitude, it is important that we understand the natural attitude that it modifies.

In *Ideas I* §§27–30, Husserl offers the following phenomenological description of how we experience the world in the natural attitude. Typically, I find myself attending to some particular entity (or entities) that stands immediately before me. But my attention may equally drift away from the entities immediately present at hand to other entities within my field of view, whose presence I may have been previously aware of, but only in a vague fashion. Alternatively, my attention may drift onto other entities that are not present in my visual field at all but which I am conscious of as being out there in the world. In the latter case, I say that I am just 'thinking about' them: 'I can let my attention wander away from the writing table which was just now seen and noticed, out through the unseen parts of the room which are behind my back, to the verandah, into the garden, to the children in the arbor, etc.' (*Ideas I* 51f.). What this illustrates is the way in which consciousness is able to roam throughout the world to all the things that it already understands to be there ('co-present') in the world.

In a distinctive way, then, the world of the natural attitude is that which 'is there' – *beginning* with my immediate surroundings but *extending* infinitely beyond my own direct experience. In this connection, Husserl speaks of a 'horizon' or 'constant halo around the field of actual perception' which extends to infinity, albeit with increasing indefiniteness and obscurity as we heed to objects further removed from our present experience. Likewise, every 'Now' is experienced as having a temporal 'horizon' receding into the past and into the future. And just as I am able to turn my regard to any point in space, so am I able to cast my mind to any point in time, albeit with more or less clarity about what might be found there and then. In short, in the natural attitude, 'I am conscious of a world endlessly spread out in space, endlessly becoming and having endlessly become in time' (*Ideas I* §27, 51).

The world of the natural attitude is the world that 'is there' – not just 'for me' but independently of me. It is that of which I am conscious as the 'wherein' of my existence and of every existent entity – a 'wherein' which extends beyond my immediate field of experience, which remains when I close my eyes, which was there before I existed, which will continue to be there after I am gone, and which I share with others. In short, the world has the sense of being the 'universal horizon' of existent being. Or, put the other way around, real (existent) being is that which *is there* in the world. The common element to all 'natural' experiences, then, is their relatedness to objects *as* objects *within the world*. Everything that I perceive or think of *as real* is thought of *as* belonging to a wider world of which I am always indirectly and vaguely conscious. In other words, essential to the natural attitude is the *positing* of the world itself (not just individual entities) as independent of my experience of it, as extending beyond my field of spatial experience, as extending beyond my temporal experience, and so forth. This 'positing' of the world, which sets up the 'universal horizon', is what Husserl calls 'the *general positing which characterizes the natural attitude*' (*Ideas I* 57).

Let me tease this out a little further. Husserl is suggesting that the natural attitude – that is, our everyday mode of being – is built around a tacit 'positing of' or 'belief in' the world *as* an independent horizon of being. It is this fundamental and unspoken 'positing' of the world as the domain of the real that makes it possible for the things we encounter in our waking experience to be experienced *as* things *in the world*. The significance of this observation for Husserl is hard to overestimate. It implies that, contrary to what we might have thought, the *reality* of the entities that we experience in the world is *not* something that the objects of experience simply impresses upon us. Rather, it is only because we tacitly 'place' the objects we experience 'in the world' that we experience them *as* entities in the world. What Husserl is describing here is something akin to the paranoiac who *believes* that people are out to kill him, and who *therefore*, given the slightest reason for suspicion, will see people on the street *as* killers. Likewise, it is only by *assuming* in advance, as it were, that our experience will be experience of objects existing independently of us (i.e. 'in the world') that we predispose ourselves to discover such objects in fact. Were it not for these expectations and assumptions, we would not immediately and habitually encounter the world of experience as the real world. Curiously, then, what makes natural experience the kind of thing that it is – namely, an experience of factual existence – has nothing to do with the actual entities that we experience in it and everything to do with the 'frame' around the experience, as it were.

But the 'frame' – that is, the world *qua* 'horizon' of real being – is something that is precisely *not* experienced. We never perceive space and time. We never perceive causality. We never perceive actuality. We only perceive individual spatial entities, temporal entities, caused entities, actual entities, etc. Nevertheless, we experience these characteristics ('categories') as basic features of the world. The structures of spatiality, temporality, causality, actuality, and so forth, are *constitutive* of natural experience without themselves being objects of natural experience. Thus, the 'general positing of the natural attitude' is unlike a regular 'belief' in the existence of this or that entity. So, for instance, if I posited the existence of white elephants, this would be empirically verifiable. But the 'positing' of the world *precedes* all empirical experience; it cannot be empirically confirmed or denied. However, as we shall see, this does not imply that the positing of the natural world is unquestionable.

THE LIMITS OF NATURALISM AND EMPIRICISM

Once the natural attitude has been analysed in this way, it is possible to show the intimate relationship between it and the natural sciences. The natural sciences, on Husserl's view, consist in nothing other than the development and rationalization of the world discovered in the 'natural attitude':

> To cognize 'the' world more comprehensively, more reliably, more perfectly in every respect than naïve experiential cognizance can, to solve all the problems of scientific cognition which offer themselves within the realm of the world, that is the aim of the *sciences belonging to the natural attitude*. (*Ideas I* §30, 57)

Thus, the 'positing' of the natural world is the foundation upon which natural science is built. Natural science *gives itself over* to the world of the natural attitude in an unspoken and unquestioning assumption that it exists independently and is an authority in all matters of fact. It puts to one side questions concerning the experience of the world and simply takes reality at face value. It asks about the objects that are given, not about the nature of their 'givenness'. It asks about real objects, not what it means to be a 'real object'. Hence, natural science naïvely or 'dogmatically' presupposes the natural attitude: 'Natural cognition begins with experience and remains *within* experience' (*Ideas I* 5).

For Husserl, this is entirely fitting and, moreover, practically necessary. On one hand, it is entirely fitting for the various sciences to accept at face value the 'evidence' available to them within the domains of enquiry to which they have been assigned. On the other hand, a division of labour must be respected, whereby the natural sciences undertake their researches dogmatically while philosophy takes up those dogmatic assumptions as matters to be scientifically investigated (*Ideas I* §26). The 'science of the dogmatic attitude' are thus contrasted with 'philosophy', which is to be a non-dogmatic or 'critical' science concerned with epistemological, ontological and sceptical problems. We must therefore look to philosophy for the clarification of natural experience, not the natural sciences. But, in that case, it falls to philosophy to extricate itself from the natural attitude and to take up a suitable vantage point from which to investigate natural experience as such.

Husserl constantly stresses the remoteness of the phenomenological attitude from our normal way of thinking and the difficulty involved in achieving this new attitude. In his view, the prevalence of natural science is partly to blame for this difficulty. Indeed, despite the legitimacy of the natural sciences, their very success has been responsible for retarding the emergence of transcendental philosophy. How so? The dominance of the natural sciences has led to the rise of a 'naturalistic constriction' or 'prejudice': the refusal to recognize any form of enquiry as legitimate that is not an empirical enquiry into real being (*Ideas I* §19).[4] Consequently, the world discovered through the natural attitude is regarded as coextensive with the possible objects of scientific research. (Psychologism is one possible outworking of this position.) But, when it is decided in advance that there are no matters for legitimate scientific research beyond those available to empirical investigation, the charter of philosophical research (which includes, for example, study of 'the natural attitude' and 'the world') is abrogated: 'In the natural attitude nothing else but the natural world is seen. As long as the possibility of the phenomenological attitude has not been recognized . . . the phenomenological world had to remain unknown, indeed, hardly even suspected' (*Ideas I* 66). As a result, the naturalistic prejudice has the effect of *entrenching* us in our natural attitude and *blinding* us to the need for a science of transcendental consciousness (it also brings about serious problems for the idea of 'pure' or 'eidetic' sciences such as mathematics and geometry, as we saw in Chapters 1 and 2). The challenge for transcendental philosophy, therefore, is double: it must overcome not only our everyday absorption in the natural attitude but also the naturalistic prejudice which reinforces that hegemony. In the following section, Husserl's strategy for achieving the phenomenological attitude is explained.

THE 'RADICAL ALTERATION' OF THE NATURAL ATTITUDE

'Instead of remaining in this [natural] attitude', Husserl writes, 'we propose to alter it radically' (*Ideas I* §31, 57). Phenomenology emerges as a science through this alteration. Already this signals that phenomenology will differ from the natural sciences by *not* being a science *belonging to the natural attitude.* It will have an entirely new 'attitude' or orientation. In this respect, it will be comparable to arithmetic which, as mentioned above, has its distinctive 'attitude' through which it discloses the domain of arithmetic objects. How then does Husserl propose to alter the natural attitude?

The natural attitude, as we have seen, consists in a comportment towards a totality of real being, a totality to which I belong. Certain entities may pass in or out of the world, entities may be shown to exist when they were thought not to, and vice versa – but this does not disturb the fundamental positing of the world of real being *as such.* Quite the contrary: judgements concerning 'existence' or 'non-existence' are simply judgements that something is or is not to be found in the natural world. The idea of the natural world is pre-supposed as the horizon within which something is or is not. Consequently, even the sceptic who denies the existence of all things implicitly *leaves intact* the 'general positing' of the world, which is retained as the horizon *within which* he finds himself unable to posit anything at all. Hence, the quest to alter the natural attitude finds no assistance from this variety of scepticism. If the general positing of the natural world is to be altered, then a more radical stance must be developed.

How then is the phenomenologist to escape the natural attitude? To answer this question, Husserl invokes a quite subtle analysis of the act of 'doubt'. He starts from some observations concerning ordinary acts of doubt and then applies these to the general positing of the natural attitude. What happens when we attempt to *doubt* the existence of some entity? The attempting to doubt does not yet involve a revision of our beliefs about the existence of the entity in question; we have not yet decided that the entity does not exist. Nevertheless, something is altered in the way we relate to the entity in question: the straightforward giving-oneself-over to the experience of the entity as something real is disrupted. That is to say, the *positing* which is characteristic of our natural experience is, in this case, *suspended* or *parenthesized.* The positing of the entity itself comes under review; and, even though it is not yet abandoned, it assumes a problematic hue.

The 'radical alteration' of the natural attitude that Husserl proposes is the result of universalizing this act of 'attempting to doubt'. What happens, he asks, when we attempt to doubt the world as a whole? It is important to stress that Husserl is not interested in whether the world is *in fact* doubtful (he does not think it is). What he is interested in is the *effect* of *attempting* to doubt. The very attempt to doubt changes the way we relate to the world, even as we hold on to it *as* the world. Without yet deciding anything to contradict our natural presumption about the world as 'being there' (*da-sein*), the positing of the world is 'parenthesized' – i.e. it is no longer allowed to be taken for granted. The general positing of the world is thus drawn out of its obscurity and is made problematic. In this way, without having yet decided anything to the contrary, the attempt to doubt '*effects a certain annulment of positing*' (*Ideas I* 58): 'the positing undergoes a modification: while it in itself remains what it is, *we, so to speak, "put it out of action", we "exclude it", we "parenthesize it"*. It is still there, like the parenthesized in the parentheses, like the excluded outside the context of inclusion' (*Ideas I* 59). The positing – and therefore natural experience itself – remains, but in limbo, as it were. This limbo state, in which the *positing* of the natural world *itself comes under scrutiny*, is what interests Husserl. What Husserl is interested in, therefore, is not so much 'the last man standing' once all dubitable objects have been excluded (contra Descartes), but rather the putting of all experience 'in parentheses' so that we comport ourselves to it in a new fashion:

> With regard to *any* positing we can quite freely exercise this peculiar εποχή, *a certain refraining from judgement which is compatible with the unshaken conviction of truth, even with the unshaken conviction of evident truth*. The positing is 'put out of action', parenthesized, converted into the modification, 'parenthesized positing'; judgement simpliciter is converted into the '*parenthesized judgement*'. (*Ideas I* 59f.)

What this 'parenthesizing' amounts to may not yet be entirely clear. Nonetheless, it should be apparent that whatever 'putting out of action' means, it cannot mean the bald negation of the general positing of the world. On the contrary, as I mentioned above, for Husserl the natural conception of the world is precisely the most essential presupposition of the natural sciences, whose legitimacy he never questions. Nevertheless, irrespective of the practical necessity – or, if you like, the transcendental validity (in the Kantian sense) – of the 'general positing which characterizes the natural attitude', this curious 'general positing' itself calls for philosophical investigation, and this is what Husserl is attempting. Husserl's aim, then, is not to deny the world but *to make it the object of philosophical reflection*:

> If I do that, as I can with complete freedom, then I am *not negating* this 'world' as though I were a sophist; I am *not doubting its factual being* as though I were a skeptic; rather I am exercising the 'phenomenological' εποχή which also *completely shuts me off from any judgment about spatiotemporal factual being*. (*Ideas I* 61)

The phenomenological *epoché* entails *abstaining* from all judgements that rely upon the general positing of the world. In other words, one enters into the field of philosophical enquiry by staying aloof from all positive affirmations of the real world – including even the tacit affirmations that are interwoven in ordinary perception. If the phenomenologist refuses to affirm the existence of the world, then, this is not because it is in doubt but because reticence on such matters is what makes philosophical reflection possible. Making 'existential' judgements falls outside the domain of properly *philosophical* enquiry. Likewise, when Husserl goes on to say that the world has its 'origin' in consciousness, he cannot be taken to mean that consciousness 'creates' the world or 'brings it into existence'.[5] Once again, this would be to make a judgement regarding the existence of the real world; it would amount to the (bizarre) hypothesis that the world of real entities exists because I think it into being. Such a crude idealism simply *contradicts* the theories of natural science rather than *suspending* them. The meaning and effect of this suspension will be further clarified below.

FROM PSYCHOLOGICAL TO TRANSCENDENTAL CONSCIOUSNESS

In *Ideas I*, having introduced the idea of 'the phenomenological *epoché*' (§32), Husserl goes on to enact the *epoché* in two phases: the first phase fails fully to throw off the natural attitude, and the second successfully breaks free from it.[6] We may call these the psychological (§§34–46) and the (properly) transcendental reductions (§§47–62).

The connection between these reductions and the 'radical alteration' of the natural attitude as it is described above is not immediately clear. When the phenomenological *epoché* is introduced,

Husserl focuses on altering our view of the *world*. In the enactment of the *epoché*, however, he focuses instead on altering our view of *consciousness*. Nevertheless, these two 'paths' to the phenomenological attitude can be viewed as commensurate and mutually interpreting. For their part, the more 'psychologically' oriented chapters, which we shall consider presently, are particularly important for clarifying the difference between the empirical ego (of psychology) and transcendental ego (of phenomenology).

In the first ('psychological') phase of enactment, the idea of a 'reduction to consciousness' is taken to mean the exclusion of anything 'outside of me', leaving only mental acts ('in me'). The result is the isolation of the mind and mental phenomena, i.e. the subject matter of *psychology*. Thus, psychology rests upon a 'reduction' of sorts: it brackets out all aspects of real being except psychical being, i.e. that which is 'immanent' to the conscious experience of human beings. All that remains is the psyche and its psychical acts. And, according to Husserl, this domain of being can quite legitimately be made the subject of either an empirical science (called 'empirical psychology'), or an 'eidetic' science (called 'pure psychology').[7] The former science investigates the empirical laws that govern the psyche, whereas the latter develops a 'regional ontology' of psychical being – that is, it determines the stock of basic concepts relevant to the empirical description of 'any psychical phenomenon whatsoever', and determines the eidetic laws relating those basic concepts to one another. (Husserl's own earlier 'descriptive psychology' had been a psychology of the 'eidetic' variety, in the tradition of Locke, Stumpf and Brentano.)

Husserl emphasizes, however, that mental phenomena considered in this fashion continue to be understood as 'real worldly occurrences' (*Ideas I* 64); the psychologist investigates the psyche as a natural phenomenon. To this extent, the psyche is an entity discovered *in the natural attitude*, and psychology is a science of the natural attitude and not yet of the phenomenological attitude. Psychology does not envisage the more radical possibility of a suspension of the natural attitude as such.

Husserl contends, nonetheless, that a further 'reduction' is possible which would be more radical than the 'psychological reduction'.[8] This second ('transcendental') phase of reduction is inaugurated when psychology discovers that its basic distinction between the *outer* object (physical) and the *inner* object (psychical/mental) breaks down. To illustrate this, Husserl uses a rather complex series of arguments (§§38–46) which brings out and contrasts two conceptions of 'immanence'. The first conception of 'immanence' (the sense employed by the psychological reduction) is built upon the spatial metaphor of being 'in me' (i.e. a 'really inherent component of consciousness') rather than 'outside me'. Husserl argues that this first distinction between immanence and transcendence is conceptually dependent upon the natural attitude and remains within the natural attitude: 'the psyche' is a *part* or *moment* of real human being conceived as a 'psychophysical' whole (*Ideas I* §53, 124). Hence, even once it is 'reduced', the psyche remains implicitly understood *as* an abstract part of the real world. Herein lies the reason why psychology remains caught in the natural attitude. By contrast, the second, more sophisticated, conception of 'immanence' bears within it no logical connection to the real world at all. Its idea of 'immanence' turns upon a distinction between two modes of *evidence* or *'given-ness'*. Specifically, it opposes that which is given 'adequately' and indefeasibly to that which is given 'inadequately' and defeasibly. Whatever is given without leaving room for doubt or revision is 'immanent'; everything else is 'transcendent'.

Applying the evidential test rather than the interiority test, Husserl finds a *new way* of marking out the sphere of consciousness. The sphere of consciousness discovered by this new method consists in the 'sphere of pure evidence' (*IP* 7). This leaves nothing more and nothing less than *the stream of conscious experience itself* as its *residuum*. The real world is left behind – including even the particular human being whose stream of consciousness this may be. As such, Husserl finds that it is possible to disregard the psyche ('man's mental activity as *his* activity is no absolute datum') and still affirm an independent sphere of given being ('the truly absolute datum is the *pure phenomenon*') (*IP* 5). Or, to make the same point another way: 'Certainly a consciousness without an animated organism and, paradoxically as it sounds, also without a psyche, a consciousness which is not personal, is imaginable' (*Ideas I* §54, 127). When even the connection to a living person is excluded from the conception of consciousness, the 'psyche' gives way to 'transcendental subjectivity': a stream of consciousness which is no longer an abstract part of the world – indeed, which is no part of the world at all. All traces of naturalism are thus cast off.

THE ANNIHILATION OF THE WORLD

To focus this reduction, Husserl introduces a thought experiment concerning 'the annihilation of the world':

> In our experiencing it is conceivable that there might be a host of irreconcilable conflicts not just for us but in themselves, that experience might suddenly show itself to be refractory to the demand that it carry on its positings of physical things harmoniously, that its context might lose its fixed regular organizations of adumbrations, apprehensions, and appearances – in short, that there might no longer be any world. (*Ideas I* §49, 109)

That is, it is conceivable that our experience may dissolve into an incoherent mess which no longer had the character of being experience *of* a regular world of nature. As a thought experiment, this hypothesis demonstrates nothing about matters of fact. It does, however, lead to certain philosophical or 'in principle' conclusions about the essential nature of 'world', and, more importantly, about the essential nature of consciousness:

> [I]t then becomes evident that *while the being of consciousness, of any stream of mental processes whatever, would indeed be necessarily modified by the annihilation of the world of physical things its own existence would not be touched* ... Consequently *no real being*, no being which is presented and legitimated in consciousness by appearances, *is necessary to the being of consciousness itself* (in the broadest sense, the stream of mental processes). (*Ideas I* §49, 110)

Thus, it is logically possible, Husserl argues, to consider the totality of experience *apart from* the positing of any factual being, including human beings. Unlike 'the psychical' and 'the physical' under the psychological reduction, 'transcendental consciousness' and 'real world' exhibit a *radical separability*. This observation establishes what Husserl calls the 'essential detachableness of the whole natural world from the domain of consciousness' (*Ideas I* §46, 104).

At this juncture, psychology discovers that the very phenomena it initially considered as phenomena belonging in a certain sense *to the world* – i.e. *qua* psychical phenomena – can equally be examined without any reference to the world. When this realization is made, psychology's own subject matter explodes the category of 'real being' and shows itself to constitute a novel domain of being, one which *survives* the suspension of belief in the natural world. Suddenly before us is a '*new region of being never before delimited in its own peculiarity* – a region which, like any other genuine region, is a region of *individual* being' (*Ideas I* 63f.). This new region demands its own non-natural (i.e. transcendental) mode of investigation. Accordingly, psychology flips over of its own accord into transcendental phenomenology:

> [Consciousness] *has, in itself, a being of its own which in its own absolute essence, is not touched by the phenomenological exclusion.* It therefore remains as the '*phenomenological residuum*', as a region of being which is of essential necessity quite unique and which can indeed become the field of a science of a novel kind: phenomenology. (*Ideas I* 65f.)

Let me attempt to explain this argument by using an illustration. The thought of 'the annihilation of the world' works like the flicker on a TV screen. To enter into the illusion of watching TV we must *forget* that we are watching *a* TV, i.e. a box with a series of rapidly changing coloured dots and sounds. Normally, we accomplish this act of 'forgetting' so habitually that we don't even notice that we do it. But when the TV starts to flicker, the happy illusion is shattered and the technology itself (the 'wizardry') becomes all too conspicuous. The portal into another world reverts once again to being a simple box filled with a few circuits and a glass tube. In a similar fashion, for Husserl, the mere suggestion of the possibility that the world may be an illusion introduces a flicker. It suddenly *makes conspicuous* the fact that the real world has *appeared* to us all along *as* the real world; and now this appearing itself comes into relief. The thought experiment unsettles our natural attitude just enough to disrupt our immersion in daily life and to bring daily life itself to our attention. When that fleeting moment of perspective is achieved, Husserl has succeeded in showing us the world in a new way: namely, as a correlate of conscious experience. The mere thought of the annihilation of the world thus establishes the critical or ironic distance between the individual and the world necessary for the world as such to be made into a theme for investigation. The 'radical alteration' of the natural attitude that transcendental philosophy requires is thus effected, and a new attitude is born, the 'phenomeno-logical attitude'. It adds to our repertoire a new 'attitude' alongside the 'natural' and 'natural scientific' attitudes, a new 'way of looking' which enables us to see things we had previously overlooked. It is not without justification then that the French phenomenologist Maurice Merleau-Ponty writes: 'True philosophy consists in relearning to look at the world.'[9]

TRANSCENDENTAL SUBJECTIVITY AS 'ABSOLUTE SUBSTANCE'

The consequences of Husserl's transcendental reduction are as radical as they are subtle. As Timothy Stapleton notes, the transcendental reduction 'inverts the whole–part relationship, so that after its performance, the ultimate horizon is subjectivity or consciousness'.[10] That is to say, consciousness is no longer viewed as a part of a worldly 'whole'; instead, it is viewed as a 'whole' of which the world is a part. Consciousness is now *everything*, not just 'a little *tag-end of the world*' (*CM* §10, 24); and the world is now something essentially related, i.e. 'relative', to consciousness. In short, after the transcendental reduction, what remains is *absolute* consciousness and the *relative* being of the world (*Ideas I* §§54–55). 'From this point on,' notes Ricoeur, 'nature is no longer just dubitable, it is also contingent and relative; consciousness is no longer merely indubitable but also necessary and absolute.'[11]

Husserl comments on the 'veritable abyss' that 'yawns between consciousness and reality' (*Ideas I* 111) and the 'fundamentally essential difference between *being as mental process* [*Erlebnis*] *and being as a thing*' (*Ideas I* 89; translation modified). In this regard, his account recalls Descartes' fundamental ontological distinction between 'extended being' (*res extensa*) and 'thinking being' (*res cogitans*). However, rather than regarding the 'essential difference' as a difference between two kinds of substance, as Descartes had, Husserl takes it to be a difference between *absolute* and *relative being* – or, to say the same differently, between *substance* and a *moment* of that substance. The 'absolute gulf' which separates the two is the gulf between that which is ontologically *independent* and that which is ontologically *dependent*. This is the lesson of the hypothetical 'annihilation of the world'. All objectivity, therefore, has its 'origin' in transcendental subjectivity. And with this we have reached

Husserl's ultimate determination of the being of consciousness: no longer considered as *object*, but as *subject* and as *absolute substance* – in the sense that 'it needs nothing in order to be' (*nulla re indiget ad existendum*).[12]

Thus, while both psychology and phenomenology take consciousness as their object, their respective ontological conceptions of it differ at the most fundamental level. Psychology views consciousness as one real being among others, whereas phenomenology views it as the primal region – the region out of which all others 'originate'. The psychologist views the ego as a component of the real world; the phenomenologist views the ego as the 'origin' of the world (although not in the existential sense, as discussed above). The phenomenologist no longer posits acts of consciousness as matters of fact belonging to the world but considers them in utter indifference to the natural world as absolutely evident being. Phenomenology thus treats the *same* subject matter as psychology, but within a radically altered frame of reference.

Taking consciousness in radical separation from the natural world and in accordance with the phenomenological 'frame of reference' does not leave phenomenology trapped in a solipsistic sphere. On the contrary, as I reflect on it, I find that within this 'solipsistic' sphere is included the *appearance* of the whole 'external' (natural) world. Absolute consciousness is not an enclosed, solipsistic sphere, but 'is in a sense all things'.[13] The world as it is experienced in the stream of consciousness is not just a meaningless flow of shapes, colours and sounds. It is a flowing stream of *objects* coming in and out of view: now a person . . . now the words on a page . . . now a watch. . . now a thought. Even after I 'exclude' the world as a reality beyond my sphere of experience, I still strangely find that I have the world of objects and a relation to them. That is, transcendental subjectivity 'includes within it' people, things, ideas, etc. The existent entities are not themselves contained in consciousness, and yet the *experience* of them *as* existing things remains. So, to the sphere of pure evidence, which is the residue after the 'transcendental reduction', belongs the *whole world* – only now I refrain from judging whether it exists and consider it solely as it is experienced.

This idea of consciousness as a vast and inexhaustible field of givenness goes well beyond Descartes' own conception of the ego. Descartes did not see that the solipsistic ego already 'possesses', in a curious fashion, the whole world. It is not simply an *ego cogito* but an *ego-cogito-cogitata* (*CM* §21, cf. §14). Husserl's idea of subjectivity thus comes closer to the Leibnizian 'monad', which, though 'windowless', contains or reflects within it the entire universe. Indeed, this term is explicitly adopted by Husserl in his *Cartesian Meditations* – although not without reservations (see *CM* §33, §60 and, especially, §62). In any case, the subject's 'possession' of the world is precisely what becomes *thematic* thanks to the transcendental reduction.

The consciousness experience of the world which remains after the transcendental reduction is given the title 'intentionality'. The 'intentional' structure of transcendental consciousness is the primary object of interest for Husserlian phenomenology. Phenomenology is not about bridging the gap from these objects-as-experienced to the real world of objects beyond my experience. (This would assume the existence of a world beyond transcendental subjectivity, which is the very thing phenomenology disallows itself for the sake of opening up its new domain of scientific research.) Rather, phenomenology is about staying with the conscious experience of the world itself, tarrying awhile, observing it in all its variety and in all of its dimensions, and then describing it according to its structures. In short then, the transcendental reduction leads directly to the central topic of phenomenological research: intentionality.

NOTES

1 Indeed, methodological expositions and clarifications are a recurrent feature of all his published works after the *Logical Investigations*. The result is an apparently endless series of 'introductions' to phenomenology, which gives the impression that Husserl had become paralysed and unable to proceed to the next step of actual concrete research. In fact, this was not the case. The voluminous unpublished manuscripts in the Husserl Archives testify to the ceaseless labour Husserl devoted to his concrete phenomenological investigations throughout this post-turn period (from roughly 1906). These studies are still today being sorted and selectively published. Methodological clarifications and substantive research, it seems, could happily develop side by side.

2 The Greek term '*epoché*' simply means 'suspension' or 'cessation'. For an illuminating discussion of the origins of the notion in ancient scepticism, see Klaus Held, 'The controversy concerning truth: Towards a prehistory of phenomenology', in *Husserl Studies* 17.1 (2000): 35–48.

3 In addition to this diverse set of metaphors, Husserl developed at least three distinct ways of introducing the transcendental reduction at a heuristic level. Iso Kern, for example, has identified what he calls the

'Cartesian', the 'Kantian (or ontological)' and the 'psychological' ways to the transcendental phenomenological reduction. See Iso Kern, 'The three ways to the transcendental phenomenological reduction in the Philosophy of Edmund Husserl', in Frederick A. Elliston and Peter McCormick (eds), *Husserl: Expositions and Appraisals* (South Bend, IN: University of Notre Dame Press, 1977), pp. 126–49.

4 See also Edmund Husserl, 'Philosophy as rigorous science', in *Phenomenology and the Crisis of Philosophy*, trans. Quentin Lauer (New York: Harper & Row, 1965), pp. 79ff.

5 It is sometimes said that Husserl's conception of 'constitution' tended towards this stronger sense of 'object-creation' as his thought developed into the 1920s. For example, Alfred Schütz writes:

> But unobtrusively, and almost unaware, it seems to me, the idea of constitution has changed from a clarification of the sense of being, into the foundation of the structure of being; it has changed from explication into creation (*Kreation*). The disclosure of conscious life becomes a substitute for something of which phenomenology in principle is incapable, viz., for establishing an ontology on the basis of the processes of subjective life. (*Collected Papers*, Vol. 3 [The Hague: Martinus Nijhoff, 1970], pp. 83–4)

However, it is debatable whether such a shift actually occurred in Husserl's later writings. Indeed, it seems to me entirely possible to read Husserl as continuing to use the term 'constitution' in almost exactly the same sense given to it in *Ideas I*. His ideas about how constitution *occurs* did most certainly change, but that is another matter (see Chapters 10 and 11).

6 Commentators disagree over which sections of *Ideas I* should be regarded as comprising the transcendental reduction. Most agree that the sections explicitly entitled 'reductions' (§§56–62) do not exhaust the matter. Ricoeur, for instance, argues (following Eugen Fink) that the whole of *Ideas I* should be read as the description of the reductive path to transcendental subjectivity, and he even questions whether we have fully completed the series even by Parts 3 and 4 of the text. See Paul Ricoeur, 'An introduction to Husserl's *Ideas I*', in *Husserl: An Analysis of his Phenomenology* (Evanston, IL: Northwestern University Press, 1967), pp. 13–34. The article on which Ricoeur bases his argument is Eugen Fink, 'Die phänomenologische Philosophie Edmund Husserls in der gegenwärtigen Kritik,' *Kantstudien*, 38 (1933): 319–83.

7 On the distinction between empirical and eidetic science, see Chapter 2.

8 Husserl does not use the phrase 'psychological reduction' as such in *Ideas I*, although he does talk of a 'psychological attitude' (*Ideas I* 126). The phrase does, however, appear in Husserl's *Encyclopaedia Britannica* article (Draft E) (see *Psychological and Transcendental Phenomenology and the Confrontation with Heidegger (1927–1931)*, ed. and trans. Thomas Sheehan and Richard E. Palmer [Dordrecht: Kluwer, 1997], p. 188).

9 Maurice Merleau-Ponty, *Phenomenology of Perception*, trans. Colin Smith (New York and London: Routledge, 2002), p. xxiii.

10 Timothy J. Stapleton, *Husserl and Heidegger: The Question of a Phenomenological Beginning* (Albany, NY: State University of New York Press, 1983), p. 80.

11 Paul Ricoeur, *Husserl: An Analysis of his Phenomenology* (Evanston, IL: Northwestern University Press, 1967), p. 17.

12 Cf. *Ideas I* §49, 110:

> *Immanental being is therefore indubitably absolute being in the sense that by essential necessity immanental being nulla 're' indiget ad existendum. / In contradistinction, the world of transcendent 'res' is entirely referred to consciousness and, more particularly, not to some logically conceived consciousness but to actual consciousness.*

13 As Heidegger was fond of reminding his readers, this is in fact an ancient insight. Parmenides, for instance, had asserted that 'being and thinking are the same' and Aristotle had written that 'the soul is in a way all existing things' (*De Anima*, G 8, 431 b 21). See, for example, Heidegger's draft of the *Encyclopaedia Britannica* article on 'Phenomenology', in Husserl, *Psychological and Transcendental Phenomenology*, pp. 107–16.

PART 2

PHENOMENOLOGICAL TOPICS

CHAPTER 5

THE STRUCTURE OF INTENTIONALITY

THE IDEA OF INTENTIONALITY

Having isolated and attended to the field of 'pure consciousness' or 'transcendental subjectivity' by the transcendental reduction, what does Husserl discover there? He finds consciousness *directed beyond itself* to a vast array of objects. That is, within the field of 'pure consciousness', he finds both *acts of consciousness* and *objects of those acts* – e.g. acts of perceiving and, along with them, things perceived, acts of remembering and things remembered, acts of meaning and things meant, and so forth. This pattern is, for Husserl, the principle characteristic of conscious experiences (*Erlebnisse*).[1] It is given the name 'intentionality'. To say that consciousness is 'intentional', then, means that consciousness is always 'directed' toward an object: consciousness is always consciousness *of something*.[2]

The analysis of consciousness as 'intentional' is something for which Husserl is famous. But he did not discover this phenomenon. The term itself stems from scholastic philosophy. But Husserl's use of the term was inspired by his teacher, Franz Brentano, who had developed a model of the psyche based on the concept of 'intentionality' in the late nineteenth century. Psychology, Brentano argued, cannot orient itself by the natural sciences, but needs to come to grips with the unique character of its object of study, and it is the doctrine of 'intentionality' that provides the key: the distinctive feature of psychical phenomena, in contradistinction to physical phenomena, is an inherent *having-of* or a *directedness-towards* an object.

Husserl recognized Brentano's advances but saw several pernicious equivocations in Brentano's doctrine of intentionality and set about revising them.[3] In the course of developing this revision, he formulated a more fine-grained and enduring analysis of the phenomenon of intentionality and its essential structures. For Brentano, there were three basic kinds of intentional (psychical) acts: presentations, judgements and desires. But Husserl refused to impose an artificial limit on the number of classes of intentional act. Also, as I shall discuss more fully below, he attempted to give a clearer account of what Brentano imprecisely called the 'mental inexistence' of the intentional object. So, while Brentano reinvigorated interest in the doctrine of intentionality, it was Husserl who for the first time elucidated the nature of intentionality by achieving a clear and distinct apprehension of the phenomenon and thematizing it in a coherent fashion.[4]

THE CRITIQUE OF REPRESENTATIONALISM

To start from a view of consciousness as 'intentional' is to reject the widely held view that consciousness is something like a self-enclosed room or box. On the latter interpretation, the 'mind' is thought of in spatial terms: as confined to the space of the brain, as it were. The problem for this view is how to account for the mind's experience of things 'outside' its sphere. Countless solutions have been offered to this problem. I shall mention just two basic and common ones.

(1) The common-sense realist holds that we are conscious of the external world because the world simply streams into the mind via the senses. But this view runs aground once it is recognized that the mind is not literally a physical space (like a camera) into which sense-data can 'stream' – the mind is not the eyeball or the eardrum. Moreover, much of our mental life is occupied with imagined objects and ideal objects, and surely these are not 'streaming in' via the senses?

(2) A more sophisticated version of the box-interpretation of consciousness is offered by the 'representationalist' theory. There are several variations on the representationalist theory, but essentially this view consists in the idea that sense-data allow the mind to *reconstruct* a representation of the outside world. Consciousness, then, 'experiences' the world indirectly via these representations. But, on closer inspection, this more sophisticated form of realism also seems implausible. Most seriously, it seems to be incapable of accounting for truth: how can I know that my representations are *true* representations of the world if I never have access to the things

themselves against which to measure them? If the representationalist is right, then we live exclusively in a world of 'copies' or 'imitations' without ever seeing the 'originals'. Thus, we are deluded in thinking that we experience the world, and in fact possess no criteria for judging truth.

Husserl provides further conceptual grounds for rejecting the representationalist's position. The idea of a 'representation' works perfectly well to characterize the relationship, say, between a portrait and the person portrayed, but only because we can experience *both* objects and establish the relation of 'representation' between them. The very idea of 'representation' breaks down, however, when it is applied to the objects of experience because it can never be properly established as a relation. That which is purportedly represented can never be pointed out as such. And, if I can point out the represented object, then the represented object must also be a representation standing in for something else, and so forth, *ad infinitum*. In other words, the representationalist theory leads to an infinite regress (*LI* II 593f.).

Thus Husserl rejects both the common-sense realist view and the representationalist view. A conscious experience, he argues, is neither a real or causal relationship between things in the world, nor a subjective representation of the world. Rather, an act of consciousness is something in which a genuinely *transcendent object* is itself presented or 'given'. For instance, a perception is a consciousness of something in the world and not merely of a representation of something in the world. Simply stated, consciousness reaches to the things themselves and not just to poor shadows of reality.

Furthermore, Husserl claims that his rejection of the box-interpretation of consciousness is not just one more theory among others: anyone who reflects upon their own conscious experience will see that there is nothing 'room-like' about it:

> But experience is not an opening through which a world, existing prior to all experience, shines into a room of consciousness; it is not a mere taking of something alien to consciousness into consciousness . . . Experience is the performance in which for me, the experiencer, experienced being 'is there', and is there *as what* it is, with the whole content and the mode of being that experience itself, by the performance going on in its intentionality, attributes to it. (*FTL* 232–3)

'Intentionality' names this mind-transcending character of consciousness which means that the world 'is there' for me *directly*. The idea of intentionality thus provides a way out to those philosophers of mind who have tied themselves up in knots trying to solve difficulties arising from the presuppositions of their own theories. The phenomenon of intentionality, which was there all along for anyone to observe, cuts the knot.

What makes this analysis of consciousness particularly attractive is that it affirms the common-sense idea that consciousness genuinely reaches outside itself to the transcendent world of things, while at the same time insisting that this transcendence is a 'performance' of consciousness (although not one that we are necessarily cognizant of or wilfully bring about). Consciousness is a genuine encounter with the world, but an encounter that must be 'achieved' through the constitution of its object. The apparently passive 'receptivity' of conscious experience is made possible, on this analysis, by the synthesizing activity of consciousness. Thus, the intuitively plausible aspect of the common-sense realist's position is recouped within a 'critical' (i.e. Kantian) framework.[5]

This critique of representationalism was one of the first fruits of phenomenological analysis. By simply going 'back to the things themselves', a longstanding philosophical dispute had apparently been overcome. Such early breakthroughs lent much weight to Husserl's claims that all philosophical questions could be rigorously and authoritatively investigated by going 'back to the things themselves'. But to show that this is not just another piece of 'word magic', we must examine in more detail Husserl's analysis of 'intentionality'. How is consciousness intentional? What goes to make up an 'intentional' relation to an object? What does it mean to 'reach' to the world? In what sense does consciousness 'have' its objects?

INTENTIONALITY IN THE *LOGICAL INVESTIGATIONS*

The 'intentional act' or 'lived experience' (*Erlebnis*) must, for Husserl, be understood as a unified whole. Nevertheless, it is possible to abstract various distinct aspects or components that make up its structure. Husserl's terminology for these components shifts over the period between the publication of the *Logical Investigations* (1900/01) and *Ideas I* (1913). The bulk of this book is expressed in the terminology presented in the latter text. But it may be worthwhile to set out briefly the terminology of the early text.

The same object can be 'intended' in many different acts. For instance, one can imagine the Eiffel Tower, delight in the Eiffel Tower, remember it, see it, etc. According to Husserl's account, the very same object is intended in each of these acts: namely, the Eiffel Tower itself (*LI* II, Inv. V §11). The difference between these acts relates, in the first instance, to the '*quality*' of the act. Here the idea of 'act quality' refers to the kind of comportment found in the act, e.g. imagin*ing*, delight*ing*, remember*ing*, see*ing*. The notion of 'act quality' is akin to the contemporary notion of 'propositional attitude', although it is somewhat broader in scope in so far as it applies not only to thoughts but to real things and states of affairs. And just as the 'propositional attitude' is today distinguished from the 'propositional content', so Husserl distinguishes the 'act quality' from the act's '*matter*'. The 'matter' of the act is 'that element in an act which first gives it reference to an object, and reference so wholly definite that it not merely fixes the object meant in a general way, but also the precise way in which it is meant' (*LI* II, Inv. V §20, 589). As its 'matter', the intentional act contains within it an 'interpretative sense' (*Auffassungssinn*) which directs it towards some transcendent object, and which also gives to the 'presentation' of that object its particular character. For Husserl, some 'interpretive sense' is involved irrespective of whether the object in question is thought, perceived, judged, loved, etc. Thus, when Husserl speaks of the 'matter' of an act, he is not referring to the sensuous contents of conscious experience (the 'sense-data' or 'phenomenal qualia'); he is referring to the *meaningful* aspect of the objects that we experience. The 'matter', therefore, is understood as an ideal 'meaning' or 'sense' (*LI* I 290).

What then of sensations? These are regarded by Husserl as belonging on the 'act' rather than the 'matter' side of the ledger. They belong to the concrete contents of the psychical act's temporal phases. Nevertheless, he stresses that sensations are not themselves intentional. Only when they are 'bestowed with sense' do they become a part of an intentional act, thus becoming 'sensuous qualities' *of* some object (*LI* I, Inv. I, 309f.). When this occurs, sensuous content, whether the product of perception or imagination, fills out (as it were) the presentation of the object intended.

In summary, then, the intentional act unifies sensuous content under a meaning-content ('matter') which presents an object with a define interpretative sense or character, and it comports itself towards that object in one way or another ('quality'). So, for example, in a perception of the Eiffel Tower, my streaming sensations are unified in such a way that they present an object which I see as a physical object, namely, as the Eiffel Tower.

NOESIS–NOEMA TERMINOLOGY

With the appearance of *Ideas I*, not only is the above terminology superseded but the analysis of intentionality is rendered more complex. Nevertheless, rough equivalents to the concepts of 'act quality', 'matter' and 'sensuous content' can be found amongst the new terminology. In *Ideas I*, Husserl calls the act of consciousness (e.g. the perceiv*ing*) the '*noesis*', the intentional object (e.g. the object as perceived) the '*noema*' and the raw sensuous elements '*hyletic data*' or 'sensuous stuff'. 'Noesis' correlates roughly to the 'quality', 'noema' to the 'matter' and 'hyletic data' to 'sensations'. More specifically, 'noesis' refers to the '*way*' something is intended in conscious acts, i.e. the act with respect to its specific quality (e.g. as a perceiving, wishing or valuing). 'Noema' refers to the correlated object in the '*how*' of its being-intended (e.g. the perceived *qua* perceived, the wish-object *qua* wish-object, the valued *qua* valued).

Consequently, one can speak of 'noetic' analyses, which look at the structure of *acts*, and 'noematic' analyses, which look at the structure of *objects*. The two are always correlated: the way the same object is given (the noema) differs according to the type of act (the noesis). For example, perceiving the Sydney Harbour Bridge is a different kind of experience-of-the-Harbour-Bridge than remembering the Sydney Harbour Bridge. Quite palpable differences in the 'mode of givenness' of the object are identifiable in each experience. The analysis of *how* conscious acts 'present' objects in such different fashions belongs to 'noetic' analysis. The analysis of the differences in the object presented (notwithstanding that the same object is 'given' in each case) belongs to 'noematic' analysis. In this regard, the same object can be 'given' in consciousness with a great many experiential variations: not just *as* near/far, dim/bright, moving/stationary, etc., but also *as* an imagined being, a material being, a person, etc. All these variations are variations in the noema of the act, the 'object-side' of the act.

The same object can be intended with the *same* sense in different acts (e.g. I see the glorious Sydney Harbour Bridge; I think about the glorious Sydney Harbour Bridge). On the other hand, the same object can be intended in the same kind of act with *different* senses. For instance, a piece of fruit may now be perceived as something desirable, later as something repulsive (perhaps because I am feeling off-colour); and yet it remains the same object. Husserl clarifies with ever-increasing precision after the publication of *Logical Investigations* that the *same* object can be given with differing interpretations. For this reason, the selfsame object must be distinguished not only from the act in which it is intended, but also from the characteristics of its 'noematic sense', its meaningfulness as an object. In this connection, the selfsame object is called the noematic 'core' or 'core-stratum' of the noema and its meaning-characteristics are called the 'full noema' (*Ideas I* §91, 221). With this more nuanced terminology it is possible to distinguish the object (noematic core) from the 'how' of its appearing (full noema) within a perception as such; for instance, to distinguish the Sydney Harbour Bridge from its curvature or its gloriousness. In this case, the Harbour Bridge itself is the 'noematic core', constituted as 'the substrate X' which is the bearer of properties (i.e. curvature or gloriousness) given in the full noema (*Ideas I* §131, 313). Thus within one and the same noema the 'object simpliciter' and the 'object in the How of its determinations' are given together (*Ideas I* §131, 314). In Fregean terms, we might say that within the appearing of the perceived object are present *both* the 'sense' (*Sinn*; i.e. full noema) *and* the 'reference' (*Bedeutung*; i.e. noematic core).

NOEMATIC AND REAL OBJECTIVITY

Intentional objects or 'noemata' are what Ricoeur calls 'the objective face of the subjective process'.[6] Thus, through the transcendental reduction, Husserl purportedly discovers something like an 'objectivity-within-subjectivity'. Once this dimension of conscious life is brought into view, we can begin to see how transcendental phenomenology might be able to develop an account of the 'mystery of cognition': through this 'objectivity-within-subjectivity', consciousness is already related to the world – it already 'transcends' itself.

We have seen that Husserl distinguishes three basic moments in the intentional act: (1) the intending itself (*noesis*); (2) the sensuous material (*hyle*); and (3) the object as intended (*noema*). But while all three moments are found within conscious experience, only the first two are said to have '*real*' (*reell*) existence in the stream of consciousness.[7] For this reason, Husserl denotes the former as the 'components proper of intentive mental processes' and the latter as their 'intentional correlate' (*Ideas I* §88, 213). This means, for Husserl, (1) that the object of a conscious act is not *really* inherent in consciousness, i.e. it does not *exist* in the mind (contra naïve idealism);[8] but equally (2) that the object of an intentional act is not something to which consciousness stands in a *real* relation – as if the object and consciousness were two things in the world (contra naïve realism). Rather, (3) the object is 'in' consciousness precisely and only as an *intended* or *meant* object. Specifically, a relation to the object is achieved in an act of consciousness – an (objectifying) 'intentional act' – by means of an *idea* or a *sense* (*Sinn*). In an act of perception, for example, a unified sense is bestowed upon the real ('hyletic') contents of consciousness (the colours, the sounds, etc.), thus unifying a mental process and allowing an experience of the perceived object to occur. Consciousness thereby encounters ('constitutes') its object. In short then, the object as it is investigated by phenomenology is taken as an ideal unity *constituted* in consciousness, but not *existing* in consciousness.[9]

However, this 'noematic objectivity', this 'objectivity-within-subjectivity', requires further elucidation. It has the odd characteristic of neither belonging to the stream of consciousness as such, nor straightforwardly to sphere of transcendent real being. As Jacques Derrida explains:

> Noema, which is the objectivity of the object, the meaning and the 'as such' of the thing for consciousness, is neither the determined thing itself in its untamed existence (whose appearing the noema precisely is), nor is it a properly subjective moment, a 'really' subjective moment, since it is indubitably given as an object for consciousness. It is neither of the world nor of consciousness, but it is the world or something of the world *for* consciousness.[10]

Husserl confesses that this 'world *for* consciousness' is a difficult and somewhat precarious phenomenon to conceptualize. He himself remarks:

At first glance it would seem to be something obvious: Any consciousness is a consciousness of something, and the modes of consciousness are highly diversified. On approaching more closely, however, we became sensible of the great difficulties involved. They concern our understanding of *the mode of being of the noema*, the way in which it is 'implicit' in the mental process, in which it is 'intended to' in the mental process. Quite particularly they concern the clean separation of those things which, as its really inherent components, belong to the mental process itself and those which belong to the noema, which must be assigned to the noema as its own. (*Ideas I* §96, 234; my emphasis)

It is one thing to say that consciousness 'has' its object; it is quite another to say what this 'having' amounts to. How are we to understand this 'noematic' object which remains after the real object is 'bracketed'? Admittedly, this is one of the most difficult aspects of Husserlian phenomenology, and it has brought many a shrewd commentator to grief. I suggest that it can perhaps best be understood along the following lines.

It appears at first as though we are dealing here with two 'objects': a really transcendent object and a quasi-transcendent 'objectivity-within-subjectivity', i.e. an object outside consciousness and a subjective representation of it which survives the transcendental reduction. There even appears to be a terminological distinction provided for this dichotomy: 'the object which is intended' (i.e. 'objective' object) as opposed to 'the object as it is intended' (noema; i.e. 'subjective' object) (*LI* II, Inv. V §17, 578). However, Husserl denies that there are here *two* objects, one transcendent and one immanent. In fact, he regards this interpretation as a catastrophic lapse back into representationalism (*Ideas I* §90). If one insists on treating the intentional object (noema) and the actual object as non-identical, then one 'fall[s] into the difficulty that now *two* realities ought to stand over against one another while only *one* <reality> is found to be present and even possible'. Inspection of the act of perception itself, however, demonstrates that

I perceive the physical thing, the Object belonging to Nature, the tree there in the garden; that and nothing else is the actual Object of the perceptual 'intention'. A second immanent tree, or even an 'internal image' of the actual tree standing out there before me, is in no way given, and to suppose that hypothetically leads to an absurdity. (*Ideas I* §90, 219)

In other words, the actual object cannot be opposed to the perceived object; they are one and the same. It is precisely the actual object that appears.[11]

Therefore, the phenomenologist cannot say: 'the object that I am talking about – the intentional object – is not at all the real object'. This would be both illegitimate and untrue. It is illegitimate because the transcendental reduction precludes the phenomenologist from opposing the intentional object to the actual object *qua* something real, for this would require straddling both the phenomenological and the natural attitudes. On the other hand, it is untrue because the subject matter of phenomenological enquiry *is* precisely *the actual object* – in so far as it is something that appears. Thus, the phenomenological *epoché* does not prevent the discussion of real objectivity; it only prevents it being discussed *naturalistically*. Instead, transcendental phenomenology investigates real objects *qua* objects for consciousness. In short, the intentional object *is* the actual object *in so far as it enters into the purview of phenomenological research* (or, in so far as it enters into the purview of *consciousness* – this amounts to the same thing). To regard the tree treated by phenomenology as a separate object to the one treated by the natural sciences is like regarding the tree investigated by the botanist as a different tree to the one investigated by the physicist. These various sciences treat the same object according to different aspects of its being.

Nevertheless, the way in which the phenomenologist approaches the actual object is admittedly radically different to the way the botanist or physicist approaches it. The physicist, for instance, isolates, measures and idealizes the physical properties of the actual object. The phenomenologist, on the other hand, isolates and investigates the *relatedness* of the object to the consciousness experience of it:

> 'Transcendental' reduction exercises the εποχή with respect to actuality; but what it retains of <actuality> includes the noemas with the noematic unity included within them themselves and, accordingly, the mode in which something real is intended to and, in particular, given in consciousness itself. (*Ideas I* 239)

Phenomenology remains within this strictly circumscribed frame of reference. Husserl and his critics often talked past each other because they failed to understand each other on this point. Ultimately, this self-limitation even prevents Husserl from taking sides on the question of realism/idealism. Far from resolving the dispute (as he sometimes claims to have done), his own *epoché* prescribes an ambivalence with respect to the issue. Husserl's critics (including some of his own students; e.g. Roman Ingarden and Hedwig Conrad-Martius), however, read the phenomenological reduction as an argument for an idealist metaphysics and, in protest, insist that the existence of the external world be affirmed. Husserl, I suggest, would counter that to affirm the existence of the external world would be dogmatically to presuppose the meaning of 'existence' and 'world' – the very things his phenomenological method attempts to study. He could not give such an affirmation – not because it would be impossible to give, but because to give it would require stepping out of the phenomenological attitude and no longer speaking from within the circumscribed field of competence that he possesses as a philosopher. His critics, in turn, hear such statements as equivocations and attribute to Husserl a veiled idealism. Such misunderstandings continue to this day.

HUSSERL AND THE KANTIAN 'THING-IN-ITSELF'

Apart from the misguided criticisms of Husserl's supposed idealism discussed above, there is another, perhaps more serious, criticism that has been directed towards Husserl's transcendental phenomenological account of objectivity. We might call it 'the Kantian objection'. In essence, this criticism maintains that by identifying intentional objectivity and actual objectivity, Husserl drains the object of its *being*. Put another way, it claims that the transcendental *epoché* forces Husserl to abstain from recognizing the one thing that gives real being its reality: its existence over and above the sphere of consciousness. The implication is that Husserlian phenomenology renders itself incapable of fulfilling the task of *ontological* clarification that it sets for itself.

The foremost proponent of this objection is Paul Ricoeur, who articulates it in explicitly Kantian terms.[12] What Husserl lacks, he argues, is an ontology – by which he means a recognition of the 'in-itself' over against the 'for me'. In other words, for Ricoeur, there is something *indispensable* about the Kantian distinction between the thing-in-itself and the appearance of the thing:

> First, let us take account of the function of the positing of the thing-in-itself in relation to the inspection of phenomena as Kant sees it. There is no knowledge of being. This impossibility is somehow active and even positive. In spite of the impossibility of knowledge of being, *Denken* [i.e. thinking] still posits being as that which limits the claims of the phenomena to make up ultimate reality. Thus, *Denken* confers on phenomenology its ontological dimension or status [i.e. as *finite* knowledge of *transcendent* reality] . . . This structure in Kantianism has no parallel in Husserlian phenomenology. Like the neo-Kantians, Husserl lost the ontological dimension of the phenomenon and simultaneously lost the possibility of a meditation on the limits and foundations of phenomenality.[13]

Notwithstanding the epistemic emptiness of Kant's thing-in-itself, for Ricoeur it is a vital part of any workable account of objectivity. We need to posit the thing-in-itself over and above the phenomenal object, otherwise we fall into contradiction. The fact that Husserl excises such an ontology from his phenomenology, in Ricoeur's opinion, deprives it of the all-important *limit* on knowledge which is constitutive for our apprehension of the world as *beyond* us and of our subjectivity as *finite*. It is this deficiency in Husserl's account, he argues, that leads him ever closer to subjective idealism.

Husserl agrees with Ricoeur and Kant that it is essential for the possibility of empirical knowledge that a distinction be drawn between the thing-(in)-itself and the appearances of the thing. But this condition is adequately fulfilled, he suggests, by Kant's enigmatic 'transcendental object = X' (*Ideas I* §143). Moreover, in the idea of the 'transcendental object = X', it seems, Kant had already identified the *positing* that is essential to the synthetic activity of consciousness. As Ricoeur himself reports, for Kant the *regularities* of the phenomenal object are enough for it to be set over against oneself as an independent objectivity and in distinction from the succession of representations.[14] So out of the succession of representations emerges the unitary 'object of experience' (cf. *CPR* A 191); but, simultaneously, the phenomenon is a representation *of* a transcendental X (non-empirical object) (*CPR* A 109). The relation of consciousness to the real object, then, occurs through this unifying synthesis in my representations (which Husserl would call 'constitution'). The non-empirical intention to the transcendental X unifies experience into experience of an empirical object. The phenomenon and the in-itself thus *refer to each other*. The conditioned and unconditioned mutually imply each other (*CPR* B xx). As we shall see, this analysis bears a strong resemblance to Husserl's own phenomenological account.

Notwithstanding these insights, Husserl criticizes Kant's account for overstepping the line in two respects:

(1) In addition to the idea of the 'transcendental object = X', Kant introduces a metaphysical account of the 'thing-in-itself' as that which is known in the creative intuition of God (*intuitus originarius*) (*CPR* B 72). Debate continues over how to interpret Kant on this point, but it seems that the phenomenological interpretation of the transcendental object (i.e. as the 'transcendental object = X') is thus supplemented – and, in Husserl's opinion, obfuscated – by a second, dogmatic interpretation (as the object known by God). For Husserl, in contrast to the 'transcendental object = X', the idea of the 'thing-in-itself' has no evidential warrant:

> [the world] was, for the subject, never given otherwise than in this subjective milieu, and in purely intuitive description of the subjectively given there was no in-itself that is not given in subjective modes of the for-me or for-us, and *the in-itself appears as a characteristic in this context and has to undergo therein its clarification of sense*. (*KITP* 11; my emphasis)

Kant's additional positing of an existent and essentially hidden 'thing-in-itself' – if, indeed, this is what the concept denotes – is therefore superfluous. Thus, what Ricoeur takes to be the essence of Kantianism, Husserl interprets as its most glaring inconsistency.

(2) Kant lapses into metaphysical speculation because he lacks methodological consistency. Specifically, he confuses his discovery of the *positing* of the transcendental object, which is constitutive for objective knowledge (*CPR* A 254f, B 310f.), with the need to *participate in* this positing himself by explicitly affirming the existence of the in-itself. In Husserlian terms, at this point Kant fails to see the difference between the 'parenthesized' positing and the positing

itself. In also positing the 'in-itself', he steps out of the transcendental attitude and back into the natural attitude:

> In contradistinction to such errors we have to abide by what is given in the pure mental process and to take it within the frame of clarity precisely as it is given. The 'actual' Object is then to be 'parenthesised' . . . [We] do not tolerate any judgement which makes use of the positing of the 'actual' physical thing, nor of the whole 'transcendent' Nature, or which 'joins in' <that positing>. As *phenomenologists* we abstain from all such positings . . . Rather we contemplate them; instead of joining in them, we make them Objects, take them as component parts of the phenomenon. (*Ideas I* 219f.)

Again, this does not mean that Husserl is opposed to the 'positing' that belongs to the natural attitude. He merely regards it as methodologically necessary that all such positing be 'parenthesized' if philosophical research is to be carried out rigorously. When this principle is not respected, philosophical confusions and spurious concepts abound. The Kantian confusion illustrates, for Husserl, the consequences of just such a transgression.

HUSSERL'S REINTERPRETATION OF THINGHOOD

Once Kant's confusion is identified, the question then becomes how the distinction between the appearance and the thing itself (*die Sache selbst*) might be understood without transgressing the bounds of phenomenological evidence, i.e. without positing an essentially inaccessible thing-*in*-itself (*Ding an sich*). How is the 'in-itself' to be philosophically accounted for as something that appears 'for-me'? What does it mean for something to appear as a transcendent object? Once the metaphysical concept of the thing-in-itself is done away with, is it still possible to conceptualize the difference between the thing as it appears and the thing as it is in itself? That is, can Ricoeur's objection be met by the phenomenologist on his or her own terms? Husserl does his best to demonstrate how these demands can be fulfilled. Indeed, he gives extremely detailed and multifaceted answers to these questions, answers which he never ceased to revisit and revise. Unravelling Husserl's answers will occupy us further in the next chapter. In the final pages of this chapter, however, allow me to briefly preview the main lines of his response.

Thinghood or 'real objectivity' is analysed by Husserl in connection with the act of perception: the real (existent) thing, he argues, is the object that can be perceived.[15] If this phenomenological definition of real being is granted, then the question of existence becomes a question of understanding what it is to be a *perceived object*. Husserl's analysis runs along the following lines.

Careful reflection upon the perception of physical things reveals that perceived objects show themselves in endlessly altering ways. When I see a physical object, I only ever see it in 'profiles' or 'adumbrations' (*Abschattungen*), in a certain light, from a certain angle, from a certain distance, and so forth (*Ideas I* §41). Each momentary profile, however, implies an infinite number of possible further profiles of the same entity. This infinite set of possibilities of perceiving a thing *structures* the act of perception. That is, the perception of a thing involves a process of *anticipation*, in which new aspects are expected to be given, and *fulfilment*, in which new aspects are intuitively given, which by and large conform to my expectations. The temporal series of such 'partial acts' makes up the one intentional act, the perception of the thing.

The perceived object, for its part – i.e. the thing we actually see or attend to – is none of these profiles, and yet it is perceived in and through each of these profiles. The object is the unifying correlate of this potentially infinite series of intentional acts of anticipation and fulfilment in which possibilities of perception are progressively intimated and confirmed. The physical object is that which is 'the same' throughout the continually changing perceptual act:

> [W]e may handle the thing from all sides in a *continuous perceptual series*, feeling it over as it were with our senses. But each single percept in this series is already a percept of the thing. Whether I look at this book from above or below, from inside or outside, I always see *this book*. It is always one and the same thing, and that not merely in some purely physical sense, but in the view of our percepts themselves. (*LI* II 789; cf. *Ideas I* 87)

For example, I walk into a room and notice a lamp. Immediately, I see the lamp and not merely an aspect-of-a-lamp. As I approach it and it is given to me in new ways, my experience of it conforms to my expectations of a lamp-thing. I know then that I was right to identify it as a lamp from the very beginning. Each temporal phase of perception merely confirms the perception and increases the evidential givenness of the thing itself.[16]

The perceived thing, then, is not built up from a collection of sense impressions like pieces of a puzzle. Indeed, the adumbrated visual sensations are never attended to as such; e.g. I immediately hear the person speak, not the bare sounds streaming into my ears. Such sensations are only abstract parts of the perceptual act in which the object is intended 'through' them. Nor is the perceived thing some 'substrate' hidden behind the veil of sense impressions. Rather, the thing is that selfsame object which is straightforwardly and immediately perceived (i.e. intended) in and through every moment of the perception. Thus, Husserl agrees with Kant that the essence of perception includes the 'positing' of some object ('X') which is the non-sensuous unifying principle of act of perception. Indeed, the distance between Husserl's account and Kant's at this point is very small. For instance, Husserl writes: '*Sensations*, and the acts "interpreting" them or apperceiving them, are alike experienced, *but they do not appear as objects*: they are not seen, heard or *perceived* by any sense. *Objects* on the other hand, appear and are perceived, but they are not *experienced*' (*LI* II 567). What Husserl provides, however, is precisely an analysis of the *object* (noema) as it is constituted in and through the synthetic acts of consciousness (noesis). In so doing, he shows that the object X is itself *constituted* by consciousness (in this case, in the act of perception). He shows, in other words, that the positing of the transcendental object, whose necessity is demonstrated by Kant, is itself nothing more than a structural component *of* the act of perception. Furthermore, it is precisely this 'X' that *appears* in the act; it does not remain hidden as Kant sometimes intimates. The thing-(in)-itself is nothing other than the posited 'unity of sense' which binds together the succession of conscious experiences into the perception of *an* object. This is what Jean-Paul Sartre lauds as the fundamental insight of 'modern thought' (by which he means Husserlian phenomenology), namely, that 'the appearance does not hide the essence, it reveals it; it *is* the essence. The essence of an existent is no longer a property sunk in the cavity of this existent; it is the manifest law which presides over the succession of its appearances, it is the principle of the series.'[17]

Husserl is thus able to reject the doctrine of Kantianism that empirical knowledge is *not* knowledge of the thing-in-itself. On the contrary, we do have knowledge of the thing as it is in itself – not because we have godlike intuition, but because the object of experi-ence *is* the object itself and not a stand-in for it (i.e. a 'representation'). And yet, as I discuss more fully in the following chapter, because the thing itself is never fully given but only given in profiles, our know-ledge of reality remains *partial* and *defeasible*. There remains, then, a 'limitation' to our empirical knowledge on Husserl's account, despite its supposedly fatal 'disontologizing of reality'.[18] In other words, Ricoeur's concern that an epistemological hubris would follow from a rejection of the Kantian 'thing-in-itself' proves to be unfounded. The epistemological limitation that he seeks to impose is already built into the essential structure of perception itself; it does not need to be imposed metaphysically (*Ideas I* 90f.). In short, then, Husserl's analysis of thinghood preserves the insights of Kant's theo-ry, and does so within a strictly transcendental-phenomenological framework.

In this chapter, I have introduced Husserl's basic analysis of the structure of the intentional act and discussed at some length what it means for an intentional object to be 'constituted' within conscious-ness *as* something transcendent to it. This led us to focus on Husserl's analysis of the act of perception. But, this is only the beginning of Husserl's studies into the intentional acts of consciousness. If 'inten-tionality' is 'the name of the problem encompassed by the whole of phenomenology' (*Ideas I* 349), then the 'problem' named by it is manifold. Indeed, it is as variegated as the life of consciousness itself. It is not surprising, then, that Husserl's investigations into intention-ality shoot out in several directions at once. He seeks to understand the noetic and noematic structures belonging to each of the various kinds of intentional act: presentation, remembrance, imagination, time-consciousness, empty signifying, consciousness of another per-son, consciousness of social realities, and so forth. He has a particu-lar interest, however, in the intentional acts through which reasoning and scientific thinking take place, and these are the subject of our deliberations in the following two chapters.

NOTES

1 The term '*Erlebnis*' is variously translated as 'experience' (Findlay), 'lived experience' (Churchill) and 'mental process' (Kersten).

2 'In perception something is perceived, in imagination something is imagined, in a statement something stated, in love something loved, in hate hated, in desire desired, etc.' (*LI* II, Inv. V §10, 554).

3 Space precludes an exposition of Husserl's critique of Brentano. Explicit engagements with Brentano occur in various places throughout Husserl's opus, but the most important of these are (1) *LI* II, Inv. V, Chapter 2 ('Consciousness as intentional experience'); (2) the appendix to the same text entitled 'External and internal perception: physical and psychical phenomena'; and (3) *Ideas I*, §85 ('Sensuous *hyle*, Intentive *morphé*').

4 Here I am following the appraisal of Martin Heidegger in *The Basic Problems of Phenomenology*, trans. Albert Hofstadter (Bloomington, IN: Indiana University Press, 1982), p. 58.

5 As will be clear to those familiar with Kantian philosophy, Husserl's concept of intentionality echoes the Kantian doctrine of the 'receptivity' of intuition and the 'spontaneity' of understanding, both of which are necessary for empirical knowledge: 'Thoughts without contents are empty, intuitions without concepts are blind' (*CPR* A 51, B 75). However, Husserl does not assign sensibility and understanding to separate 'faculties'. On his account, 'aesthetics' and 'logic' are more intimately intertwined, as will become clear.

6 Paul Ricoeur, *Husserl: An Analysis of his Phenomenology*, trans. Edward G. Ballard and Lester E. Embree (Evanston, IL: Northwestern University Press, 1967), p. 9.

7 'These so-called immanent contents are therefore merely intended or intentional, while truly *immanent contents*, which belong to the real make-up [*reellen Bestande*] of the intentional experiences, are *not intentional*: they constitute the act, provide necessary *points d'appui* which render possible an intention, but are not themselves intended, not the objects presented in the act' (*LI* II 559).

8 It should be noted that Brentano, following the scholastic formula, had already designated the object of consciousness as having 'mental inexistence'. The challenge, however, is to give a precise explanation of what 'mental inexistence' might mean. As Husserl writes: 'it is an immense step to go from seizing upon a distinction pertaining to consciousness for the first time to its right, phenomenologically pure, fixing and correct valuation – and precisely this step, which is decisive for a harmonious, fruitful phenomenology, has not been effected' (*Ideas I* 218).

9 For a helpful blow-by-blow explication of these basic distinctions, see Dan Zahavi, *Husserl's Phenomenology* (Stanford, CA: Stanford University Press, 2003), pp. 13–22.

10 Jacques Derrida, 'Genesis and structure', in *Writing and Difference*, trans. Alan Bass (London: Routledge, 1978), p. 163.

11 The same point is made in *Logical Investigations*; see *LI* II 595f.

12 See Ricoeur, 'Kant and Husserl' in *Husserl: An Analysis of his Phenomenology*, pp. 175–201.

13 Ibid., pp. 186–7, 190.

14 Ibid., p. 189.

15 Husserl defines 'real object' as 'the possible object of a straightforward perception' (*LI* II, Inv. VI §47, 791; cf. *Ideas I* §42).

16 The spectre of failed perception (hallucination or mistake) also belongs essentially to perception and it too is a function of the act's 'intentional' character. It is the fact that we *anticipate* certain perceptions of the object that makes the experience of surprise or failure possible. And yet it is this same feature of perception which also demonstrates that the condition for the possibility of a sensuous experience *of* an object (i.e. perception) is a *directedness* towards the object over and above the mere sensations.

17 Jean-Paul Sartre, *Being and Nothingness*, trans. Hazel E. Barnes (London: Routledge, 1969), p. xxii.

18 Ricoeur, 'Kant and Husserl', p. 193.

CHAPTER 6

INTUITION, EVIDENCE AND TRUTH

Husserl's conception of intentionality is initially developed in the context of a 'pure phenomenology of the experiences of thinking and knowing [*Denk- und Erkenntniserlebnisse*]' (*LI* I 249). Such a task is the subject matter of the six investigations that make up the *Logical Investigations*. At issue in these investigations is the clarification of the structure of the intentional acts basic to thinking and knowing, and central to this task is the analysis of *intuition, evidence* and *truth*. In this chapter, I aim to elucidate Husserl's analysis of these phenomena. I occasionally draw upon his later work on these same problems, but this presentation follows in its main outlines the Sixth of the *Logical Investigations*.

INTUITION AND EVIDENCE

Evidence (*Evidenz*) means, for Husserl, a cognition or act of knowing in which the object in question is given with 'insight' (*Einsicht*).[1] What then is this 'insight' which marks off evidence from non-evidence? It is initially glossed as 'an immediate intimation of truth itself' (*LI* I, Proleg. §6, 61). An evidence, then, is something that brings the fact of the matter to our immediate apprehension. It resolves what is in question. To this extent, an evidence is something basic, i.e. something which verifies and not something which needs to be verified.[2] But this only tells us what evidence achieves, not what it is or how to determine what counts as 'an immediate intimation of truth itself'.

Let me begin by discussing the traditional doctrine of evidence which Husserl most vehemently rejects. Husserl goes to great lengths to refute the idea that evidence is a 'feeling' that accompanies ideas and marks them out as true.[3] Evidence, he argues, is to be differentiated from the conviction that something is true. Husserl voices two main objections to the feeling-theory of evidence. These oft-repeated refutations of the psychological account of evidence, incidentally, add another string to the bow of the critique of psychologism discussed in Chapter 1:

(1) Feelings or affects accompany many beliefs. This is not an uncommon experience. However, we can experience strong feelings of certainty in connection with the most vague and unsubstantiated ideas, or conversely strong feelings of uncertainty with respect to perfectly accurate judgements (*Ideas I* 40). This indicates that evidence itself must be something separate from the feeling of certainty and something by which we can adjudicate between feelings of certainty, i.e. by which we can *discover* that our convictions were mistaken or well-placed. Conviction and evidence, therefore, cannot be conflated.

(2) To identify evidence with conviction or feeling is to make evidence an irrational psychological phenomenon. It is to render evidence 'subjective' and to deny what is most essential to it: namely, that it makes manifest what is *objectively* the case. By making evidence an essentially private experience, the feeling-theory removes matters of evidence from the sphere of public debate. The end of this road is relativism. But evidence is not an affect; it is a rational and objective ' "experience" of truth' (*LI* I 194). Only thus is it able to fulfil the role required of it as adjudicator over convictions.

So how does Husserl explain the idea of objective evidence? His fundamental move is to ally the idea of evidence with the phenomenon of 'seeing' (*LI* I 195). As Emmanuel Levinas remarks:

> Husserl was looking for the primary phenomenon of truth and reason, and he found it in intuition, here understood as an intentionality which reaches being. He found it in 'vision', the ultimate source of all reasonable assertions. Vision has 'justification' as its function, because it gives its object in a direct manner; inasmuch as vision realizes its object, it is reason.[4]

Literal seeing is, for Husserl, the paradigm example of evidence. But, as Levinas notes, the proper concept to describe justificatory vision in the broadest sense is 'intuition' (*Anschauung*). This distinction will become important as we proceed.

From the outset, let it be said that 'intuition' in the Husserlian sense has nothing to do with special cognitive powers purportedly possessed by women, mystics and sleuths. There is nothing magical or mystical about 'intuition' in Husserl's sense. It is a commonplace occurrence and one that happens in almost every waking moment. 'To intuit' simply means 'to look at' or 'to observe something first-hand': 'We use the expression "to see" here in the completely broad sense which implies nothing other than the *act of experiencing things oneself*, the fact of having seen things themselves' (*EJ* §88, 348). Thus Heidegger, for instance, glosses Husserl's idea of 'intuition' as the 'simple apprehension of what is itself bodily found just as it shows itself'.[5]

Husserl's definition of intuition is somewhat broader than the standard Kantian definition. In Kant's philosophy, intuition is syn-onymous with sensibility. That is, intuition is the faculty that repre-sents the data that we involuntarily receive from our senses. For Husserl, by contrast, the term 'intuition' is given the full range to which we ordinarily apply the verb 'to see': I *see* the cat; I *see* that the cat is mottled; I *see* the solution to the maths problem; I *see* what the problem is with the broken kettle; I *see* that I was wrong; I *see* what you mean; I *see* what you are going through; and so forth. In most of these examples, the verb 'see' does not mean 'perceive' in the literal sense. It has a broader sense. Indeed, the verb 'to see' is here used of several *different* intentional acts. Some intend sensuous objects (i.e. Kant's 'objects of experience'); others do not. Husserl's claim is not that these diverse experiences can all be described as though they were completely alike. Nevertheless, these experiences all have some-thing in common: they are 'firsthand' experiences of the object in question – and this is what Husserl means by 'intuition'.

EVIDENCE AS FULFILLING INTUITION

'Evidential' acts are understood by Husserl to be acts in which the object in question is given with 'intuitive fullness'. In a word, evi-dence is provided by '*fulfilment*' or '*fulfilling intuition*'. But the idea of 'intuitive fullness' or 'fulfilment' can only be understood if we first consider its counterconcept: the empty meaning-intention (*LI* I 280–82):

(1) More often than not, we speak or think about objects without any image or perception of them. This is what Husserl calls 'meaning-

intention' (*Bedeutungsintention*) or 'empty intending' (*Leermeinen*). In such acts, the object in question is meant, and yet is not present – not even recollectively or imaginatively. Now, when I utter a proposition in the absence of its referent, 'the expression functions significantly, it remains more than mere sound of words' (*LI* I 280). An intentional relation to the object in question is achieved by my referring to it. And yet, the merely signifying act 'lacks any basic *intuition* that will give it its object' (*LI* I 280; my emphasis). When I verbally communicate to someone that there is an accident further up the road, for example, I am not sharing a visual image that I have seen, but expressing an intelligible fact. What gets communicated in discourse, therefore, are meanings, not sensations or intuitions.[6] Likewise, speech and other signs can be *comprehended* even if I have no intuitive familiarity with the subject matter being discussed (*LI* I, Inv. I §§19–20).

In meaning-intention, then, the intended object is endowed with a richness of meaning but not with the intuitive character of something imagined or perceived. The meaning-intention, it could be said, *anticipates* the 'in person' givenness of its intended object. However, the meaning given to the intended object(s) prior to their being experienced 'in person' may or may not be accurate (*LI* II 694f.). Until proof is adduced, Husserl states, we cannot claim knowledge; we operate in the realm of 'inauthentic' (*Uneigentlich*) or 'signitive thinking' (*LI* II, Inv. VI §§17–20). In signitive thinking, one deals with meanings in abstraction from any sensuous or intuitive constraints. This can be very useful, but it also has its dangers. On the one hand, many complex operations of thought are made possible by sign-thinking. It makes possible, for example, counting beyond ten. Beyond this number, which is roughly the highest number of entities we are able to grasp intuitively, we rely on signs and understanding the meaning of those signs. Thus, the whole enterprise of mathematics operates in the realm of 'inauthentic' thinking. On the other hand, inauthentic thinking allows judgements to be formed which have no basis in fact. In the absence of first-hand experience, I can easily make specious claims and pass these off as truths. Herein arises the possibility of false assertion and rumour.[7] The aim of science, by contrast, is precisely to ground its assertions *evidentially* and to disseminate only demonstrably true propositions. I shall return to this ideal of science below.

(2) What signitive acts characteristically lack is the certification of

a 'fulfilling intuition'. When an anticipation or meaning-intention is fused with an intuition of the thing itself, we have a 'fulfilment' (*Erfüllung*). In intuitive fulfilment, 'the draft it [i.e. the meaning-intention] makes on intuition is as it were cashed' – so much so that 'it readily seems as if the expression first got its meaning here, as if it drew meaning from the act of fulfilment' (*LI* I 294f.). What occurs in a fulfilling intuition then is a marriage of meaning and meant: the sense posited in the act of meaning is matched in the first-hand experience of the thing or state of affairs in question. The *same* object is intended in the *same* way – only now it is given in a different mode, namely, *in person*. It sometimes occurs that intended objects are given in imagination or recollection, and here we have to do with a *mode* of intuition, to be sure (*Ideas I* §99). But only when an object comes to be given *in person* – that is, 'bodily' (*leibhaftig*), 'in the flesh', *in propria persona* (*LI* II 608f.) – is an intention genuinely 'fulfilled'. In contrast to the former 'representational' (*vergegenwärtig*) modes of intuition, this is said to be a 'presentational' (*gegenwärtig*) mode of intuition – or, more precisely, an 'originary presentive intuition' (*originär gebende Anschauung*) (*Ideas I* §24, §136). The expression 'originary' again denotes the fact that the thing *itself* is present to an immediate seeing; it gives itself (*Ideas I* 36). Only this kind of intuitive grasping allows 'inauthentic' (*uneigentlich*) thinking to become 'authentic' (*eigentlich*).

Additionally, when the fulfilling intuition perfectly or completely fulfils the meaning-intention, it is said to offer '*adequate*' evidence. In this case, we have absolute evidence, or evidence in the strict sense (*Evidenz*) (*LI* II, Inv. VI §38). It is not always the case, however, that the fulfilling intuition reaches this standard of evidence. For instance, Husserl notes that physical objects are always and for essential reasons given '*inadequately*'. The very 'adumbrated' structure of the perceptual act, as discussed in the previous chapter, means that the intuiting of the physical object is an infinite task. The perceptual object continually exceeds or transcends the act in which it is given. Thus, even 'originary' intuition of the physical object never has the 'all-at-once' character necessary to confirm *definitively* the meaning-intention. The intuition of the entity and the entity intended never fully coincide. The object that is present is never present in the full and strict sense. We can, however, obtain ever-increasing levels of intuitive familiarity with the thing, and this confirms and expands the evidence we do possess. Inadequate evidence is regarded by Husserl as evidence in the loose sense.

The essentially perspectival character of perceptual givenness is contrasted, for example, with the non-perspectival bodily givenness of the contents of consciousness themselves in acts of 'reflection'. For the most part, lived experiences (*Erlebnisse*) are simply *lived through*; we are usually caught up with whatever we have regard to, and thus for the most part have no regard to our experiences themselves. However, according to Husserl, it is an eidetic law that any mental process (*Erlebnis*) can become 'regarded' or 'reflected upon' (*Ideas I* §77). When this occurs, I catch myself in the act, as it were, and am then able to objectify that act. In reflection, conscious acts are given *immediately*, not in 'profiles'. This does not mean that the apprehension of mental acts is always clear and distinct, but it does mean such acts can, in principle, be given adequately (*Ideas I* §§67–69).[8]

In deference to these phenomenological differences in modes of evidential givenness, Husserl finds himself restating the Aristotelian idea of the 'regionality of evidence': namely, the idea that to the various kinds of object belong their own proper *modes* of evidence. Aristotle writes: 'It is the mark of an educated mind to expect that degree of precision in each kind of study which the nature of the subject at hand admits: it is obviously just as foolish to accept arguments of probability from a mathematician as to demand strict demonstrations from an orator.'[9] Likewise, Husserl repudiates the tendency common among rationalist philosophers to recognize as 'true' knowledge only that which is known with apodictic (indubitable, mathematical) certainty. It is simply unreasonable, for example, to expect incontrovertible certainty regarding matters of fact. Apodictic certainty is impossible in matters of fact because matters of fact are given evidentially in an 'adumbrated' and therefore 'inadequate' fashion. But there is no *deficiency* in this state of affairs; this type of evidence *is* the apposite modality of evidence for this kind of enquiry. Nor is this a fault of our 'finite' cognitive faculties. It belongs rather to the essential structure of perceptual objectivity *as such*:

> [S]omething such as a physical thing in space is only intuitable by means of appearances in which it is and must be given in multiple but determined changing 'perspective' modes and, accordingly, in

changing 'orientations' not just for human beings but also for God – as the ideal representative of absolute cognition. (*Ideas I* 362)

It should be mentioned that there are, in addition, certain perfectly intelligible meaning-intentions that are incapable of being fulfilled, even by God. One of Husserl's favourite examples is the 'square circle'. He denies that this is, strictly speaking, a meaningless (*Sinnlos*) expression – we can, after all, understand it. Instead, we ought to say that it exhibits 'the *a priori* impossibility of a fulfilling sense' (*LI* I 294). That is, the meaning-intention that intends a square circle will, for essential reasons, never achieve an intuition or 'realization' of its object. For Husserl, this is simply a function of the fact that 'the realm of meaning is . . . much wider than that of intuition' (*LI* II 824).

But, the main point here is that each and every kind of evidence is a more or less complex *cognitive achievement* in which one 'sees' first-hand how things stand with respect to the matter at hand. In short, the alternative to regarding evidence as a *feeling* (i.e. as a remote intimation of how things stand) is to regard it as a *seeing* – an immediate apprehension of the things themselves.

THE CONCEPT OF TRUTH

Once this idea of intuition is in place, Husserl's concept of truth can be straightforwardly explicated. In all knowing, Husserl discerns what Ricoeur has called the 'original dialectic of sense and presence'.[10] That is, knowledge begins from an empty cognition, presumption or thought and then finds itself confirmed or contradicted by an act of 'seeing' (i.e. intuiting). Even when knowledge first arises unexpectedly (as it were) in an act of perception, a *coincidence* between a meaning and an intuiting is present. Husserl's idea of truth, therefore, rests upon this structure of presumption or meaning and fulfilment: a meaning is *confirmed* (or perhaps *disappointed*) in an act of evidential intuition. Truth, then, has at least three moments: (1) the meaning-intention; (2) the fulfilling intuition; and (3) the 'identification' or 'synthesis' of the two.

The revolutionary aspect of this concept of truth is its ingenious reinterpretation of the old scholastic formula '*veritas est adaequatio rei et intellectus*' ('truth is the correspondence of thought and thing').

Epistemologists had puzzled for centuries over the problem of how a thought and a thing could be seen to correspond given that (1) this presupposes equal 'access' to both thoughts and things as they exist in themselves, and (2) thoughts do not resemble things in any obvious sense. Husserl, in one brilliant stroke, resolves both difficulties: (1) consciousness directs itself 'intentionally' to both thoughts and things as a matter of course; (2) thoughts and things, when understood phenomenologically, are not so radically heterogenous – they are simply the respective objects of two kinds of intentional act. Specifically, a thought is the object of an empty intending, and a thing is the object of a fulfilling intuition. From here it is not difficult to see that a 'correspondence' can occur when the same object is given in these two different 'modes' – when 'the same objective item which was "merely thought of" in symbol is now presented in intuition, and . . . is intuited as being precisely the determinate so-and-so that it was at first merely thought or meant to be' (*LI* II 694). The 'correspondence' necessary for truth, therefore, is not found in a comparison between a thought and a thing *per se*, but in discovering a coincidence between an object intended emptily and the same object intuited originarily: 'the *intellectus* is in this case the thought-intention, the intention of meaning. And the *adaequatio* is realized when the object meant is in the strict sense *given* in our intuition, and given as just what we think and call it' (*LI* II 762). In this way, Husserl reinterprets the classical definition of truth. His could still be called a 'correspondence theory of truth', therefore, provided that his phenomenological reframing of the question is born in mind.

Husserl goes on to tease apart several equivocations to which the concept of 'truth' is prone. In an important passage of the Sixth Logical Investigation (§39), he distinguishes the following four senses of 'truth':

1. The 'truth' of some matter is what we grasp when we perceive the *identity* of the object as meant and the object as bodily given. 'Truth' in this first sense is the existence (as it were) of a coincidence between the object meant and the object given. The *experience* of truth is the *intuition* of the state of affairs *that* the one is coincident with the other. That is, what we recognize in an 'experience of truth' is not just the object-meant or the object-perceived but the *coincidence* of the two. We have a second-order intuition, as it were, of the agreement between the two component acts (i.e. the meaning and fulfilment). (What is here called a 'second-order intuition' is more

precisely described as a 'categorial intuition', but more is said about such acts in the following chapter.)

2. 'Truth' can also denote *the relationship of coincidence* itself, which characterizes experiences of truth in the first sense. Truth can be said to reside in this relationship of coincidence or 'adequation'.

3. 'Truth' can denote the object about which the true judgement is made. Here, the true is *the thing itself*, defined as that which is given in an 'originary presentive intuition', i.e. in an 'in person' (*leibhaftig*) seeing. Or, put slightly differently, according to this third sense of truth, the truth is the 'perceived thing' as opposed to 'thought thing'; or, more broadly, the 'intuited thing' as opposed to the 'merely intended thing'. In contemporary parlance, we come close to this definition of truth when we refer to physical things as 'the evidence'.

4. 'Truth' can denote the 'rightness' of the act in which a state of affairs is correctly judged. This fourth conception of truth parallels the Aristotelian one: a sentence is true if it says what is actually the case, and false if not.[11] When we say that a judgement is 'true', this means that it does indeed direct us to the thing itself as it really is. But what it means for a judgement to 'direct us to the thing itself as it really is' is what Husserl explicates in definitions (1) and (2). In other words, Husserl makes the 'truth' pertaining to judgement secondary to the 'truth' pertaining to the act of identification.[12]

It is a noteworthy feature of Husserl's analysis of truth that he thus sets truth in a broader context than judgements and propositions. Truth is no longer understood as a feature *of* propositions or judgements. It is now seen as an *intuitive* or *perceptual* phenomenon that is not confined to propositions or linguistic expressions *per se*. The primary locus of truth, for Husserl, is not the proposition, but the act of identification itself which occurs in lived experience. Propositional truth thus comes to be understood by Husserl as a *derivative* phenomenon whose possibility rests on the more primordial pre-thematic 'experience of truth'. Heidegger makes much fuss about this feature of Husserl's analysis. Glossing Husserl's account, he says that, when we intuit anything originarily, it is a 'living in the truth'.[13] We 'live in the truth' continually every day without it necessarily being made *thematic* in linguistic assertions. However, Heidegger's expression would not, I think, be wholly endorsed by Husserl. It is true that the latter sometimes speaks of the perceptual fulfilling-intuitions as themselves 'acts of identification', and therefore, by implication, as experiences of truth (*LI* II 696). In this sense we 'live in the truth' in our everyday perceiving. But Husserl clarifies that, strictly speaking, an experience of truth does not occur until the agreement (i.e. identity) is explicitly 'noticed', i.e. made the object of an intentional act of identification (*LI* II 697, 766).

Husserl divides the four senses of 'truth' enumerated above into two pairs. Senses (2) and (4) relate, he says, to the structure of the intentional act; senses (1) and (3) relate to its objective correlates. The two 'objective' senses of 'truth' are interpreted by Husserl as names for *being*, that is, ' "being" in the sense of truth' (*LI* II 768). Here Husserl is alluding to Aristotle's discussion of the 'manifold senses of being'. Aristotle famously remarked that 'being is said in many ways' and proceeded to tease apart the ambiguities of the verb 'to be'. Husserl is suggesting that he has isolated the very origin of 'being' in one of the senses discussed by Aristotle, namely, being in the sense of 'truth' (*ens tanquam verum*). Specifically, Husserl claims, 'being-true' refers to the identity of object meant and object given. In his reading of this section of the *Logical Investigations*, Heidegger suggests that here Husserl achieves more than he himself realizes.[14] In point of fact, Husserl's truth$_1$ and truth$_3$ succeed in explicating not one but *two* of the manifold senses of being: truth$_1$ explicates 'true being' and truth$_3$ 'actual being'.[15] The latter provides the meaning of 'is' in the sense of 'is actual' or 'exists', and the former provides the meaning of 'is' in the sense of 'is true'.

However, even if Heidegger is right, these are only two of the 'manifold' senses of the verb 'to be' enumerated by Aristotle. Aware of this, Husserl expressly notes that his discussions to this point have not yet touched upon the sense of 'to be' found in assertions of the form '*S* is *P*', i.e. the 'copula' (*LI* II 766f.). This further sense of being – 'is' as it is used to relate or link subject and predicate – becomes a theme in the following chapter. As we shall see, Husserl has a strikingly original interpretation of this sense of 'being' too, one which is bound up with his analysis of the phenomenon of 'categorial intuition'.

THE PRINCIPLE OF ALL PRINCIPLES

The analyses outlined above are fundamental to the development of Husserl's 'theory of science' (*Wissenschaftslehre*). They lay the groundwork for an account of scientific thinking and knowing in general. In this final section, I would like to bring out the relevance of the preceding discussions for Husserl's idea of science.

The idea of science, on Husserl's interpretation, has two basic components: (1) Sciences are bodies of interconnected truths (*LI* I, Proleg. §62); that is, sets of true propositions that cohere in an 'ideal fabric of *meanings*' (*LI* I, Inv. I §29, 325). Sciences are logically organized and interrelated propositions, grounded in a set of basic laws or axioms. The coherence of any such theoretical discipline is governed by the laws of logic, i.e. the laws that pertain to the inter-relations of meanings (relations of entailment, non-contradiction, formalization and generalization, etc.). (2) But sciences are not only defined by the theoretical unity of the propositions that make them up; they are also defined by their pretensions to *truth*. The interconnection of truths must correlate to the way things stand in the world. For this reason, science is defined by the principle of *evidence* (*Evidenz*): that is, the commitment to regard as true what there is evidence to believe is true, and nothing else besides (*LI* I, Proleg. §6, 62).

At this point, I would like to leave aside the first component and concentrate upon the second, i.e. the principle of evidence. Now that we have put in place the concepts in which Husserl couches this principle, it is possible to discuss it in detail. The principle of evidence itself is summarized in the slogan 'back to the things themselves' (*auf die 'Sachen selbst' zurückgehen*; *LI* I 252) or 'to the things themselves!' (*zu den Sachen selbst*). However, it is given more precise formulation by Husserl, most famously in this passage from *Ideas I* (§24):

> The principle of all principles: *that every originary presentive intuition is a legitimizing source of cognition*, that *everything originarily* (so to speak, in its 'personal' actuality) *offered* to us *in 'intuition' is to be accepted simply as what it is presented as being*, but also *only within the limits that in which it is presented there*. We see indeed that each <theory> can only again draw its truth itself from originary data. Every statement which does no more than confer expression on such data by simple explication and by means of significations precisely conforming to them . . . serve[s] as a foundation. (*Ideas I* 44)

The principle states that propositional statements can be regarded as scientific only in so far as they are demonstrably drawn from the relevant evidential sources. Simply put, science is not to be occupied with its own musings, completely disconnected from experience; rather, scientific questions are to be answered based upon the evidence and without straying beyond it. At its foundations, then, scientific enquiry requires *descriptive* and *demonstrative* labour.

The 'principle of all principles' gives a precise sense to the notion of 'evidence' along the lines discussed above: evidence is *originary presentive intuition*. This means that only the object given in an 'in person' or 'bodily' (*leibhaftig*) fashion counts as evidence in the pregnant sense. It is noteworthy, however, that there is no mention in this definition of the ideal of complete adequation, which marks out 'evidence in the strict sense' (*Evidenz*). To do so would have implied that only disciplines capable of achieving the stricter standard of evidence could qualify as sciences. As it stands, the principle is broad enough to serve as a universal criterion of science. It does not discriminate against sciences whose proper standard of evidence is 'inadequate' in the Husserlian sense of the term. Both 'adequate' and 'inadequate' evidence are admitted as 'legitimizing source[s] of cognition'. The scientific standard is 'originary' or 'bodily' givenness, not adequation. For those sciences whose objects do not admit of adequate fulfilment, the achievement of ultimate truth presents itself as an idea in the Kantian sense: a necessarily unrealizable goal, but one towards which our efforts tend.

Sometimes, Husserl also articulates his principle of all principles in the form of a prohibition. In such a form it states that all dogmatic constructions and all received theories are to be avoided. He calls this corollary of the principle of evidence 'the principle of freedom from presuppositions' (*LI* I 263). To cite just one instance, Husserl writes in the *Logical Investigations* that 'meanings inspired only by remote, confused or inauthentic intuitions – if by any intuitions at all – are not enough: we must go back to the "things themselves" ' (*LI* I 252).

The principle of evidence in its positive and its prohibitive form is applied by Husserl to phenomenology itself. This is what certifies the status of phenomenology as a 'rigorous science'. On one hand, the prohibitive form of the principle manifests itself in what calls in *Ideas I* 'the philosophical εποχή [bracketing]': 'Formulated explicitly, the philosophical εποχή that we are undertaking shall consist of our *completely abstaining from any judgement regarding the doctrinal content of any previous philosophy and effecting all of our demonstrations within the limits set by this abstention'* (*Ideas I* §18, 33–4). This abstention does not preclude the discussion of judgements passed down by the tradition – it is permissible to speak of these as historical facts. But it does deny to them any authority in resolving philosophical questions. They remain mere theories until legitimating evidence is adduced in support of them. Enforcing this abstention has strategic importance in the field of philosophical research. The philosophical *epoché* establishes, against the influence of received traditions, an autonomous space of thinking from which critique and theoretical innovation are possible. As Heidegger explains:

> The phenomenological maxim '*to the matters themselves*' is addressed against construction and free-floating questioning in traditional concepts which have become more and more groundless. That this maxim is self-evident, that it nevertheless has become necessary to make it into an explicit battle cry against free-floating thought, characterizes the very situation of philosophy.[16]

It is worth reiterating and clarifying before moving on that the philosophical *epoché* is not be confused with the transcendental or eidetic reductions; it is antecedent to both.[17] Indeed, as I have mentioned, it is nothing peculiar to phenomenology but applies equally to all sciences.

On the other hand, phenomenology takes up for itself the directive to go 'back to the things themselves'. In this way, Husserl's principle demands an evidence-based, and even 'positivistic' style of philosophical method. This Husserl proposes to carry out through an isolation of the sphere of transcendental being via the transcendental reduction (a sphere in which adequate evidence is possible). Remaining strictly within the limits of this sphere, the goal is then to undertake the 'descriptive and demonstrative labour' demanded by the principle of all principles. The result should be a body of knowledge (eidetic in character) regarding the sphere of transcendental subjectivity.

As it stands, however, the analysis of intuition offered so far is not even comprehensive enough to account for the evidential acts operative in *empirical* science, let alone *pure* sciences such as phenomenology. We have so far introduced only two forms of presentive intuition: straightforward perception and reflection (the latter mentioned only in passing). Yet, as we shall see, empirical science requires what Husserl calls acts of 'categorial intuition'. And, to complicate matters further, eidetic or pure science requires yet another form of intuition called 'ideation' or 'eidetic seeing'. Without an explanation of how these two forms of *non-sensuous* intuition can also be 'originary' and 'presentive', the principle of all principles would prove to be extremely narrow in scope indeed. If Husserl is to provide a comprehensive 'theory of science' which explicates the possibility of scientific thinking in all its diverse forms, his theory of intuition clearly needs to be expanded. These matters are made all the more pressing by the fact that phenomenological research *itself* is one of the sciences whose legitimacy cannot be certified according to the principle of all principles until the evidential acts it utilizes are shown to be 'legitimizing source[s] of cognition'. In the next chapter, therefore, I discuss these more sophisticated forms of intentionality and intuition.

NOTES

1 It should be noted that, in *Ideas I*, Husserl comes to reserve this term *Einsicht* (insight) and its cognate *Einsehen* (intellectual seeing) for acts of evidence that have a pure, apodictic character (see *Ideas I* 330).

2 Husserl nevertheless acknowledges that evidences can also be confirmed or amplified by other evidences. On this point, see his discussions in *Ideas I* §138 and §151.

3 See *LI* I 193–6; also *LI* II 769; *IP* 47f. and *Ideas I* §21.

4 Emmanuel Levinas, *The Theory of Intuition in Husserl's Phenomenology*, trans. André Orianne (Evanston, IL: Northwestern University Press, 1995), pp. 89–90.

5 Martin Heidegger, *History of the Concept of Time: Prolegomena*, trans. Theodore Kisiel (Bloomington and Indianapolis, IN: Indiana University Press, 1985), p. 47.

6 Indeed, sensuous ('hyletic') impressions can never be communicated as such; the sensuous impression of an entity is always an essentially individual experience. Words themselves are sensuous, to be sure, but they do not resemble the objects they describe.

7 This aspect of Husserl's account has many similarities with Heidegger's more widely known notion of 'idle talk' (*Gerede*). See Martin Heidegger, *Being and Time*, trans. John Macquarrie and Edward Robinson (Oxford: Basil Blackwell, 1962), p. 35.

8 Husserl also acknowledges that fulfilling-intuition of objects of reflection is complicated by requiring a certain *synthesis* (*Ideas I* §78). A synthesis

is required by the fact that the moment in which we 'catch ourselves in the act' is only one temporal phase of that act, and so does not immediately give the *whole* act to our reflective regard. In order to grasp an intentional act as a whole, reflection must supplement the lived experience present 'just now' with recollections and anticipations of the act as it was and will be experienced. The apprehension of a mental act, therefore, is temporal in a way that the apprehension of, say, a mathematical object is not. This has implications for the kind of evidence reflection yields. These remarks receive greater elaboration in Husserl's writings on 'time-consciousness' (see Chapter 8). In any case, Husserl still accords a higher level of evidential status to acts of reflection than acts of perception.

9 Aristotle, *Nichomachean Ethics*, 1094 b 24–7. Cf. *Ideas I* §138.

10 Paul Ricoeur, *Husserl: An Analysis of his Phenomenology*, trans. Edward G. Ballard and Lester E. Embree (Evanston, IL: Northwestern University Press, 1967), p. 6.

11 Aristotle, *Metaphysics*, 1011 b 25–30.

12 From Husserl's list is absent a fifth conceivable meaning of 'truth' which his analysis makes comprehensible: namely, truth as the *interpretive sense itself* (i.e. noematic sense) inherent in the correct act of judgement. This sense of truth would correspond to the propositional content of the assertion or judgement. Here we would be calling 'true' the *meaning* which is seen to be fulfilled in the act of identification or adequation. It could be that this is what Husserl intends in definition (4), albeit conflating the intentional with the interpretive sense of the act. In any event, the distinction I am making is present elsewhere in Husserl's account; see, for example, the discussion of knowledge as grasping the matter according to its 'concept' in *LI* II 696f.

13 Heidegger, *History of the Concept of Time*, p. 52. Theodore Kisiel highlights the usage of similar expressions in the work of Emil Lask, who was also heavily influenced by Husserl's analysis of truth (see Theodore Kisiel, *The Genesis of Heidegger's* Being and Time [Berkeley and Los Angeles, CA: University of California Press, 1993], p. 34).

14 See Heidegger, *History of the Concept of Time*, pp. 49–54; and for a discussion, Daniel O. Dahlstrom, *Heidegger's Concept of Truth* (Cambridge: Cambridge University Press, 2001), pp. 65–73.

15 Heidegger, *History of the Concept of Time*, pp. 53f.

16 Ibid., p. 76.

17 In a marginal note in his 'D' copy of the text, Husserl writes that the 'philosophical *epoché*' is 'not to be confused with that *epoché* which, as a method, shapes philosophy itself; cf. phenomenological reduction' (*Ideas I* 34).

CHAPTER 7

CATEGORIAL INTUITION: SYNTHESIS AND IDEATION

Perception alone does not account for the breadth of experiences that we enjoy every day. For example, the experience of other people, the experience of oneself, of states of affairs, of empirical truths, of essential truths, of value, of beauty, of time passing – none of these experiences can be classed as a straightforward (sensuous) perception. And yet, each involves, in some sense, a 'presenting' or 'giving' of some object. Husserl takes the view that each of these experiences (and many more besides) requires its own phenomenological analysis – that is, an analysis of the way in which its object comes to be 'constituted' or encountered within conscious life. For reasons of space it would be impossible to deal with the full breadth of Husserl's studies. In the chapters ahead I consider a selection of them: the experiences of time, self, others, the lifeworld and the 'real' world of science. In this chapter, however, I focus on two of the most basic non-sensuous experiences addressed by Husserl: the 'synthetic' intuition of states of affairs, and the 'ideative' intuition of essences. In the *Logical Investigations*, Husserl groups these two kinds of intuitive act together under the heading 'categorial intuition'.

THE PROBLEM OF CATEGORIAL INTUITION

It is a novel feature of Husserl's epistemology that he believes even simple acts of objectification can either achieve or fail to achieve their 'adequation', and to this extent they can be true or false (*LI* II 767f). The received wisdom states that sees truth and falsehood only appear for the first time where a *relation* is asserted (i.e. in 'relational' acts). Husserl takes the standard view to be unnecessarily restrictive. Even 'non-relational' acts, such as the presentation of an individual object, can in principle be seen to be true or false, and can thus count as 'evidences'. So, for example, the meanings 'car', 'brown', 'upholstery' and 'warm' all intend individual objects whose bodily givenness would confirm these 'nominal acts'. In each case, an 'identity' could be grasped between object meant and object given, and we would have an 'experience of truth' (see Chapter 6). Nonetheless, Husserl recognizes that, for the most part, we do not posit individual things or properties of things in isolation. Instead, we articulate propositions or judgements concerning *relations or states of affairs*, e.g. 'the car is brown', 'the car's upholstery is warm', etc. For this reason, any account of 'truth' has to explain how we achieve 'evidence' or 'fulfilling intuition' with respect to these kinds of 'relational' or 'multi-rayed' acts.[1] As we shall see, this is by no means a straightforward matter. Husserl dedicates an entire section of the Sixth Logical Investigation to addressing this question ('Sense and Understanding', §§40–66), and it is a topic to which he frequently returns throughout his career.

The term 'state of affairs' (*Sachverhalt* or *Sachlage*) is of central importance in what follows, and it requires some explanation. 'State of affairs' denotes the way things stand. States of affairs are those realities (loosely speaking) that we refer to by propositions such as '*S* is *P*' or '*A* and *B* stand in relation *R*'. If the state of affairs is as it is asserted to be, then the proposition is true. In this connection, the proposition is 'the truth-bearer' and the state of affairs is 'the truth-maker'.[2] Or, put the other way around, the state of affairs is what we typically 'express' in perceptual propositions; e.g. 'the candle is on the dining table'. The assertions that usually count as 'knowledge' concern *states of affairs*: e.g. the moon is full; 20 million people live in Australia; Napoleon was defeated at Waterloo; blue colours are called 'blue' in English; this is a book; A is not ~A; the global economy is becoming increasingly integrated. In short, our *knowledge* of the world concerns *states of affairs*, not entities *simpliciter* (*LI* I, Proleg. §6).

There is a puzzle, however, concerning states of affairs. It is one thing to explain how states of affairs can be *intended* in expressive acts – this is taken care of by the idea of 'interpretive sense' or 'noematic sense': the inherent 'matter' or 'noema' in a meaning-intention allows an object to be intended with a complex meaning of the type found in categorial judgements. It is quite another thing, however, to explain how such a meaning-intention might find a *fulfilling intuition.* What in intuition corresponds to the categorial judgement to make it true? Or, put the other way around, what in perception are we expressing when we say, for example, that the paper *is* white? This is an ancient philosophical problem known at least since Plato.[3] Allow me to explain the difficulty in more detail.

Grammatically speaking, nouns and modifiers correlate to real objects (e.g. 'paper') and moments of real objects (e.g. 'white') respectively; these elements of assertions have perceptible objective correlates. But even the simplest propositions appeal to more than mere sensuous objects of these kinds. Assertions contain other puzzling meaning-elements that do not find simple correlates in experience: particles, connectives, relations, the copula, universals, etc. Husserl describes these as the 'surplus of meaning' in assertions (*LI* II, Inv. VI §40, 775). These surplus elements refer to components of the state of affairs that are not *seen* in the literal sense. For example, the relation 'bigger than' cannot itself be seen, yet it is integral to the state of affairs that *a* is bigger than *b*. Or, take the following example. The assertion 'the door is red' is not made true by there being a door and redness. It is made true by a door, redness and the door *being* red (*LI* II, Inv. VI §43, 780). And yet where is this '*being*-red'? It is not literally seen:

> The 'a' and the 'the', the 'and' and the 'or', the 'if' and the 'then', the 'all' and the 'none', the 'something' and the 'nothing', the forms of quantity and the determinations of number, etc. – all these are meaningful propositional elements, but we should look in vain for their objective correlates (if such may be ascribed to them at all) in the sphere of *real* objects, which is in fact no other than the sphere of *objects of possible sense-perception.* (*LI* II 782)

Thus, states of affairs may have individual entities as their terms, but states of affairs are not themselves entities. On this point, Husserl agrees with Kant's famous pronouncements that 'being is absolutely imperceptible' and that 'being is not a real predicate' (*CPR* A 598/B 626; cf. *LI* II, Inv. VI §43). How is it then that we 'perceive' not just individual objects but *states of affairs*? How are states of affairs intuited?

On the one hand, Husserl declines to posit a faculty of 'intellectual intuition', i.e. the ability to apprehend non-sensuous (e.g. logical) objects via a form of intuition which sees beyond the sensuous realm to a transcendent realm of 'rational truths'. For Husserl, the idea of 'intellectual intuition', found in differing forms in Descartes, Leibniz and Spinoza, is nothing more than a licence for metaphysical invention. It does nothing to *explain* genuinely our intuition of states of affairs, which (initially at least) has nothing to do with a realm of 'rational truths' and everything to do with the contingencies *of this real world*. Whatever the answer to the puzzle, it cannot surrender the connection between states of affairs and sensuous objects. Indeed, Husserl reiterates the Kantian point that there can be no validity to knowledge claims if they do not ultimately refer to sensuous intuition: 'It lies in the nature of the case that everything categorial ultimately rests upon sensuous intuition, that a "categorial intuition", an intellectual insight, a case of thought in the highest sense, without any foundation of sense, is a piece of nonsense' (*LI* II, Inv. VI §60, 817f.).

On the other hand, Locke's solution is equally problematic: the non-sensuous components that belong to states of affairs cannot be explained by looking to the inner workings of the mind, e.g. by assuming that 'logical' components are psychical phenomena. If the 'logical' components of states of affairs were merely products of the human mind, then they would constitute a class of objects that could be found amongst the inventory of one's inner, mental world, i.e. found by 'inner perception'. But this is not at all what we find to be the case. Husserl's point is pithily stated by Heidegger: 'When I examine the immanence of consciousness, I always find only the sensory and objective, which I must take as "immanently real" [*reeles*] components of the psychic process, but I never find anything like "being", "this", "and".'[4]

Having ruled out two traditional solutions to the problem at hand – i.e. intellectual intuition (rationalism) and inner perception (empiricism) – how does Husserl propose to proceed? We must recognize, he claims, that the 'surplus' elements of meaning refer to a class of *objects*: 'categorial forms'. These are the various logical forms that may be found to apply to perceptual objects: e.g. relation, number, conjunction, predication. Now these categorial forms, as I have mentioned, do not 'exist' in quite the same sense that real objects do. The car's *being*-brown, for instance, is itself neither a physical thing (like the car) nor a property of a thing (like the brown). Ontologically, Husserl takes states of affairs to be 'ideal complexes' rather than 'realities'. To mark this difference, entities are said to 'exist' or 'be', whereas states of affairs are said to 'hold', 'subsist' (*bestehen*), or 'be the case' (*LI* II 768f.). But just because states of affairs are not 'real' objects does not mean they are any less 'actual' or 'objective'. They are certainly nothing like fictions or mere thoughts. On the contrary, they belong in some sense to the fabric of the actual world in which we live.[5] Far from being 'merely subjective' phenomena, Husserl avers, categorial forms belong to the truly objective dimension of reality. (At this point, the argument dovetails with the critique of the psychologistic tendency to collapse logical objects into mental phenomena; see Chapter 1.)

Furthermore, Husserl finds himself forced to conclude that categorial forms are *intuitable*: 'there must at least be an act which renders identical services to the categorial elements of meaning that merely sensuous perception renders to the material elements' (*LI* II 785). Indeed, is it not the case that there are acts in which I *see* the car, and also acts in which I *see* that the car is red? Thus, it would seem that, even if there are theoretical difficulties associated with explaining acts of 'categorial intuition', there are certainly no practical difficulties in carrying them out: such acts are accomplished unproblematically in virtually every waking experience. In other words, we habitually 'see' more than is sensuously encountered in immediate perception. Thus, we must admit both 'sensuous intuition' *and* 'categorial intuition'. The question is how to understand the latter *qua* intentional act.

It is at this point, incidentally, that Husserl parts ways with Kant, for whom the categories are derived from the forms of judgement (i.e. pure structures of thinking), quite apart from intuition. Husserl counters that the *forms of judgement* ('signification categories') derive their legitimacy from categorial intuition in which *logical forms* ('logical categories') are first given, not the other way around.[6] Hence, rigorous research into the categories can and must go back to the things themselves, i.e. the categorial forms, and not content itself with basing its studies in the (conventional) forms of judgement.

THE INTUITION OF CATEGORIAL FORMS (SYNTHETIC ACTS)

How then does Husserl understand the phenomenon of 'categorial intuition'? In contradistinction to perceptual acts, which are 'straightforward' or 'simple', acts of categorial intuition are said to be 'multi-levelled' or 'founded' acts. Whereas simple perceptual acts give their object 'in one blow' (*LI* II, Inv. VI §47, 788), categorial intuitions occur when objects given in simple perceptual acts are themselves taken up and observed in terms of their 'categorial' or 'logical' relation. To put it simply, this means that categorial intuitions piggy-back, as it were, on other intuitive acts and thereby enjoy a previously unknown perspective on objective being. Let us pause over this for a moment.

The categorial act relies on preceding acts in which individual objects have already been constituted. For example, the act of intuiting that the door is red relies upon prior acts of simple sense-perception in which the door and the red are objectified. The categorial intuition, for its part, then takes up the objects so constituted and interprets them with respect to their relation. The categorial act *synthesizes* the pre-given objects under some categorial form. By synthesizing the objects contained in prior acts, the categorial act intends a *new* object – e.g. not just the door or the red, but now a *relation* which pertains to those pre-given objects: namely, the door's *being*-red. The objects are combined under a categorial form – in this case '*S* is *P*':

> What we have are acts which, as we said, *set up new objects*, acts in which something *appears as actual and self-given*, which was not given, and could not have been given, as what it now appears to be, in these foundational acts alone. *On the other hand, the new objects are based on the older ones, they are related to what appears in the basic acts.* Their manner of appearance is essentially determined by this relation. We are here dealing with a sphere of objects, *which can only show themselves 'in person' in such founded acts.* (*LI* II, Inv. VI §46, 787f.)

In short, the objects given already in sensuous perception are taken up in a 'logical' act in which they are combined under some categorial form. The result is that something implicit in the straightforward perception is now presented objectively. Some truth about the world is disclosed that previously had not been seen.

In so far as they bring together multiple objects, categorial acts are characterized by Husserl as 'synthetic' acts. The 'synthesis' that occurs in such acts, however, is different in kind to the synthesis that occurs in straightforward acts of perception. In the perceptual act, as we have seen, an individual object is constituted through a series of partial acts. This series may entail massive complexities, but it remains never more than a variegated intention towards an *individual* object. In the categorial act, by contrast, an object is constituted through bringing together two or more objects already constituted in acts of the single-levelled variety. This may be a much simpler operation than the straightforward act of perception, and yet because it constitutes a new, non-sensuous object, it involves a step 'upwards' towards a higher level of objectivity and therefore counts as a 'multi-levelled' act.

The resultant categorial objects can themselves be taken up into higher-level categorial acts (e.g. I see that the red door needs a new coat of paint). This possibility of iteration allows for a 'ladder' of categorial acts that build upon one another. Only at the top of such a ladder can certain truths 'show themselves'. Consider, for example, the doctor's judgement that her patient is suffering from bronchitis. For such a state of affairs to be evident (i.e. intuited), a certain collection of symptoms would have to be observed in conjunction. This requires a synthetic act of categorial intuition. But this would already require a series of lower-level categorial acts; e.g. each of the symptoms would have to be observed individually. To observe each of symptoms would, in turn, require further categorial acts; e.g. the doctor would have to observe that the patient's breathing is abnormal (i.e. related in the mode of 'comparison' to normal breathing) and is accompanied by a certain kind of cough, and so forth. Without establishing this 'ladder' of founded acts – e.g. if I didn't have the expertise to recognize such symptoms and to look for this particular conjunction of symptoms – the relevant categorial object (i.e. the patient's *having* bronchitis) would not be 'observed'. But, on the basis of this interconnected series of observations, the doctor's hypothesis (meaning-intention) is confirmed (intuitively fulfilled).

As this example intimates, there are many kinds of logical act, e.g. acts of conjunction, predication, quantification, causation. Indeed, there are as many logical acts as there are logical or categorial forms. Husserl recognizes that to each categorial form there corresponds an act of categorial intuition and that each of these is a unique cognitive achievement admitting of phenomenological analysis. There is no single phenomenological analysis that can explain categorial intuition; categorial intuition is a genus under which fall a multiplicity of intentional acts. Husserl never claims to have presented an exhaustive analysis of these acts, but he does provide certain illustrative studies.

For instance, in the Sixth Logical Investigation (§48), the act is described in which the state of affairs of the form '*A is or has a*' or '*a is in A*' is intuited. '*A*' here is a term standing for a perceived object, and '*a*' is a property of it. Now, the object *A* is perceived as a whole in an ordinary perceptual act 'in straightforward fashion'. That is, it is constituted as the unifying correlate of a flux of sensuous appearing. The sensuous property *a* can likewise be attended to as the object of a separate perceptual act. But if we remain at the level of sensuous perception, we can never grasp the fact that *a* is a *property of A*. To grasp this relation between *a* and *A* requires a new and different kind of act which allows the perceptual object *a* to appear *as* a 'moment' or 'partial-intention' belonging to the total percept of the object *A*. In this case, the job of the categorial act is to bring into relief the *part–whole* relationship between the perceived object and one of the sensuous (hyletic) elements of the very flux in and through which the perceived object had been perceived. *A* is grasped as a whole, *of which a* is a part.[7] Thus, the form '*A is or has a*' becomes the object of a new act which includes, as it were, both *A* and *a* as its terms. A new (categorial) object is thus constituted without losing from sight *A* and *a*. The *relation* is now the intentional object of the categorial act, but *A* and *a* are said to be 'co-intended'.

Little reflection is required to realize how complex are the acts of thinking that make up our everyday lives – let alone the acts accomplished in the course of scientific research. The sophisticated propositions of science do not find their evidential fulfilment immediately in bare sense-perception. They find their intuitive fulfilment in equally sophisticated strata or dimensions of objective being, strata made intuitively manifest by complex sequences of categorial acts. Husserl sees it as a central task of phenomenology to study these acts individually and in their interconnection. Only a full analysis of categorial intuition could account for the range of evidence available to scientific rationality.[8] Nothing short of a comprehensive analysis of such acts could serve as the theory of 'Reason and Actuality' (*Ideas I*, Part Four). There is, however, another variety of categorial act that needs to be introduced in this context in order to complete this overview of the basic non-sensuous intuitions upon which science is built: eidetic seeing.

IDEATIVE ACTS

In almost every perception of a physical thing, one is *also* conscious that the thing is such and such a thing. One sees not just the thing, but sees it in terms of What it is. For example, I see a cup and am aware that it is a cup. Now, there is a difference between seeing a thing as a cup and considering the idea 'cup' as such. Nevertheless, it is perfectly possible to turn my attention away from this cup to consider the idea 'cup'. So, if you were to ask me a series of questions about this cup, I could give you some answers; but equally, if you went on to ask me to define what makes a cup what it is, I could speak with some degree of cogency on the matter. Clearly the discussion would have shifted gear, as it were, but it would be no less meaningful. This shift, by which the *idea* becomes the topic of conversation rather than the real objects to which it applies, is what Husserl calls 'ideation' or 'eidetic seeing' (*Wesenserschauung*; *Ideas I* 8).[9]

I mentioned above that a body of knowledge consists of 'categorial judgements', not mere 'sensuous judgements'. Some categorial judgements concern real objects or sets of real objects, e.g. 'all polar bears are white'. Other categorial judgements, however, concern ideal objects or 'essences', e.g. 'the number 3 is prime'. No matter how complex the chain of foundations, no synthetic act alone will yield knowledge of ideal objects *per se*. To reach the sphere of ideal objects – specifically, the sphere of 'material essences'[10] – ideal objects need to become objectified in their own right. This is only achieved when 'eidetic seeing' is employed. No other categorial act (e.g. the 'synthetic acts' discussed above) can account for the possibility of *evidential intuition* in matters of eidetic judgement. Eidetic seeing is, therefore, the condition for the possibility of all regional eidetic sciences, including phenomenology itself. For this reason, Husserl singles out the act of eidetic seeing, of all categorial acts, for special investigation.

Ideation begins with individual objects, but does not remain there. It diverts attention away from entities entirely so as to consider in isolation the idea or *universal* under which those *particulars* may be subsumed. The universal is uncoupled from the individual object or state of affairs in which it is founded, and is contemplated in itself. For instance, it might begin with a cup, but only as a launching-point for a consideration of the idea 'cup' with complete indifference as to the existence of cups and contingent facts about them. All factual information concerning actual entities 'falls out' of ideative acts, as it were, leaving only the essential make-up of such entities, i.e. that set of predicates and laws that necessarily govern objects of that species.

This feature sets ideation apart from ordinary synthetic acts. In synthetic acts, a 'logical' object (such as a relation) is intended, but the intention does not lose sight of the individual objects to which the logical form is said to apply. For instance, if I assert that the candle is on the table, then I am asserting a categorial form (the positional relation of being-on), but I am asserting it *of* the two real objects given in the foundational acts (the candle and the table). The candle and table are, as Husserl says, 'co-intended'. In ideative acts, by contrast, an essence is objectified in such a way that no individual objects are co-intended: 'the objects of the founding acts do not *enter into* the intention of the founded one' (*LI* II 799f.). Hence, the essence is considered in isolation, as an idea in its own right, and not just in so far as it characterizes certain real objects. We might say, then, that synthetic acts intend multiple objects *by means of* a categorial form – hence intending a categorially 'formed' state of affairs – whereas ideative acts intend a single object: the essence or form itself. Therefore, ideation has no necessary connection to categorial objects *per se*. It is true that ideation can be applied to categorial objects; yielding, for example, the ideas 'and', 'on', 'after', etc. However, as the examples above show, ideation can equally be applied to individual objects; yielding, for example, the ideas 'cup', 'yellow', 'heat'.

In the *Logical Investigations*, synthetic and ideative acts are lumped together under the heading of 'categorial intuition'. But, as Husserl came to recognize, ideation is a considerably more complex intuitive act than ordinary acts of synthesis. In *Ideas I* and subsequent writings, therefore, synthetic and ideative acts are treated quite separately.[11] Ideative acts are unusual amongst categorial acts for the way they treat their founding acts. The 'foundation' that other presentive acts offer to ideation is that of *arbitrary examples*. For the purposes of ideation, *imagined* particulars of the relevant universal will serve just as well as founding acts as *perceived* instances:

> The Eidos, the *pure essence*, can be exemplified for intuition in experiential data – in data of perception, memory, and so forth; but it can equally well be exemplified in *data of mere phantasy*.

Accordingly, to seize upon an essence itself, and to seize upon it *originarily*, we can start from corresponding experiencing intuitions, *but equally well from intuitions which are non-experiencing, which do not seize upon factual existence but which are instead 'merely imaginative'*. (*Ideas I* §4, 11; cf. §70).

In the natural sciences, grounding experiences can never be exchanged for imaginary ones (*Ideas I* 16). The result would be merely imaginary experiments yielding imaginary results, i.e. most likely falsehoods. But, because the sciences of essences are interested only in *possibility* and not *actuality*, they can do without actual experience and make do with imagination alone. Indeed, in eidetic sciences, '*free phantasies* acquire *a position of primacy over perceptions*' (*Ideas I* §70, 158f.).

In writings after the *Logical Investigations*, this observation concerning the usefulness of imagination is incorporated into Husserl's analysis of the intentional structure of eidetic seeing.[12] Husserl comes to the view that the thing itself of an ideative act, i.e. the essence, is brought to intuitive givenness through the imaginative process of 'free variation'. Through a series of examples, varied in every conceivable way, an element of similarity can be identified and evidentially confirmed. One sees 'red', for example, when one identifies that which is common amongst a variety of sensuous intuitions of something red. In the categorial act of comparison, the invariant element itself emerges (i.e. redness) (*EJ* 348). A determination of what is invariant is thus reached through fantasy which arbitrarily varies the given exemplar:

[B]y an act of volition we produce free variants, each of which, just like the total process of variation itself, occurs in the subjective mode of the 'arbitrary'. It then becomes evident that a unity runs through this multiplicity of successive figures, that in such free variations of an original image, e.g. of a thing, an *invariant* is necessarily retained as the *necessary general form*, without which an object such as this thing, as an example of its kind, would not be thinkable at all. While what differentiates the variants remains indifferent to us, this form stands out in the practice of voluntary variation, and as an absolutely identical content, an invariable *what*, according to which all the variants coincide: *a general essence*. (*EJ* §87, 341)

The quality of the evidence provided by this method of variation does not rest on it being carried on infinitely, but in it having the character of being 'infinitely open': that is, that it could be carried on infinitely in the same arbitrary fashion. The 'arbitrariness' here is important. It signifies the difference between naming that which is common to a certain set of empirically familiar particulars and delimiting the ideal extension of the *eidos* as such. For example, the redness which is common to five or six red things is not the ideal extension of 'red' as such; redness as such is grasped when the examples are seen to be arbitrary particulars. Only in this way does the object transcend empirical generality and become a purely grasped universal which enjoys complete indifference to its actual particularizations.

Such is the method of the geometer, for example, who uses sketches of figures as arbitrary particulars of essences. The sketching of particulars (figures) may facilitate the attaining of intuitive clarity in the apprehension of the universal. But the reliance on sketches also restricts the geometer in a way that he is not restricted in free phantasy in which he can alter figures at will and run through variations ('phantasy-constructions') (*Ideas I* 159). Likewise, the philosopher may use perceptions and representations as exemplars to 'fertilize one's phantasy'. In this connection, Husserl points to history and poetry as sources that might provide provocative descriptions and thus advance our imagination beyond its current capabilities.

But what is essential here is the imagination and variation which the examples initiate, for it is through the course of variation that the invariant comes to be intuited with evidence. The intuition of particulars needs to be cultivated in order to provide sufficient exemplars for the determination of the essence to be made with maximum clarity. Only clearly seen examples (particulars) can yield clearly seen essences. On this basis, however, it is possible in principle for consciousness to achieve an *adequate* intuition of an essence (*Ideas I* 67f.): '*perfectly clear seizing-upon* ... allows for an *absolutely certain* identifying and distinguishing, explicating, relating, and so forth, thus allowing for effecting all "logical" acts "with insight" ' (*Ideas I* 156; emphasis altered). This is remarkable because 'absolute certainty' (apodicticity) is not a standard of evidence attainable in the straightforward perception of a thing, nor in the intuition of an empirical state of affairs. As Husserl admits, however, the intuition of essences is a very difficult matter and one in which further degrees of clarity and distinctness are often possible (*Ideas I* §§67–69).

The whole gamut of judgements belonging to the sphere of understanding or rational thought are grounded on synthetic and ideative acts. The foregoing analysis of these concepts has only touched upon the most essential points of Husserl's quite extensive studies – and only those studies from the early and middle periods. These, however, are not Husserl's final word on the nature of rational thought. He continually revisited territory covered in his earlier work, and in the final years of his life his thinking on this topic underwent another significant revision. Indeed, as I discuss in Chapter 11, his later 'genetic' studies of scientific consciousness take up a more thoroughly *historical* perspective on the achievement of scientific knowledge and, in the process, acquire a more critical tone with regard to modern science.

NOTES

1 On the terminology of 'single-rayed' and 'many-rayed' acts, see *LI* II 622–4 and 632–5. 'Single-rayed' acts intend an individual object, whereas 'many-rayed' acts intend multiple objects at once. Husserl notes, however, that consciousness tends to continually collapse its syntheses into new, more semantically complex objects (633). For instance, the many-rayed judgement that *the door is red* becomes a single-rayed apprehension of the *red door*. On this transformative operation, see also *Ideas I* §119.

2 I owe this formulation to Dermot Moran, *Introduction to Phenomenology* (New York: Routledge, 2000), p. 112.

3 See Plato, *Theaetaus*, 185a–186e.

4 Martin Heidegger, *History of the Concept of Time: Prolegomena*, trans. Theodore Kisiel (Bloomington and Indianapolis, IN: Indiana University Press, 1985), p. 59.

5 It becomes apparent at this point that 'ideality' functions as something of a 'catch-all' term for Husserl. Anything that is not real – barring absolute consciousness itself – is regarded as a kind of 'ideal object'. And yet very different kinds of object fall into this category: states of affairs, propositional contents (meanings), essences, concepts, natural laws, eidetic laws, and so forth.

6 On these distinctions, see the discussion in Chapter 2.

7 Husserl stresses the centrality of part-whole (i.e. 'mereological') relationships to the understanding of logical forms. Though it is difficult to generalize, he typically defines categorial relationships in terms of the way in which they relate pre-given objects *as* parts and/or wholes. This

explains why the Third Logical Investigation is devoted to the theory of parts and wholes.

8 The most extensive treatments of scientific rationality in the published works of Husserl, apart from those in the *Logical Investigations*, are found in *Experience and Judgement* and *The Crisis of the European Sciences*.

9 The most detailed and advanced analysis of the act of eidetic seeing amongst Husserl's published works is found in *Experience and Judgement* (§§80–98, esp. §§86–89).

10 Material essences are the species and genera to which individual objects belong. They are differentiated from formal essences, i.e. logical forms. For a more detailed discussion of these distinctions, see Chapter 2.

11 In *Ideas I*, for example, synthetic acts are dealt with primarily in §§118–123, and eidetic seeing is discussed in §§1–26 (esp. §§3–4) and §§69–75. Likewise, in *Experience and Judgement*, synthetic acts are treated under the heading of 'Predicative (Receptive) Experience' (§§22–46), and eidetic seeing later under the heading of 'The Constitution of General Objectivities' (§§86–93).

12 The discussions of ideation and the consciousness of universalities in the *Logical Investigations*, which appear primarily in Inv. II ('The Ideal Unity of the Species and Modern Theories of Abstraction'), are quite limited in scope and are far surpassed even by the discussions in *Ideas I*, but most certainly by the analyses in *Experience and Judgement*. Nevertheless, Husserl voices no criticisms of these earlier studies, for example, in the preface to the second edition of 1913.

CHAPTER 8

TIME-CONSCIOUSNESS

Husserl begins his lectures on the phenomenology of internal time-consciousness (1905–10) by recalling St Augustine's famous remark: 'What then is time? Provided that no one asks me, I know. If I want to explain it to an enquirer, I do not know.'[1] Idle speculation will not reverse this ignorance. Here, as always, Husserl argues, we must start from concrete experience and consider that concrete experience in the phenomenological attitude. Both the problem of time and its proper analysis arise for Husserl out of his prior interest in the concrete experience of perception, and so it is here that we must begin in our examination of his phenomenological analysis of 'time-consciousness'.

THE HORIZONAL STRUCTURE OF INTENTIONAL EXPERIENCE

Crucial to Husserl's account of the perceptual act is the idea that each moment in the perception is accompanied by an understanding that its object may yet be given in further aspects or 'adumbrations'. The thing itself is not exhausted by the aspect of it that is currently given: 'There belongs to every external perception its reference from the "genuinely perceived" sides of the object of perception to the sides "also meant" – not yet perceived but only anticipated' (*CM* §19, 44). In a sense, then, every moment of a perception is haunted by an infinite series of further possible perceptions of the object. Some of these 'possible perceptions' may have already been *actualized* in prior moments of the same perceptual act; however, most of them are merely *anticipated*. The act of perception is *structured* by moving within this interconnected '*horizon*' (*Horizont*) of possible perceptual aspects of the object. What this observation implies is that the intentional act of perception always 'has an eye to' that which is not currently the focus of its immediate sensuous intuition; what is immediately intuited in the present moment is tacitly projected against a background of that which is currently absent or hidden. The background is always also 'there' too, although not as the object of our immediate attention. Husserl will say that the background is 'co-intended' but not 'objectified'.

Our consciousness that the present contents of experience *stands within* a context of other possible contents is what Husserl calls 'horizon-consciousness' (*CES* 237). The horizonal 'halo' of which I am conscious represents that to which I may divert my attention (*Ideas I* 52). This 'halo' includes, for instance, the *parts* of the object that I am currently attending to. So, for example, as I observe a table, the halo or co-intended horizon would include also the grain of the wood which may, in the next moment, become the direct object of my perceptual gaze. Initially, I perceive the thing as a whole, but then the perception is modified as I turn my attention to various parts of the whole. Throughout such a sequence of perception, the same object is intended, but in different aspects and within increase levels of first-hand familiarity. But, of course, horizons of possible perceptions extend beyond the singular object currently before me. Other objects belonging to the background of my current perception can come into the foreground. From the table I may turn my attention to the room in which it is situated, then to the block of land, to the neighbourhood, to the city, and so on. As you will recall, Husserl's definition of 'the natural idea of the world' is simply the consequence of extending one's 'horizonal consciousness' as far as possible: the world is the world-horizon, i.e. the universal horizon of possible objects implied in any act of perception (*Ideas I* §27; cf. Chapter 4, pp. 59–61).

How does this relate to the question of time? Husserl notices that the remarkable and fundamental 'horizonal' structure of experience seems to bear an intrinsic and essential connection to temporality. The 'possible perceptions' that accompany perception at every turn are possible *future* experiences, or perhaps possibilities already realized in *past* experiences. This is even more clearly the case within the simple act of perception itself. I *anticipate* that further adumbrations of the physical thing will appear in a continuum as I move around the thing or the thing changes position. In this context, the horizonal structure of my intention is precisely correlated to the predictable temporal experience of the thing. In so far as I intend the thing as it actually is, my temporal experience will conform to my anticipations. If my anticipations are disappointed, then I find myself surprised, and am forced to set up a new horizon of anticipations (*Ideas I* 102). This analysis is illustrated by Descartes' famous description of the square tower which I first see as round. But as I move closer, I see that I was mistaken; it was round all the while. This illustrates also, incidentally, that it is only in a temporal act structured by anticipations that I can be *mistaken*. The horizonal structure of perceptual acts is the condition for the possibility of being correct or mistaken. Indeed, every encounter with physical objects is regulated by this dialectic of anticipation and fulfilment; this is what makes it possible to experience *objects* (which always means *unities*) rather than just an endless flux of sensations.

On the basis of these interrelations between intentionality and temporality, Husserl sees that to penetrate more deeply into the workings of the remarkable and fundamental 'horizonal' structure of intentional experience requires coming to grips with the 'temporal' structure of experience. The temporal character of all experience thrusts itself to the fore as potentially one of the most fundamental of all phenomenological themes – indeed, 'perhaps the most important in the whole of phenomenology'.[2]

Before launching into Husserl's analysis, however, it is worth clarifying the ambiguities in the phrase 'the temporal structure of experience'. Husserl distinguishes three meanings:

(1) The object of a perceptual act is itself 'temporally structured'. That is, the perceived object is 'in time' and may either be static or perhaps undergoing some alteration or movement over its temporal phases. It may come into being or pass out of being. It may also be simultaneous with, prior to, or after other objects/events. The 'temporal structure' at stake here is the temporal structure of the world in general. Husserl calls this 'cosmic' or 'objective time': the measurable, datable, linear, intersubjective dimensionality in which worldly events occur and objects exist. 'Objective time' is the temporal dimension of the world-horizon. By convention, it is measured in years, months, days, hour, etc., and we refer to it relatively as 'past', 'present' and 'future'.

(2) The *experience* of temporal objects, however, also has 'temporal structure'. Acts of consciousness unfold in temporal phases. Hence, to speak of 'the temporal structure of experience' can also

mean to speak of the structure governing the unfolding phases of some intentional act. This may be called the 'subjective' side of the question of temporality. In this connection, Husserl speaks of the 'subjective', 'pre-empirical' or 'phenomenological time' in contrast to 'objective time'.

(3) Crudely put, Husserl's interest lies in how 'objective time' comes to be experienced or 'constituted' within 'subjective time' (*PITC* 22). However, as we shall see in due course, Husserl questions whether it is coherent, in the final analysis, to construe lived experience as itself *temporal*, even in the 'subjective' sense. To be sure, lived experience can be considered in its subjective temporal unfolding. But is the conscious subject to whom transcendent and immanent temporal unfoldings are given itself temporal? Husserl argues that the consciousness by which an act of consciousness is 'reflectively' constituted as an immanent temporal object cannot itself be equated with that temporal unfolding act. To avoid an infinite regress, then, both transcendent and immanent temporal objects must be constituted within a *non-temporal* 'absolute consciousness'. Absolute consciousness, for its part, names the 'living present' (*der lebendige Gegenwart*): the temporalizing form of consciousness itself (*Zeitbewusstsein*; time-consciousness). It is this structure that makes possible the temporal flow of conscious experience; time-consciousness is constituting consciousness. I shall say more about this difficult idea below. But, for now, let it be said that we have here introduced a *third* sense of 'temporal structure', namely the structure of the 'living present' *per se*.

In summary, therefore, Husserl seeks to understand objective time in terms of its constitution in subjective time, and then to investigate the origin of subjective time in absolute consciousness. I shall follow this broad progression as we proceed.

THE CONSTITUTION OF TEMPORAL OBJECTS

If we habitually experience and understand 'objective time', then 'objective time' must be something *for* consciousness; consciousness must somehow experience the world *as* temporal. But how?

Husserl first asks us to consider the experience of objects whose essential character is to have duration, e.g. melodies, uttered sentences, a sprint or a game of chess (*PITC* §7). Take a melody, for instance. It could never be a timeless entity, given all at once (as it were). A melody collapsed into one temporal moment would be a chord (and even here we are assuming some temporal duration). A melody is, by its very essence, something that unfolds over time and is only perceived as the melody that it is when the *whole* temporal sequence is perceived 'together' in some sense. In other words, the perception of a melody requires a unified intentional act which takes in or objectifies a temporal manifold. But this requires further explanation.

How are such 'temporal objects' (*Zeitobjekte*) experienced? What does it mean to 'perceive' an entity which is given over a period of time? Experience of such objects would be impossible, Husserl claims, if consciousness were only ever consciousness of the punctual now. The consciousness of a melody, by definition, is consciousness of something which is not confined to the punctual now. At any particular moment during our hearing of a melody, it is somewhat past, somewhat present and somewhat future – and all together. It is not the case that, say, at the beginning of the second bar of music, the first bar of the melody is still *present* to me any more than the bars yet to be played are present to me. And yet, at each moment during the listening, I am *hearing* the melody, not just *this* note. Is this talk of 'hearing the melody' merely a figure of speech? Do we ever truly hear a melody, or do we only ever hear the note sounding *now*? Husserl defends our common-sense belief that we do indeed hear melodies and not just notes. When we say that we are hearing the melody, we mean precisely that we are attending to a singular melody which unfolds over a period of time. The melody as a whole is the 'intentional object' of our act of listening, just as the physical thing as a whole is the 'intentional object' of our act of seeing.

For Husserl, the fact that we genuinely *perceive* temporal objects exhibits a peculiarity of consciousness: it is constantly reaching *beyond* the punctual now in order to perceive objects with temporal 'breadth'. But how are we to make sense of this achievement? How does consciousness reach beyond the now to intend something which only exists over a duration? Franz Brentano had asserted that this achievement is a function of imagination. Only what is now is perceived, and what is just-past and what is not-yet are supplemented by the faculty of imagination (*PITC* 29–34). Husserl regards this as an untenable interpretation. The components of a temporal object that are not present now (e.g. the past and future notes of the melody) do not have the character of 'imaginary objects'. Only one 'object' is apprehended in a perceptual act, e.g. the melody itself. The individual notes belong to *phases* of the singular object, the unfolding melody. So, strictly speaking, Brentano errs in thinking of past and future components or phases as 'objects' in their own right, objects which would need to be posited by something like an act of imagination (*PITC* 36ff.). Instead of thinking of the non-present phases of the melody as products of imagination, Husserl suggests it is more accurate to think of them in terms of memory and expectation. This last point, however, requires further elaboration and refinement.

Husserl, pursuing a Jamesian observation, insists that consciousness of what is just-past and what is not-yet accompanies every moment of perception like a 'fringe' or 'halo'.[3] Every moment of perception includes a *'primal impression'* (*Urimpression*)[4] of the hyletic data (sounds, colours, etc.) that make up the current phase of the perception. But, crucially, it also incorporates a *'retention'* of past phases of the perceptual act and an anticipation or *'protention'* of future phases of the act. The 'retained' phases are co-given with the now, although with the index of being 'just past'; and, likewise, the 'protended' phases are co-given, although with the index of being 'not-yet'. The retentions and protentions are not the past and future phases themselves, but are the retention *of* past phases *in the present* and protentions *of* future phases *in the present*. Husserl explains:

> In this way, it becomes evident that concrete perception as original consciousness (original givenness) of a temporally extended object is structured internally as itself a streaming system of momentary perceptions (so-called originary impressions). But each such momentary perception is the nuclear phase of a continuity, a continuity of momentary gradated retentions on the one side, and a horizon of what is coming on the other side: a horizon of 'protention', which is disclosed to be characterized as a constantly gradated coming.[5]

Throughout the perception, as Husserl says, the now-phase is constantly 'running off' (*ablaufen*) into retentional modifications. The 'living present' is constantly having its content displaced by a new primal impression. Each now-phase runs off into being a past phase, and the retentions of previous past phases are passed down the line, as it were. Husserl likens the now-phase and the retained past phases to a comet and its tail: the primal impression is ever new, but as it renews itself it draws behind it the remnants of what is displaced (*PITC* 52). As more and more phases are intuited and retained, the act of perception constantly enlarges itself with regard to its first-hand acquaintance with its object. Over the duration of the act, the intuitive givenness of the transcendent object accumulates – until, of course, the retained phases are so remote as to be intuitively empty, hence losing their status as evidentially 'originary'.

As the constant running off occurs, ever-new primal impressions are also continually being greeted *as* fulfilments or disappointments of our expectations or 'protentions'. As the act unfolds, therefore, expectations and understandings of what is being perceived may need to be revised. Consequently, it would be a mistake to think of the primal impression as merely the passive reception of sensations. What is really occurring in the moment of 'primal impression' is the *fulfilment* or otherwise of a protention. This is what allows every sensation to be experienced as imbued with meaning. Likewise, retentions of the primal impression are more accurately thought of as memories of fulfilled protentions, not as memories of sensations *per se*. When I am surprised by some turn of events, it is because something happens to break a run of fulfilled expectations. It is not against a backdrop of retained sensations that the surprise shows itself, but of retained fulfilments.[6]

To illustrate these ideas, consider again the hearing of a melody. In moment t_1, the first note of the melody is given while, at the same time, further notes are anticipated. In moment t_2, the first note is now intended as something just past (retained) and no longer has the character of actually sounding. Meanwhile, the next note is sensuously given as the now-phase; and, again, further notes are anticipated. Skipping to the final moment of the melody, the final note is heard to sound while the series of previous notes is retained as having preceded this present note in precisely the sequence in which they had 'run off'. By the end of the melody, all the preceding phases (belonging to moments t_1, t_2, t_3, ... t_n) have passed over into retention. The melody is now intended to as an intuitively given whole, notwithstanding that the earliest phases may now only be retained in an almost completely 'empty' (*leer*) fashion. It is important to emphasize, however, that it is not the case that the perception of the melody is only possible once it is past. On the contrary, the melody as a whole is perceived (or rather is *being* perceived) in every moment of the performance; only the contents and extent of what is yet to come and what is already past change as the act unfolds.

THE DOUBLE INTENTIONALITY OF CONSCIOUSNESS

In reality, of course, the phases of perception are not numerically distinct. These are abstractions from what presents itself in a continuum. Nevertheless, the example just given illustrates that no moment in a perception is isolated from the horizon of past and future moments. Each now-phase given in a 'primal impression' is apprehended *as* the present phase of a temporal sequence through *being accompanied by* retentions and protentions of past and future phases. Beneath the surface of an intentional consciousness, then, is a *relating* or *synthesizing* that constantly knits together the current sensuous impression with the appearance-phases that have come before and shall come after so that the primal impression appears *as* the now-phase of the object's appearance. The now-phase only counts as the *present* profile of the object because consciousness construes it *as* a phase within a temporal series. The continual relating of phases constitutes the awareness of a temporal *flow*, and makes the now-phase appear *as* the now-phase of a temporal unfolding. What the phenomenon of 'relating of phases' represents, therefore, is the consciousness *of* temporal succession in every moment of the intentional act. Hence, Husserl speaks of both a 'transverse intentionality' (*Querintentionalität*), which relates consciousness to a transcendent object, and a 'longitudinal intentionality' (*Längsintentionalität*), which continually relates and synthesizes the temporal phases of an act (*PITC* 107–8).

As the foregoing remarks suggest, transverse and longitudinal intentionality are intertwined (*PITC* 109): there can be no relation to the object without the temporal 'phasing' of its appearance; and, there can be no relation of phases into a temporal order if they are not construed as phases in the appearance of some enduring object. The punctual now alone does not suffice to constitute the givenness of a perceptual object. This is obviously the case for temporal objects of the kind discussed above. Without the longitudinal intentionality of time-consciousness, all that could be given of a temporal object is a series of impressions, like frames of a film-reel: sequential, yet isolated and without any intrinsic interconnection. Thus, the knitting together of temporal phases within intentional acts makes it possible for a temporally extended object (such as a melody) to be perceived *as a whole*. And, more generally, longitudinal intentionality makes it possible to identify any object as *the same* object throughout a temporal series of impressions – and this, as you will recall from Chapter 5, is the essence of the perceptual act. Confined to the punctual now, we could not be conscious of a series of impressions as a series, let alone as a series in the appearance of a singular object.

Thus, when Husserl speaks of the 'intuitive' or 'bodily givenness' of perceptual objects, he is referring not simply to the now-phase of consciousness but to the phased totality of a perceptual act. What is 'present' is not simply the primal impression but the object as it is perceived over the course of an act of perception.[7] Likewise, the very concept of real objectivity is correlated to this form of temporal synthesis: to be a real object is to be an object which coheres and endures through an act of perception (*PITC* 168). Or, put negatively, an object cannot be said to have physical reality if it cannot be seen to endure. Only on this condition can alterations be seen as the alternations *of* the selfsame object (*PITC* §41).

PRIMARY AND SECONDARY MEMORY, AND THE CONSTITUTION OF OBJECTIVE TIME

Retention is a form of memory, to be sure. However, Husserl is careful to stress that it is a fundamentally different kind of memory to the act of recollection. In recollection, we *restage* in consciousness a past perception of an object in a wholesale fashion, i.e. including the temporal halo that accompanied the unfolding of the perception the first time around (*PITC* §14). In other words, the retaining and protending that belonged to the perception is replayed, as it were, as a part of the recollection. The running-off-into-retentional-consciousness that occurred in the original act of perception is nested within the act of recollection. By contrast, retention never has the character of a 'replay'. On the contrary, it has the sense of a retaining-in-mind: it is the 'continuous shading-off' of the now into the past (*PITC* 70). Thus Husserl considers the phenomenon of retention to be of a different order to the phenomenon of recollection. Retention is a component in the originary presentation (*Gegenwärtigung*) of an object, whereas recollection is a discrete re-presentation (*Vergegenwärtigung*) of a completed act of perception.

For this reason, Husserl refers to them as 'primary memory' (i.e. retention) and 'secondary memory' (i.e. the act of recollection) (*PITC* §19). Primary memory is clearly the more radical phenomenon. It belongs to the very form of lived experience and is operative in every mode of intentionality. Recollection, on the other hand, is merely one variety of intentional act, and it refers back to the original perception of which it is a reproduction. In later studies, Husserl characterizes phenomena of the 'primary' variety as 'passive' acts of synthesis and phenomena of the 'secondary' variety as 'active', by which he means that acts of the latter kind can be enacted at will.

Recollection may be the derivative phenomenon, but with the possibility of recollection comes the possibility of *returning* to a particular 'now' any number of times. Thanks to recollection, rather than simply being experienced *once* as it flows past, a now can be considered again and again. This fact is central to the story Husserl tells about the origin of the idea of 'objective time' (*PITC* 143ff.). In recalling a past moment to mind at will, it becomes possible to take that moment as a *fixed point* in relation to which the streaming present is increasingly distant. Suddenly, rather than taking the streaming now as a reference-point, some particular now-phase is taken up as an 'objective' reference-point. Moreover, this process can be idealized and extended infinitely. The result is the projection of an infinitely extended plane of now-points existing independently of conscious experience. Thus the idea of 'objective time' is constituted.

As opposed to the time which is experienced within the form of the living present as an incessant *flowing*, objective time comes to be represented as a *stable* continuum of temporal points at which events may be located in a fixed and unchanging fashion. The now of conscious experience, the living present, is subsequently construed as a pointer moving steadily along the idealized dimension of objective time (Aristotle). And every relative temporal position which comes to givenness in an act of perception (thanks to 'longitudinal intentionality') is now also construed as a temporal position within this universal objective temporal plane. Every object of experience with its own temporal horizon can also be slotted into this wider temporal horizon. Even the act of perception itself can be situated in the frame of objective time (*PITC* 146ff.).

ABSOLUTE CONSCIOUSNESS AND THE PROBLEM OF
PHENOMENOLOGICAL REFLECTION

The analysis of time-consciousness is, for Husserl, the most fundamental of all phenomenological themes. As we have already seen, it
provides the key to understanding the subjective conditions for the
possibility of constituting any objectivity whatsoever and of objective time as such. The stream of consciousness that fills 'subjective
time', in turn, has the structure *protention-primordial impression-
retention*. This structure is what Husserl calls the 'formal structure
of the flux', or 'absolute subjectivity' (*PITC* 153, 100). The temporalizing of subjective time (i.e. the stream of consciousness) through
which objective time is constituted is itself an achievement of absolute consciousness (*PITC* 150). This 'temporalizing' is, therefore, the
'ultimately and truly absolute' stratum of being, the condition for
the possibility of intentionality (*Ideas I* 193f.).

However, herein lies a difficulty over which Husserl agonized until
the very end:[8] analyses of time-consciousness, such as those above,
assume the possibility of intuitively investigating and hence objectifying the time-constituting structures of absolute consciousness.
Now, the temporal unfolding of transcendent objects is observable,
as is the temporal unfolding of conscious acts; hence, these are
amenable to phenomenological description. But is this also true of
constituting consciousness itself, i.e. the structure of the living present (protention-primal impression-retention)? And even if absolute
consciousness could be made the object of phenomenological
investigation, would this not involve objectifying it and construing it
as a *temporal* object – that is, reducing it to an object in subjective
time? After all, as Husserl states, 'no part of what is not-flux can
appear' (*PITC* 153). In short, then, how is a phenomenology of
absolute time-consciousness possible?

The problem is further complicated, Husserl argues, because we
find in consciousness no *object* undergoing alteration, nothing
mutating in its appearance. The streaming of consciousness is nothing like a 'substance' that may undergo alteration or mutation;
it is nothing apart from continuous alteration (*PITC* §35). Properly
speaking, therefore, the stream of consciousness cannot be described
as though it were an object like any other. For this reason, Husserl
stresses that the notions of 'sequence', 'flow', 'stream', 'continuity',
'before', 'after', etc. are all metaphors when applied to pure

consciousness, and are all strictly speaking inadmissible (*PITC* §36). However, we have no choice but to describe consciousness 'in conformity with what is constituted', and this means having to borrow names from temporally constituted objects and apply them to what cannot be constituted as an object. Even to describe constituting consciousness as 'non-temporal' is, for the same reason, not entirely adequate. What is meant by this expression is merely that time-consciousness is not an object *within* subjective or objective time.

Are we then to understand the foregoing analyses of the structure of time-consciousness as a theoretical construct lacking any phenomenological basis? Not at all.[9] Despite the difficulties just mentioned, Husserl maintains that the flow of constituting consciousness is *observable* in a fashion thanks to the possibility of *reflection*. What Husserl stresses, however, is that the conditions for the possibility of reflection are quite different to those operative in the perception of a transcendent entity. The object of perception is first given through being *constituted* in the perceptual act. The object of reflection, by contrast, is always already given to consciousness before being constituted as an object.[10] Even as intentional consciousness is conscious of something transcendent, it is always already conscious of itself too. This self-consciousness which always accompanies conscious experience is 'pre-reflective' in the sense that it is operative in *every* conscious experience and does not first arise in acts of reflection. Objectifying acts of reflection are only possible because of this pre-reflective self-awareness:

> [N]o matter what else it may be intrinsically conscious of, [intentional life] is, at the same time, consciousness of itself. Precisely for that reason (as we can see when we consider more profoundly) it has at all times an essential ability to *reflect* on itself, on all its structures that stand out for it – an essential ability to make itself thematic and produce judgements, and evidences, relating to itself. *Its essence includes the possibility of 'self-examination'* . . . (*FTL* 273; cf. *Ideas I* 99, 174–5 and *Ideas II* §23)

The possibility of reflection, then, is referred to the deeper question concerning the pre-reflective self-awareness of lived experience. It is here that Husserl's analysis of time-consciousness comes into play again. Consciousness, he argues, is self-aware by virtue of the same structure by which it is conscious of transcendent objects:

namely, in the 'longitudinal intentionality' that knits together the phases that make up the subjective appearing of the object for a 'transverse' intention (*PITC* §39).[11] In this 'longitudinal intentionality', we are already *aware* of our phasing experiences. Indeed, were it not for this consciousness of our phasing experiences, they could not form the basis of an intentional consciousness of a transcendent object. But, of course, we do not usually attend to these 'phasing experiences' but rather live 'through' them. This is why they must be called 'pre-reflective'. Nevertheless, in this 'pre-reflective' fashion, absolute consciousness is already *manifest* in its intentional acts. Consciousness itself is 'manifest' without first being *constituted* as a temporal object in its own right; it is already given indirectly in the course of its directed (intentional) activity:

> The flux of the immanent, temporally constitutive consciousness not only *is*, but is so remarkably and yet so intelligibly constituted that a self-appearance of the flux necessarily subsists in it, and hence the flux itself must necessarily be comprehensible in the flowing. The self-appearance of the flux does not require a second flux, but *qua* phenomenon it is constituted in itself. (*PITC* 109–10)

In this way, as Dan Zahavi remarks, Husserl's description of the structure of time-consciousness doubles as 'an analysis of the structure of the pre-reflective self-manifestation of our acts and experiences'.[12]

Nevertheless, to make this pre-reflective self-appearance *thematic* requires a 'turn of regard' towards the relations of retention and protention in an act of reflection. This is, of necessity, a form of objectification. But because its 'object' is already pre-given, it does not require the constitution of a *new* objectivity. Reflection is rather an attending to what is already present in naïve conscious experience (*PITC* 161f.). Put another way, reflection is merely the act of making explicit that of which we are always already self-aware; subjective time and absolute time-consciousness are one and the same, albeit experienced differently. Therefore, on the basis of reflective acts, constituting consciousness can indeed be analysed in terms of its essential structures. That is, on the basis of the reflectively grasped stream of consciousness, the structure of the living present can be investigated. The 'formal structure of the flux' is nothing other than that unchanging structure governing every act given to the phenomenologist's reflective regard. Precisely this unchanging structure is the subject matter of phenomenological research into time-consciousness and has been the theme of this chapter.

However, in one final twist, Husserl concedes that in acts of reflection, the reflecting subject itself escapes objectification. Here, as always, the consciousness that is *functioning* to make consciousness thematic cannot itself be made a part of the picture. The act of reflection is only able to objectify what is accessible to it through *retention* (*PITC* 162).[13] Therefore, there always remains a blind-spot, as it were, within reflective activity: namely, the position held by the observer, i.e. the present constitutive functioning of consciousness. In short, it is impossible for the conscious experience discovered in reflection to be identical with the 'absolute stream' of the living now. The 'functioning subjectivity' remains, so to speak, 'anonymous' (*PITC* 110).[14]

Two qualifications need to be made in this connection, however. First, the intentional subjectivity grasped in reflection is nevertheless the same intentional subjectivity functioning in the present. As Husserl writes, 'the original cogito itself and the reflectively grasped cogito are one and the same and can be grasped mediately, in a reflection on a higher level, as indubitably absolutely the same . . . It is just that at one time [the constituting subject] is given, at other times not given' (*Ideas II* 108). Second, the 'anonymous' consciousness is always already pre-reflectively self-aware even when it is not 'thematically given'. Even if it is not thematically present to itself, constituting consciousness is certainly not hidden or 'unconscious'. Indeed, Husserl explicitly rejects as absurd the notion that present conscious experience is unconscious (of itself) and only becomes conscious of itself once it is past. This would simply be a denial of the phenomenon of pre-reflective self-awareness. On the contrary:

> Consciousness is necessarily *consciousness* in each of its phases. Just as the retentional phase was conscious of the preceding one without making it an object, so also are we conscious of the primal datum – namely, in the specific form of the 'now' – without its being objective. (*PITC* 162)

Not only the retained phases of consciousness but also the primal impression (now-phase) is manifest to itself. And this would be the case even apart from the 'halo' of retention and protention. However, the primal impression is only manifest as an experienced 'now' when it is experienced together with its halo of retention and protention. (This again illustrates Zahavi's point that time-consciousness and pre-reflective self-awareness are one and the same.) In conclusion, then, the 'anonymity' of absolute consciousness presents a limit to phenomenological investigation but by no means renders it impossible.

It is difficult to assess the impact of Husserl's phenomenology of time-consciousness in the field of philosophy and outside it. It is probably true to say that Heidegger's analysis of *Dasein's* 'temporality' presented in *Being and Time* has been known and read more widely.[15] But it is also true that Heidegger's own analyses are heavily indebted to Husserl's lectures on the phenomenology of internal time-consciousness, which he had access to during the period in which he wrote *Being and Time*. In any case, the phenomenological avenue of approach to the question of time has inspired some of the most daring philosophy of the last 50 years. Of the many thinkers influenced by this aspect of phenomenological thought, perhaps the most noteworthy is Jacques Derrida, whose critique of the 'metaphysics of presence' developed partly out of his reading of Husserl's writings on time.[16] But the impact of these analyses has been felt also in fields such as theology, history, literary theory and cultural theory.

NOTES

1 Augustine, *Confessions*, trans. Henry Chadwick (Oxford: Oxford University Press, 1991), Book XI, Chapter 14, p. 230.
2 Edmund Husserl, *On the Phenomenology of the Consciousness of Internal Time (1893–1917)*, trans. John Barnett Brough (Dordrecht: Kluwer, 1991), p. 346.
3 References to William James are few in light of his not insignificant influence on Husserl. The debt concerning the term 'fringe', however, is recognized. See *CES* 264 and *On the Phenomenology of the Consciousness of Internal Time (1893–1917)*, p. 155.
4 The primal impression is also called a primal sensation (*Urempfindung*).
5 Edmund Husserl, *Phenomenological Psychology: Lectures, Summer Semester, 1925*, trans. John Scanlon (The Hague: Martinus Nijhoff, 1977), p. 154.
6 For a fuller discussion of this point see Lanei Rodemeyer, 'Developments in the theory of time-consciousness: an analysis of protention', in Donn Welton (ed.), *The New Husserl: A Critical Reader* (Bloomington and Indianapolis, IN: Indiana University Press, 2003), pp. 131–9.

7   These observations bear upon the much-ventilated question of whether Husserl succumbs to a 'metaphysics of presence'. This is discussed well by Dan Zahavi, *Husserl's Phenomenology* (Stanford, CA: Stanford University Press, 2003), pp. 95–8.

8   Husserl continued to write studies of time-consciousness into the final decade of his life. These are collected in the 'C' class of manuscripts in the Husserl Archives. It appears, however, that the decisive studies are still those from the period immediately preceding the First World War (roughly 1908–11). Most of these studies are already included in the Churchill edition cited in this chapter. However, some further relevant texts can now be found in John Barnett Brough's translation of *Husserliana*, Vol. 10, *On the Phenomenology of the Consciousness of Internal Time (1893–1917)*.

9   The following analysis is indebted to the important recent work of Dan Zahavi on Husserl's analyses of self-awareness. See his *Self-Awareness and Alterity: A Phenomenological Investigation* (Evanston, IL: Northwestern University Press, 1999) and 'Inner time-consciousness and pre-reflective self-awareness', in Welton (ed.), *The New Husserl*, pp. 157–80.

10 For this reason, Husserl speaks of absolute consciousness as either 'unconstituted' or 'self-constituting'. But, as Zahavi points out, each formulation is somewhat inadequate: 'The first formulation might suggest that transcendental subjectivity does not at all manifest itself, the second that it manifests itself in the same way as objects do' ('Inner time-consciousness', p. 176, n. 39).

11 The curious interdependence between transverse intentionality and longitudinal intentionality has the consequence that pre-reflective self-awareness only exists where there is also consciousness of some transcendent object. Only under these conditions is an interrelated series of acts retained and protended and thus subjective time constituted. The unified subject only emerges (i.e. is self-conscious) where it is first conscious of something beyond itself. This provides a striking parallel to Kant's refutation of Idealism (*CPR* B 274ff.).

12 Zahavi, 'Inner time-consciousness', p. 168.

13 This does not preclude, of course, the thematization of recollected acts or imagined acts. However, for the purposes of a *science* of consciousness, it is significant that reflection can take place within the ambit of retention. Reflection is thus able to grasp that which is or can be found in the span of the 'living present', and therefore take possession of what is given originarily (*originär*; *leibhaftig*) (*Ideas I* §77). This is a significant result for the practice of phenomenology itself which, as Husserl acknowledges, 'operates exclusively in acts of reflection' (*Ideas I* 174). It means that phenomenology can, in principle, attain the highest level of evidential certainty.

14 This brings Husserl into line with the position of the influential neo-Kantian Paul Natorp, which he had previously rejected (see *LI* II 549). More is said about the non-objective transcendental ego in the following chapter.

15 See Martin Heidegger, *Being and Time*, trans. John Macquarrie and Edward Robinson (Oxford: Basil Blackwell, 1962), pp. 65–71, *et passim*.
16 See Jacques Derrida, *Speech and Phenomena*, trans. David B. Allison (Evanston, IL: Northwestern University Press, 1973).

CHAPTER 9

THE EGO AND SELFHOOD

What is the relation between transcendental consciousness and the self who I am or you are? Does Husserl have anything to say about our embodiment, our personality, our selfhood? Or, does Husserlian phenomenology remain at the level of egological abstraction? The short answer is that Husserl does develop quite a sophisticated analysis of each of these matters, and he does so, he claims, without leaving the transcendental and eidetic terrain of pure phenomenology. In fact, once we begin to examine his studies on these topics we soon find that we get somewhat more than we bargained for, as his conceptions of the ego multiply to distinguish amongst others the pure ego, the bodily ego, the psychic ego, the psychophysical whole, the person, the eidos ego and the monad. When it comes to the self, it seems, the matters for phenomenological analysis are intricate indeed. In this chapter, I discuss Husserl's analyses of selfhood and embodiment as they are developed primarily in *Ideas II*. But I begin from the notion of the transcendental ego with which we have become familiar in preceding chapters. From there, I discuss the phenomena of 'the psyche' (the object of the natural science, psychology) and then 'the person' (the subject who belongs to an intersubjective community, and who is the object of the human sciences). In the final section, I attempt to address the question of whether it is possible to reconcile this bewildering array of selves.

THE TRANSCENDENTAL OR PURE EGO

The empiricist tradition, in which Husserl was immersed in his early years, is characterized by a certain scepticism regarding the idea of the ego. Hume, for example, suggests that the ego is nothing more than an illusion, and that the self is not a subsisting identity. When I inspect my 'self' all I discover is a bundle of ever-changing perceptions. William James likewise rejects the notion of a soul-substance which persists as an identical subject of experience. Rather, the self, he argues, is simply that which is judged to be 'the self' in the opinion, as it were, of the present thought occurring in the stream of consciousness. That is, each conscious experience includes a representation of the self, of the thinker of the thought; but there is no guarantee that this representation will be identical from one moment of consciousness to another. Where a stable self does exist, this is a consequence of belonging to social contexts in which we tend to adopt certain personas that regulate our behaviour.

Under the influence of this tradition (via Brentano), Husserl found little place for the idea of the ego in his *Logical Investigations*. While he sometimes employs the term 'phenomenological ego' in this work, he uses it merely to designate the stream of consciousness itself (*LI* II 541). The phenomenological ego, then, is just the name for the unity of the stream of consciousness given in the 'living present', the unity that is achieved thanks to time-consciousness. But such a unified temporal stream is not yet a unified self or 'I'. At this stage in his philosophical development, Husserl did not see the need to speak of a transcendental 'I' to whom all experiences are given, *over and above* the stream of consciousness itself and *prior to* the objective, empirical self. Husserl could see no reason to posit the existence of a 'transcendental' or 'pure ego' in this sense.[1] It seemed to be superfluous in explaining the constitutive function of consciousness.

By the time of the second edition of the *Logical Investigations* published in 1913, however, it seems that Husserl had managed to locate the missing pure ego. In a footnote to his initial dismissive remarks, he writes: 'I have since managed to find it [i.e. the ego], i.e. have learnt not to be led astray from a pure grasp of the given through corrupt forms of ego-metaphysic' (*LI* II 549 n. 1). Husserl's change of heart on the matter of the pure ego is of a piece with his Kantian transcendental turn and his journey through Cartesian subjectivism.[2] What, after all, is the residuum of Cartesian doubt if not the 'I am' (*CM* 22)? How then, asks Husserl rhetorically, can we avoid assuming a pure ego (*LI* II 544 n. 1)?[3] Hume had rightly reacted to the 'corrupt forms of ego-metaphysic' and was again right to reject the idea of the ego as an empirical object. But, as Kant had argued, this does not preclude the possibility that the ego be conceived as a transcendental subject, i.e. a condition for the possibility of experience.

Interestingly, the point at which Husserl resurrects the transcendental ego in his philosophy appears to have lagged behind his transcendental turn by a few years. In *The Idea of Phenomenology* (1907), for example, the exclusion of 'the ego as a person' is the last mention of the ego; no phenomenologically reduced ego is spoken of (*IP* 34). By about 1910, however, Husserl had come to see that what needs to be 'bracketed' is only the *empirical* ego and the psycho-physical domain in which it exists. What remains is the *pure* ego: the 'I' *to whom* experience is given. Experience is necessarily experience *for someone*; the transcendental ego is thus irreducible (*Ideas I* 132f.). But, what is this pure transcendental ego? What does it consist in and how is it to be described?

THE PURE EGO AS SUBJECT POLE

Already in the *Logical Investigations* Husserl had offered an interpretation of words such as 'I' and 'you', labelling them 'essentially occasional expressions'. By this he means that the words shift their referent according to the occasion on which they are used. When I use the word 'I', it refers to me; when you use it, it refers to you. The sense of the word is simply 'whoever is speaking'. The word 'I', then, is the means of a signitive intentional relation directed to myself. Now, phenomenology is not conceptual analysis; the phenomenologist does not aim to gain philosophical knowledge from the study of linguistic usage but by a study of the things themselves. Nevertheless, the ever-present possibility of *expressing* experience as *my* experience (e.g. 'I perceive x') is, for Husserl, the clue pointing us to an underlying and primitive sense of the unity of all experience as my experience, a sense which precedes and makes possible such expressions.

Kant had articulated this same thought in his doctrine of 'transcendental unity of apperception' (*CPR* B 129–40; cf. A 106–30). The 'I' is not perceived as though it were an object of experience, but is 'apperceived' when we are conscious of objects. Consciousness experience only counts as conscious experience in so far as it is experience for someone; or, as Kant says, it is possible for the 'I think' to accompany all my representations (*CPR* B 131). Husserl's analysis in *Ideas I* broadly follows this Kantian line of thought. The pure ego is neither the ever-changing stream of consciousness, nor an object for consciousness like other objects. Rather, the ego is always implicitly a part of consciousness experience precisely *as the subject who is experiencing*: 'its "regard" is directed "through" every actional cogito to the objective something' (*Ideas I* 132; cf. also §80). Likewise, in *Ideas II*: 'The ego is the identical subject functioning in all acts of the same stream of consciousness; it is the center whence all conscious life emits rays and receives them, it is the center of all affects and actions, of all attention, grasping, relating, connecting' (*Ideas II* §25, 112). This ego is a component of the complex phenomenon of intentional experience. So conceived, it is the 'ego-pole' of intentional acts as opposed to the 'object-pole' (*FTL* 262). Intentional acts, therefore, are said to have the form *ego–cogito–cogitatum*, and the ego is that term from which an intentional ray is directed toward the object (*CM* §21):

> I take myself as the pure Ego insofar as I take myself purely as that which, in perception, is directed to the perceived, in knowing to the known, in phantasizing to the phantasized . . . In the accomplishment of each act there lies a ray of directedness I cannot describe otherwise than by saying it takes its point of departure in the 'Ego', which evidently thereby remains undivided and numerically identical while it lives in these manifold acts, spontaneously takes an active part in them, and by means of ever new rays goes through these acts towards what is objective in their sense. (*Ideas II* §22, 103f.)

The 'I' of the 'I think' is formally identical in every case. What makes the ego-pole identical or unitary on Husserl's account is not initially clear. In various places, however, Husserl refers this question of the unity of conscious experience to the function of time-consciousness.[4] In Chapter 8, I recounted Husserl's analyses of the way in which consciousness constitutes itself as an individual stream through the 'longitudinal intentionality' of retention and protention, and I discussed the difficulties involved in investigating the unifying function of absolute consciousness. The ego, in this context, is the absolute consciousness whose *form* ensures the unity and connectedness of streaming experiences and which makes of them a singular conscious life. The pure ego in this sense is the immutable *form* of temporalization which is the engine-room of all experience and hence the most basic function of constituting consciousness. As the ground of all experience, thought and action, this ego is the *absolute*. This is the only conception of the ego provided by Husserl which comes close to fulfilling the traditional description of the pure or transcendental ego as an invariant and subsisting identity throughout all permutations of experience. But what he is describing is emphatically not a substance, and in this he echoes the empiricist and Kantian critiques of Descartes.[5]

HABITUALITY, CONVICTION AND SELF-CONCEPTION

Absolute consciousness, in the sense just described, is in itself empty and only has content as it finds itself intentionally related to various objects: 'As pure Ego it does not harbor any hidden inner richness; it is absolutely simple and it lies there absolutely clear. All richness lies in the cogito and in the mode of the function which can be adequately grasped therein' (*Ideas II* §24, 111). However, Husserl gradually realized that it would not do to think of the pure ego as a complete vacuity or rather as only filled by its *cogitationes*. The ego must also be the bearer of certain persisting (although changeable) 'properties'. For instance, the pure ego must possess certain motivations and convictions by which to order its constituting activities. A series of retained 'convictions' and 'habitualities' must underwrite the constituting subjectivity, guiding its behaviour and thought (*CM* §§31–32). Without this more or less unarticulated cognitive framework of motivations, contingently formed though they may be, there would be no principle by which to connect together thoughts, perceptions or, indeed, actions into meaningful wholes.

Some reflection upon the act of judgement illustrates this point. A judgement posits decisively what had previously announced itself to enquiring consciousness as questionable. Which is to say that the judgement serves to increase knowledge because it is performed against the backdrop of a history of prior experiences and convictions out of which the present act is motivated. What this suggests is that the phenomenon of 'rational thought' cannot be fully accounted for on the basis of an analysis of atomized acts of judgement alone. These analyses need to be incorporated into a broader phenomenological investigation of rational thinking as the cumulative achievement of an ego's 'experience', moulded at each turn by various motivating concerns and enfolded into the ego as its 'convictions'. To understand the achievement of knowledge thus requires a description of the ego as possessing a history, habitualities and convictions, and not simply a description of its momentary acts.

How is the self with its convictions and motivations formed and maintained? For this, at least two conditions must be met: (1) The 'having' of beliefs, attitudes and habits presupposes a form of temporal self-constitution, which Husserl interprets as an extension of the *retentive* function of time-consciousness. In this connection, for instance, he considers the way in which the results of a judicative act pass over into belief and become the background conviction or perhaps the explicit premise of further acts of reasoning (*Ideas II* §29).[6] (2) The second condition is a factical history through which the ego has had the opportunity to garner experiences and to develop its own knowledge, interests, convictions and habits. Thus, the ego, as Kant maintains, is essentially dependent upon the consciousness of objects – not just in the formal sense (as a pole in the intentional relation) but also in the substantive sense. It is the 'richness' of the cogito, mentioned in the quotation above, that oils the wheels of the transcendental ego's constitutive activity and gives it 'shape' as a transcendental ego.

A third condition could tentatively be added to this list in light of the fact that these remarks edge us closer to the question of *embodiment*. Notwithstanding his insistence on the non-essentiality of the body over against absolute consciousness, a survey of Husserl's publications and manuscripts reveals that he never understood transcendental subjectivity as a disembodied phenomenon. For instance, at the time that his thought took its so-called 'transcendental turn', Husserl was already thinking about the role of motility in the act of perception.[7] The question arises here whether this recognition of the embodiment of transcendental subjectivity is inconsistent with the idea of the radical separability of the pure ego from all factuality. Does it not seem that Husserl's account overflows its own methodological bounds at this point? I shall return to this question below.

Before moving on, however, it is worth flagging another complication regarding this account of the ego: it presupposes that the ego not only develops in its cognitive life but also has a *conception* of itself as an ego so developed. It is one thing to ask how the self *of which I am self-aware* is formed by its experiences; it is another to ask how one comes to understand oneself as such an ego, i.e. who possesses knowledge, convictions, experience, etc. With this question we move from the matter of the pre-thematic development of the ego's motivations and convictions through the course of its life-experience to the thematic self-consciousness of that ego. Husserl holds these two levels of pre-reflective lived experience and reflective experience apart (*Ideas II* §58). When we form certain judgements about ourselves, these judgements can be intuitively verified like any other form of judgement. For example, the thought that I am a dutiful citizen admits of evidential fulfilment in reflection on my convictions, habitualities and behaviours. Such phenomena, which would provide the evidence for my self-assessment, are given, as it were, in a pre-thematic fashion. According to Husserl, we are already vaguely familiar with our dispositions, habits, preferences, and so forth, even if we do not usually take notice of them. When we do take these thing into consideration and constitute a sense of ourselves, then we make ourselves an object to be grasped like any other object. To this degree, the ego is 'self-constituting'. Of course, Husserl also acknowledges that the self contains many mysteries and, especially, hidden motivations. Our ability to form evidentially based and balanced judgements about ourselves is limited. Consequently, our self-conceptions are often skewed and incomplete, even to the point where our habits and behaviours contradict our idea of ourselves (*Ideas II* §56, esp. (c)). Nonetheless, reflection upon the pure ego is possible in principle.

FROM THE PURE EGO TO THE FULL HUMAN BEING

The analyses above go some way towards explaining how the transcendental or pure ego can be understood, but they do not account for the phenomenon of the 'I' in the ordinary sense(s). The everyday notion of the 'self', the 'human being' or the 'person' implies much more than the very minimal account above contains. For instance, as Husserl himself observes, the 'I' in the ordinary sense 'encompasses the "whole" man, Body and soul' (*Ideas II* 99). The transcendental subject, the 'pure ego', therefore needs to be supplemented by an account of the full human being, or, more precisely, an account of the *various* additional senses in which we conceive of the self. Husserl distinguishes four fundamentally different senses of the self as a worldly reality: (1) the self *qua* physical object or thing (*Ding*; *Körper*); (2) the self *qua* animate body (*Leib*); (3) the self *qua* psyche (*Seele*); and (4) the self *qua* person. In accordance with his phenomenological method, Husserl investigates the way in which these conceptions of the self *qua* self are *constituted* by the pure or transcendental ego: 'I as a man am a part of the content of the real surrounding world of the pure Ego, which, as the center of all intentionality, also accomplishes that intentionality by which is constituted precisely I, the man, and I, the person' (*Ideas II* §27, 116). Here I shall focus on his constitution of the 'I' as psyche and person.[8]

THE PSYCHE

Leaving aside the pure ego, then, we turn first to the self as a psyche. At this point, Husserl is aiming to clarify phenomenologically the basic concept of psychology, the sense of its region. The psyche, for Husserl, is the subject who along with the animal body makes up the *real* person existing in the natural world. Like the body, the psyche is a reality, albeit an indivisible and non-physical one. This means that it occurs within the sphere of the natural world and is encountered within that world. As such, the 'psychic ego' must be distinguished from the 'pure ego'. The psychic ego is made up of those mental states that I perceive in others or myself via certain manifestations in behaviour, speech, and so forth. The 'pure ego', on the other hand, stands beyond the world as that ego to whom the real world is given. The phenomenological question concerning the 'psychic ego', then, is the question of how a self is constituted *within* the natural attitude.

Ricoeur helpfully schematizes Husserl's analyses as follows.[9] On the one hand, Husserl traces the way in which the psyche emerges (for the natural scientist) as a strange *interiority* belonging to bodies, whether human or animal. The psyche is here the name for that animating power observed to be governing the body and its behaviour. On the other hand, he traces the way in which we recast our own immanently observed mental acts as phenomena *of* the natural world. In this second series of analyses, the ego becomes objectified or reified so as to be understood as a part of the spatio-temporal contexture. These two paths of analysis merge into one conception of the self as a quasi-natural object, subject to determinable 'natural' laws and ontologically secondary and dependent in relation to the body *qua* biological object. The psyche and its 'mental states' are taken to be an appendage to this physical object.

What allows us to view the psyche or soul as a thing belonging to the real world in this way is the *analogy* between the psyche with its behaviours and the material thing with its properties (*Ideas II* §§30–31). The 'properties' of the psyche (i.e. its mental states), it seems, are *observable* just as material properties are, albeit via different forms of observation. We experience the soul via its actions in the natural world just as, analogously, we experience the thing via its properties. The psyche comes to be posited, therefore, as the substrate to which various behaviours and acts belong. We attribute characteristics to the psyche or soul in a parallel fashion to the way in which we attribute properties to the material thing. This analogy is given further support by the fact that judgements concerning selves assume the same grammatical form as judgements concerning things: e.g. compare 'He is stacking the shelves' and 'The rock is rolling down the hill'. Thanks to this analogy between the psyche and material objectivity, then, we are able to view the 'properties' of material objects and the 'faculties', 'capabilities' and 'propensities' of the psyche as together belonging to the sphere of nature. The natural sciences and psychology, therefore, can be grouped together.

Having said that, Husserl observes that even in the case of the psyche or soul, the analogy with substance only goes so far (*Ideas II* §32). Despite the fact that the soul is essentially incarnate, it is not caught up in causal relations as physical entities are. To act on the world and to be affected by it are not synonymous with the categories of cause and effect. Moreover, the 'substance' of the psyche is never a constancy in the same sense as a material thing. Unlike the material thing, changes in the psyche are shaped by the history of its experiences and not simply by its immediate circumstances. The psyche has a 'memory' while the material thing does not. This introduces a fundamental difference between thingly and psychical reality:

> We must undoubtedly say that there is no soul-substance: the soul has no 'in itself' the way 'nature' has, nor does it have a mathematical nature as has the thing of physics, nor a nature like that of the thing of intuition . . . [And] if we call *causality* that functional or lawful relation of dependence which is the correlate of the constitution of persistent properties of a persistent real something of the type, nature, then *as regards the soul we cannot speak of causality at all.* (*Ideas II* 139f.)

The subject matter of psychology, therefore, sits precariously on the fringe of the objective world of nature known by the sciences and, indeed, threatens to outrun it. Nevertheless, the psyche or soul is 'linked to nature' through its corporeality, its being seated within a body (*Ideas II* 145). The nature of this 'link' is, of course, one of the most hotly debated topics in philosophy. Husserl speaks of the soul's quasi-nature and quasi-causality which it enjoys by virtue of being embodied and thus inserted within the natural world, occupying space and time. In this regard, he draws out a distinction between the mere body (*Körper*) and the ensouled body (*Leib*).[10] The animated body is not a mere body. It exhibits ego-like characteristics and is rightly called 'me', 'he' or 'she', even though in a certain sense it is also 'mine', 'his' or 'hers'; that is, the body *is* the person, but is equally *not* the person but only their 'possession' (*Ideas II* §21, 102). Likewise, there is no absolute division between the psyche and the body; the body always has 'psychic significance'. The whole body is the 'psychic field' of sensations through which the psyche intends the world and lives in it as a world of real objects. Conversely, we apperceive psyches by means of indications given by human bodies (*Ideas II* §45). The psyche or soul, therefore, properly conceived, is not an 'inner' phenomenon accessible to introspection alone (*CM* 119f.). Indeed, the experimental practice of psychologists already reflects this fact. The embodiment of the psyche is thus absolutely essential to the psychological conception of the self. The soul is 'bound' in each of these ways to the body.

Thus, Husserl concludes that the second kind of reality (next to material nature) is not the soul *per se* but the human being *as a whole*, a unity of body and soul (*Ideas II* 146). To speak of the soul or psyche in isolation is possible, but it is always an abstraction from this complex form of 'animal' being. Similarly, it is possible to speak of a living body in abstraction from its soul. But, again, the bodily 'I' is the empirical body 'animated' by a subject whose body we perceive it to be, and for whom the body is his or her body. There is no *Leib* without the accompanying apperception of the soul. Thus, within the realm of reality, we can speak of the region of material nature and now also of a second region, the phenomenologically distinct region of psychophysical human being (of which psychical being is an abstract part).

THE PERSON

Despite having made this distinction between the merely physical body and the animated body, we still remain, broadly speaking, in the attitude of the *natural* sciences. We have only differentiated the basic kinds of reality investigated by the physical sciences and the psychological sciences respectively. But Husserl describes a curious 'surplus' to every human being which exceeds the psychological conception of the self (*Ideas II* 147). As an initial rough description, we might call this surplus 'individuality'. What makes each human being unique is precisely their being a 'person' who has a capacity to act and to react in certain more or less intelligible ways. This is the aspect of human being of interest to the historian, for example. The historian is not interested in Napoleon's psychological states but in his opinions, motivations, his reasons for action grounded in his conception of himself, his nation, his destiny, and so forth. But here we move into a mode of investigation or 'attitude' quite distinct from that of the psychologist; we move from the 'psychological attitude' to the 'personalistic attitude'. Here we are no longer dealing with the psyche but rather with the 'spirit' (*Geist*) or 'person'. While the psyche is conceived in terms of its dependencies upon the body and the constraints laid down by its material–physiological circumstances, the spiritual ego[11] or person emerges out of a consideration of the context of intersubjectivity and is shaped and informed by social circumstances. Hence, over and above the pure ego and the human ego (the psychophysical whole), we are asked to consider also the social or personal self.

To these three conceptions of the self, incidentally, correspond the three basic sciences of subjectivity: (1) to the pure ego, transcendental phenomenology; (2) to the animal or human ego, psychology; and (3) to the social or personal ego, the human or historical sciences (*Geisteswissenschaften*). To the latter belong the sciences concerned with the world of intersubjective institutions such as family, morality, law, religion, politics, and so forth. In the late nineteenth century Wilhelm Dilthey famously articulated an account of the human sciences as distinct from the natural sciences. The natural sciences, he argued, consider phenomena only in so far as they can be *explained* by causal laws, whereas the human sciences consider the phenomena of culture and history which comprise a vast interconnected web of meaningful phenomena available to be *understood*, i.e. interpreted according to their motivations and significance. Husserl's constitutive analysis of the personal ego is an attempt to provide the fundamental philosophical groundwork for Dilthey's conception of the historical world and the human actors who live in it (*Ideas II* §48).

The psyche and the personal ego, according to Husserl, are constituted in quite different ways. The constitution of the psychic ego, as we have seen, begins with the stratum of material thinghood and proceeds through a series of founded constitutive acts to constitute the psychophysical whole as a rather unusual phenomenon bound to the body. The psychological attitude, therefore, takes its start from within a naturalistic framework and conceives of the ego as a quasi-natural object with its seat in some material entity (the body):

> All men and animals we consider in this attitude are, if we pursue theoretical interests, anthropological or, more generally, zoological Objects. We could say physio-psychic Objects, whereby the inversion of the usual 'psychophysical' indicates quite appropriately the order of the founding. (*Ideas II* 192)

In this natural-scientific conception, the ego is considered in so far as it admits of characterization within the natural world, for example, in terms of 'mental states'. Social or institutional phenomena are not out of bounds to the psychologist, but again these will only be considered in so far as they can be explained in terms of psychic facts. This inevitably squeezes out the ego in the full sense, leaving behind a naturalistic residuum.

The constitution of the personal ego, by contrast, places the person as a member of a social world, capable of agency, rational discourse, moral responsibility, etc. Here again certain characteristics of the person are *observed* through a temporally unfolding perception of bodily behaviours (e.g. she is obeying the law by walking at the pedestrian crossing). But the person is constituted in his or her 'sense' according to certain patterns of lawfulness or meaning belonging not to the laws of nature but to social conventions and practices. Thus, the 'personal ego' is only encountered by someone who is able to interpret phenomena within the horizon of practical and cultural significance. Only then is the culturally significant *act* recognized as such and, likewise, only then is the culturally significant *object* recognized. The chess set, for example, is a cultural object – it is a thing endowed with a cultural sense. As such, it is a form of 'objective spirit'. It will only be 'given' *as a chess set* to a person who is initiated into the spiritual life of a culture and who is thus able to intend the object as the spiritual object that it is.

We live in the personalistic attitude when we are oriented towards practical significance rather than theoretical observations (*Ideas II* §55). In the personalistic attitude, therefore, the world presents itself in terms of its relation to my ends or our ends. So, for instance, this thing before me is a desk and not merely a lump of wood – that is, I perceive the object not as a mere 'thing of nature' but as a 'thing of use'. Indeed, in the everyday (personalistic) attitude, the same world of nature is there for me that is there for the physicist, but as more than a mere aggregate of physical things; it is there, for example, as scenery, as a source of fuel, or as a playground. Conversely, the natural-theoretical attitude is achieved by suspending our normal teleologically occupied existence, thus draining the world of its practical significance in order to enable it to present itself as a pure and indifferent manifold of qualified substances.

For those readers familiar with Heidegger's *Being and Time*, these ideas will sound strikingly familiar. The 'personalistic attitude' is that which Heidegger calls the 'everyday' mode of being-in-the-world. And, anticipating Heidegger's analysis, Husserl speaks of the world as the 'surrounding world' (*Umwelt*; environment) for the person in this attitude (*Ideas II* §50), and of the fact that we share this world with others (*Ideas II* §51). He also insists, like Heidegger, on the priority of the personalistic over the naturalistic-scientific attitude:

> [T]he naturalistic attitude is in fact subordinated to the personalistic, and . . . the former only acquires by means of an abstraction or, rather, by means of a kind of self-forgetfulness of the personal Ego, a certain autonomy – whereby it proceeds illegitimately to absolutize its world, i.e., nature. (*Ideas II* 193)

But I shall leave the reader to investigate these connections and hidden debts more fully for him- or herself. (The notion of the *Umwelt*, however, is considered in more detail in Chapter 11 under its more familiar Husserlian title of the 'lifeworld'.)

THE INTERRELATION BETWEEN THE VARIOUS CONCEPTIONS
OF THE EGO

How are these conceptions of the ego – the psychical and the personal – to be reconciled? This is a version of the dilemma faced by all philosophers after Kant: how are the empirical self (which is bound by the laws of causality) and the noumenal self (which is free and subject to the moral law) to be reunited? Husserl's distinctive contribution is to refer this question to a phenomenological analysis of the *attitudes* (*Einstellungen*) that underlie the dichotomy, and to ask how these apparently conflicting conceptions of the ego are *constituted* within those attitudes. But, to trace forms of objectivity to their grounds in absolute consciousness is not to reconcile conceptually those object-senses. The regions of being analysed in this way remain phenomenologically (and hence also conceptually) distinct, although they are said to be 'intertwined' (*verflochten*).[12] Hence, what emerges in the present case is not a *reconciliation* or mediation of the psychical and personal egos but a *legitimation* of their respective forms of objectification.

Reality, Husserl shows us, is plural and cannot be reduced to any one kind of objectivity. Such a reductive move would be fatal for one or more of the sciences and would lead to a schism between our lived experience of the world and our theoretical conception of it. (This, of course, is a restatement of Husserl's critique of naturalism or 'scientism', to which I return in Chapter 11.) The way forward shown to us by phenomenology is to cultivate a sensitivity to the multiple forms of reality and to study their individual provenance in lived experience. This is the virtue of the phenomenological attitude: it occupies a standpoint from which the multiple kinds of reality can be investigated in their origin and meaning. But, if the recognition of the multiplicity of being is indebted to the phenomenological attitude, then this in turn gives to the transcendental ego a primacy over all others. The transcendental ego must be affirmed as the absolute ground of all forms of objectivity, including the reified self:

This whole apprehension [of Objective nature] presupposes, however, that which can never be transformed into an 'index': the *absolute subject* with its lived experiences, its intentionally meant, its acts of reason, etc., the subject *for* which is constituted the totality of nature, physical as well as animal. (*Ideas II* 180)

This is not to say that all being is reducible to the solipsistic domain of the pure ego. Husserl criticizes the naïveté of the metaphysical idealist who collapses the real ego into the pure ego just as deftly as he criticizes the naïveté of the materialist who collapses the pure ego into the real. What we are given by phenomenology, again, is not a reconciliation or harmonization of these apparently competing ideas of subjectivity but an appreciation of the logic behind the extreme objectification of the self by the natural sciences on one hand and the extreme subjectification of the self by transcendental philosophy on the other. Both logics – the logic of the natural attitude (in the broadest sense) and the logic of the phenomenological attitude – have their legitimacy. This 'genealogical' analysis of the provenance of the objectivist and subjectivist tendencies of modernity is taken up again and pursued in new ways in *The Crisis of European Sciences and Transcendental Phenomenology*. But, I shall defer a discussion of the arguments mounted there until Chapter 11.

To conclude, however, I would like to pause to consider just one complication regarding the ostensible primacy of the transcendental ego. The complication concerns the relation between the personal ego and the pure ego. One would expect from the organization of *Ideas II* that the personal ego and the pure ego would be the most distant from one another, that the personal ego would be the most sophisticated or 'highest' constituted sense of the ego, founded perhaps on the psychic ego, and thus farthest removed from its origins in simple perception. The contents of *Ideas II*, however, do not bear out this assumption. In fact, the spiritual or personal ego is treated quite separately from the psyche in terms of its constitution, and, in any event, it turns out to enjoy a much more intimate relation to the pure ego than we might expect.

The *person* that we are becomes thematized through reflection upon ourselves as the ego who is the subject of experiences, the ego-pole of intentional acts. It is possible, after all, for us to develop a sense of ourselves *qua* subjects of experience; that is, it is possible for us to reflect upon our habitualities, opinions, tendencies and to construct a 'sense' of ourselves as we consider the ways in which we have thought and acted in various past circumstances. Now, in the course of a life lived, the spiritual self so observed may change as its experience of life 'shapes it', and as its circumstances change. But this 'I' of self-observation, the spiritual self, is nothing other than the 'I' of phenomenological reflection as it finds itself *enmeshed* in the contingencies and specificities of its own life-history and in the intersubjectively mediated 'surrounding world' (*Umwelt*) through which it comes to develop as a self and to develop an understanding of itself. The intentional life of the pure ego, through the accretions of experience and the mediations of sociality, becomes the life of an individual person (*Ideas II* 259–61). Conversely, the pure ego is just *this* form of subjectivity (i.e. the person) severed from its life-context and considered in its monadic individuality.

This extremely close proximity between the personal ego and the transcendental ego has led some philosophers to question the possibility of meaningfully separating the two. Maurice Merleau-Ponty will serve here as a spokesperson for this position. His *Phenomenology of Perception*[13] is massively indebted to Husserl's analyses of embodiment and to the distinction between the naturalistic and personalistic attitudes found in *Ideas II* (and also in the *Cartesian Meditations* and elsewhere). The debt runs so high, in fact, that it is almost possible to regard Merleau-Ponty's work as a systematic defence of Husserl's ideas. The point at which he breaks with Husserl, however, is the point at which we have now arrived. The identity between the pure ego and the individual, embodied person signifies, for Merleau-Ponty, that it is impossible to 'complete' the reduction.[14] The constitution of objectivity described by Husserl is always tacitly the constitution performed by the ego who *exists* in the world. For this reason, we must conclude that the analysis of lived experience (and, for that matter, the critique of naturalism) is perfectly comprehensible from within the *personalistic* attitude.[15] In short, the phenomenological attitude is a novel and important form *of* the personalistic attitude, but it is a form of it all the same. Husserl, then, in Merleau-Ponty's judgement, simply misrecognizes the truth of his own researches in so far as he continues to insist that they proceed from a narrowly egological starting-point.

Whether or not Merleau-Ponty's criticism is trenchant, we have nevertheless clearly come full circle. The pure ego of transcendental phenomenology, we now see, is for Husserl that kernel of *personhood* which would survive the hypothetical annihilation of the world – not merely the natural world (including the body), but the social world with its ready-made meanings and hard-won interpretations of reality (*Ideas II* 311). The pure ego is that remnant of unique, first-person experience that exceeds – or, rather, precedes – even my being as a person. The task of the phenomenologist is to retrace piece by piece the emergence of those meanings that make up reality (physical, animal, psychical and spiritual) according to the essential structures of their constitution as intentional objects for the pure ego. And, in the foregoing discussions, we have filled out in broad brush-strokes two corners of this canvas: (1) the constitution of the psyche-object on the basis of an encounter with the body as a material thing; and (2) the constitution of the personal ego through the recognition of one's place in the 'spiritual' or historical world. In the next chapter, I deal with one of the main phenomenological puzzles that emerges for Husserl out of this grand project of 'constitutive phenomenology': the problem of intersubjectivity.

NOTES

1 In the writings from the mid 1920s, the term 'transcendental ego' is introduced to take over the role of the term 'pure ego'. In *Ideas II*, which is our primary text in this chapter, the term 'pure ego' is used exclusively. In each case the term refers to *constituting* subjectivity, that in and through which objects are known.

2 It is worth noting that the influences on Husserl's shift were in fact not Descartes or Kant themselves but rather the neo-Kantians, especially Paul Natorp. For details concerning Husserl's historical development in this regard, see Joseph J. Kockelmans, 'Husserl and Kant on the pure ego', in Frederick A. Elliston and Peter McCormick (eds), *Husserl: Expositions and Appraisals* (Notre Dame, IN: University of Notre Dame Press, 1977), pp. 269–85.

3 Several critics of Husserl's notion of the transcendental ego cite precisely the same arguments given by Husserl himself in his early period. The most famous example is Jean-Paul Sartre's *The Transcendence of the Ego: An Existentialist Theory of Consciousness*, trans. Forrest Williams and Robert Kirkpatrick (New York: Noonday Press, 1957). Sartre acknowledges that there is an ego for consciousness, but denies that consciousness is itself an ego or is grounded in an ego (p. 48, *et passim*).

4 For example, *Ideas I* §§80–81; *CM* §18 and §37.

5 It must be borne in mind, however, that for Husserl the form of time-consciousness is the possible object of intuitive reflection, as I discussed at the end of Chapter 8 (see also *Ideas II* §23). Thus, he rejects Kant's assertion that the transcendental subject is not capable of becoming an object of knowledge. For a more detailed discussion of this comparison, see David Carr, 'Transcendental and empirical subjectivity', in Donn Welton (ed.), *The New Husserl: A Critical Reader* (Bloomington and Indianapolis, IN: Indiana University Press, 2003), pp. 181–98.

6 For a further discussion of this point see James Mensch, *Intersubjectivity and Transcendental Idealism* (Albany, NY: State University of New York Press, 1988), pp. 309–30.

7 These reflections can be found in the lectures on 'thing and space' (*Ding und Raum*) which have been translated by Richard Rojcewicz as *Thing and Space: Lectures from 1907* (Dordrecht: Kluwer, 1997). For reasons of space, I am not able to discuss Husserl's investigations of the role of the body in the constitution of perceptual objects and his important notions of 'motility', 'the body as organ of sense' and 'kinaesthetic experience'. For an excellent introduction to Husserl's thought on these topics, I recommend Dan Zahavi's *Husserl's Phenomenology* (Stanford, CA: Stanford University Press, 2003), pp. 98–109.

8 The full set of self-determinations and their interrelations is helpfully discussed by Ullrich Melle, 'Nature and Spirit', in Thomas Nenon and Lester Embree (eds), *Issues in Husserl's* Ideas II (Dordrecht: Kluwer, 1996), pp. 15–35.

9 See Paul Ricoeur, *Husserl: An Analysis of his Phenomenology*, trans. Edward G. Ballard and Lester E. Embree (Evanston, IL: Northwestern University Press, 1967), pp. 51f.

10 To differentiate the terms, the translators of *Ideas II* use 'body' to denote the mere physical body (which remains as a corpse after death), and 'Body' to denote the ensouled body, the body of someone.

11 The term 'spiritual ego' is used by Husserl in opposition to the term 'bodily ego' to distinguish the self conceived apart from its corporeality (*Ideas II* §22, 103).

12 These ideas are developed particularly in *Ideas Pertaining to a Pure Phenomenology and a Phenomenological Philosophy: Phenomenology and the Foundation of the Sciences* (Vol. 3), trans. Ted E. Klein and William E. Pohl (The Hague: Martinus Nijhoff, 1980); and *Phenomenological Psychology: Lectures, Summer Semester, 1925*, trans. John Scanlon (The Hague: Martinus Nijhoff, 1977). For a discussion, see Ted Klein, ' "Essences and experts": Husserl's view of the foundations of the sciences', in Nenon and Embree (eds), *Issues in Husserl's* Ideas II, pp. 67–80.

13 Maurice Merleau-Ponty, *Phenomenology of Perception*, trans. Colin Smith (London: Routledge, 1962).

14 Ibid., p. xiv.

15 This is often taken to be a repetition of Heidegger's critique of Husserl, although a close reading of Heidegger's lectures will show that he also had misgivings about the idea of 'personalism'. The personalistic movement (Dilthey, Scheler, Husserl), he argued, was heading in the right direction, but remained mired in traditional conceptions of human being. See Martin Heidegger, *History of the Concept of Time*, trans. Theodore Kisiel (Bloomington and Indianapolis, IN: Indiana University Press, 1985), §13.

CHAPTER 10

INTERSUBJECTIVITY

Husserl devoted a huge amount of energy attempting to investigate phenomenologically 'intersubjectivity': our being *with others*.[1] As scholars have digested Husserl's published and unpublished writings on intersubjectivity, it has become increasingly clear that from quite early on he saw our capacity to constitute the world as intimately tied up with our being in relation to other people. By about the time *Ideas I* was published, in fact, Husserl had decisively overcome the solipsistic model of subjectivity found in Descartes and had embraced the radical notion of 'transcendental intersubjectivity'. Nevertheless, he reportedly regarded the Fifth *Cartesian Meditation* as his first successful account of the constitution of intersubjectivity.[2] For this reason, the following discussions focus on this text, which in any case is the best known and most accessible text on the topic. This chapter is divided into two halves. The first examines the theoretical context out of which Husserl's 'intersubjective turn' arises. That context comprises the questions of reality, objectivity and transcendence. As we shall see, Husserl maintains that the constitution of an object as something really transcendent and truly Objective requires that it be an object *for others* as well as for me. But this observation necessitates a transposition of phenomenological analysis into an 'intersubjective' register. As a result, the question of the constitution of the other becomes, for Husserl, a key phenomenological topic and one with which he continued to wrestle until his life's end. In the second half of the chapter, therefore, I examine Husserl's account of how our experience of the other is itself constituted and how we find ourselves within a community of egos and within a shared natural and cultural world.

THE PROBLEM OF OBJECTIVITY AND TRANSCENDENTAL
INTERSUBJECTIVITY

It could be assumed from the analyses of perception expounded earlier (in Chapter 5) that the constitution of objective, real being (e.g. material things) is possible on a solely egological basis; that is, quite apart from the existence of other minds. This, however, is not quite correct. Husserl's analysis of the act of perception explains how a physical entity can be constituted as a unity through the phases of perception, but it does not yet fully explain how that unified object comes to have the sense of an 'Objectively real' thing.[3] This strong notion of objectivity – which Husserl often denotes by the term *Objektivität* and which I, following most translations, shall signify by a capital 'O' – implies existence *in itself* and therefore that the object is *the same for all rational subjects*. Objectivity in this strong sense requires something more than the constitution of the object as a perceived or judged unity. The imagined chair, for example, is a unified intentional object, one that even gives itself in adumbrations; and yet it is not really existent. The question then is how we are to understand what is 'added' to the experience to differentiate the imaginary from the real.

The heart of Husserl's answer has already been alluded to in the previous paragraph: Objectivity in the sense of 'independent reality' has at its heart the idea of *intersubjective validity*: 'The existence-sense of the world and of Nature in particular, as Objective Nature, includes . . . thereness-for-everyone' (*CM* 92). The Objective world, then, is just that world which we *collectively* recognize as having being not just for me but also for you. Curiously, then, the weight of reality that we experience in connection with the world, Husserl is saying, is only experienced by you or me once we have some awareness of others who *also* experience the world. This requires some more explanation.

First of all, let me pause to explain the term 'intersubjectivity'. I relate to the world or worldly objects 'intersubjectively' when I take them to be objects belonging to a world shared with others. 'Intersubjectivity' or 'intersubjective experience' is that manner of experiencing the world in which one's experience is mediated by an awareness of others' experience of the same. Intersubjectivity, in this sense, is not equivalent to the experience *of* other conscious beings *per se*. Instead, it is the manner of experiencing made possible by already possessing a sense of 'being *with* other conscious beings'. The experience of other subjects – usually denoted as, 'the other' or 'the Other' – forms, if you will, the condition for the possibility of 'intersubjective experience'. I shall return to Husserl's analysis of the experience of the other below. But, for the moment, I shall stick to the theme of 'intersubjectivity'.

Why is it the case that I must have an 'intersubjective experience' – i.e. consciousness of being one ego among many – before I can have a consciousness of, say, a stone as a stone? Initially, this seems a counterintuitive claim. Husserl's argument, essentially, is as follows: The private world of the solipsistic ego is in principle inadequate to account for the kind of Objective knowledge that we are able routinely to achieve as cognitive subjects. In fact, without the inter-subjective dimension, the solipsistic subject can manage very little constitutive work. And what it is able to constitute in its absolute isolation on the basis of simply hyletic data is merely a rudimentary and even pathological version of the world. For instance, if I were to see a strange phenomenon in the night sky, I might not be sure whether to regard it as a sighting of something real or as some form of hallucination. I have no external measure to differentiate what is a 'merely subjective' experience and what is a subjective experience *of* a genuine (i.e. real) objectivity. If all experiences were like this, then the world would have quite a surreal quality to it. But, if there were others who could confirm that they too saw the phenomenon, I would have every reason to believe that there was at least some objective event that had truly taken place. This would not yet establish an explanation for the event, to be sure, but it would at least rule out the possibility that it had been a 'merely subjective' event.

Until other subjects come on the scene, then, the subject-independence or 'transcendence' of objects can never unambiguously assert itself. But, when the other does come on the scene, it becomes possible for the first time to conceive of the world as something whose existence lies beyond my own consciousness of it, i.e. as having a subject-independence that is not merely speculated about but attested to. When there are others who can attest to the appearing of an object for them, then the genuine transcendence of the object is more firmly established. Thus, the inclusion of an intersubjective dimension makes possible objective knowledge in a stronger sense than solipsistic experience could ever achieve, namely, Objective knowledge. Hence, Husserl states that 'the Objective world as an *idea* ... is essentially related to intersubjectivity' (*CM* 107f.). The same observation can also be expressed in terms of intentionality: A solitary ego's intentional act can provide 'evidence' (*Evidenz*) (as we saw in Chapter 6), but an object can only be posited as a really transcendent Object thanks to the *mediated* experience of that object *as* also given 'evidentially' to others. Thus, as Ricoeur insightfully observes, 'the constitution of the other plays the same role in Husserl that the existence of God does in Descartes in preserving the objectivity of my thoughts'.[4] That is, it establishes the possibility of secure knowledge of that which is transcendent.

Now, it is important to see that Husserl is not claiming that *only* corroborated experiences of objects count as experiences of real objects. Rather, the claim is that, in my *own* experience of an object, I cannot constitute it (i.e. encounter it) *as* a real object unless the *sense* that I bestow upon it includes some reference to its possible appearance to others. That is, the intentional relation to something real must include within it (as a 'matter of eidetic necessity', as Husserl would say) a component pertaining to its possible appearance to others. So, according to Husserl's analysis, when I see something as a real object, I am implicitly recognizing that it is something experienceable by others, even if in fact no one else *does* experience it, and even if I am not explicitly conscious of giving it such a meaning (*CM* 93). What this means is that for 'intersubjective experience', objects are endowed with an intersubjective status: as either having, possibly having, or lacking intersubjective validity. Intersubjective experience perceives objects as layered with an 'appresentational stratum' of their possible appearances to others (*CM* 125).

With the advent of intersubjective experience, what had previously formed an undifferentiated set of experiences, lacking any criterion of differentiation, suddenly differentiates itself into kinds of 'subjective' or 'objective' experience. There is suddenly a difference between the strange phenomenon in the night sky and the mere illusion of something in the night sky: one is a strange Object; the other is a delusory subjective experience. Here, of course, the terms 'subjective' and 'objective' no longer refer to structural moments of the intentional act (noesis – noema) but to *levels of intersubjective validity*. In the present context, 'subjective' and 'objective' have the sense of immanent vs. transcendent, or (mere) appearance vs. reality (*CM* 107). The more 'objective' (i.e. Objective, *Objektiv*) something is, the greater its claim to intersubjective recognition, i.e. reality. Countless confusions have arisen from the failure adequately to distinguish these two sets of meanings that have attached themselves to the terms 'subjective' and 'objective'. One of the many virtues of Husserlian phenomenology is its ability to help us clearly separate out these two semantic contexts. In light of this ambiguity, then, the subjective–objective distinction under discussion here is probably better expressed in terms of 'for me' vs. 'in itself'.

What Husserl's analysis adds to the familiar distinction between the 'for me' and the 'in itself' is the idea that the difference itself is one that is constituted *within* transcendental subjectivity – or, rather, within transcendental intersubjectivity.[5] Thanks to the mediation of a set of social possibilities – i.e. those of being shared, contradicted, described, discussed, investigated, and so forth – I am able to constitute the world *as* a public world and differentiate it from my private world (*CM* 91). Thus, 'the other Ego makes constitutionally possible a new infinite domain of what is "other": an *Objective Nature* and a whole Objective world to which all other Egos and I myself belong' (*CM* 107).

The constitution of the world of Objective Nature, for Husserl, is both a marvellous achievement and a curse. It is a curse because the idea of Objective Nature is the conception of the world characteristic of 'the natural attitude', i.e. the idea of the world with which we become so enamoured that we completely overlook our constitutive relationship to it. Thus we have arrived, via a circuitous route, back at the attitude which must be 'suspended' in order for phenomenological research to be possible. But this indicates, simultaneously, that we are now finally coming full circle and are reclaiming, as it were, those transcendencies initially refused to us by the phenomenological reduction – only now they return with their properly transcendental origins clearly in view. On the other hand, however, the natural concept of the world is a laudable achievement in its own right, for it marks the step into modern scientific consciousness. The idea of the Objective 'in itself' stands over against my personal representations and understandings of the world, and forces me into a process of rationalization, experimentation and debate in pursuit of a conception of the world that is *truly Objective* and which therefore commands rational assent by everyone (*CES* 278). My personal perceptions and judgements take on the relative validity of 'truthclaims': claimants or pretenders to recognition by the community of egos as truths, but with no intrinsic priority over any others. The consequence is the development of an ever more sophisticated 'scientific' (i.e. Objective) conception of the world.

An inevitable tendency of this process of scientific 'Objectification', however, is a steady move *away from* 'subjective' descriptions of the world as it is given in the fullness of my lived-experience *towards* a mathematized view of the world, described in terms of objective space and time. Only such objectified notions of the world can hope to attain universal assent. But, as this process accelerates, the distance between the 'true world' of science and the world of my experience (i.e. the 'apparent world') widens. My entire realm of first-person experience comes to be regarded as a mere 'veil of appearances' hiding the Objective world described by the sciences. As I discuss in more detail in the next chapter, Husserl argues that this is the source of the pervasive experience of alienation that characterized the Europe of his day.

TRANSCENDENTAL INTERSUBJECTIVITY

Husserl's realization that intersubjectivity is necessary for consciousness of genuine transcendence and Objective reality has repercussions for phenomenology itself. It implies, for instance, that constitutive analysis of even the most mundane physical thing cannot be completed without a consideration of its *constitution for and by a community of egos*. Indeed, Husserl's realization implies that there comes a point at which constitutive analysis must leave the solipsistic sphere behind, so to speak, and instead consider how the object in question is constituted by the intersubjective community. To give just one example: in light of Husserl's realization, the phenomenological account of the constitution of the psyche would have to involve a discussion of the way in which the psyche comes to be recognized as an Objective reality by an ideal *community* of psychologists, and not simply in the mind of an ideal observer. In other words, Husserl's ideas regarding the meaning of Objectivity make it imperative for phenomenology to situate its analyses within an intersubjective context. Constitutive analysis has to become 'intersubjective' if the project of transcendental phenomenology is to be completed.

What sense are we to make of this transformation of the phenomenological project? Does it entail the abandonment of the methodological foundations laid, for example, in *Ideas I*? Husserl remarks:

As beginning philosophers we must not let ourselves be frightened by such considerations. Perhaps reduction to the transcendental ego only *seems* to entail a *permanently* solipsistic science; whereas the consequential elaboration of this science, in accordance with its own sense, leads over to a phenomenology of transcendental intersubjectivity and, by means of this, to a universal transcendental philosophy. As a matter of fact, we shall see that, in a certain manner, a transcendental solipsism is only a subordinate stage philosophically; though, as such, it must first be delimited for purposes of method, in order that the problems of transcendental intersubjectivity, as problems belonging to a higher level, may be correctly stated and attacked. (*CM* 30–31)

Having come to the view that the 'transcendental' function of constitution must somehow take place between a community of egos, Husserl takes the bull by the horns and assigns to the community of egos the role previously assigned to the solipsistic constituting subject (see *CES* 179–83). With respect to this assignment, Husserl even employs the remarkable phrase, '*transcendental intersubjectivity*' (*CM* 107, *et passim*). Thus he writes: 'Transcendental intersubjectivity is the absolute and only self-sufficient ontological foundation. Out of it are created the meaning and validity of everything objective, the totality [*All*; cosmos] of objectively real existent entities, but also every ideal world as well.'[6]

Husserl's analysis of the *transcendental* function of intersubjectivity anticipates the more recent work of Karl-Otto Apel and Jürgen Habermas.[7] The point of difference, however, is that Husserl insists that the intersubjective framework be grounded in individual subjects and not be construed as a transpersonal subject itself. The transcendental ego is still regarded as the non-eliminable starting-point of phenomenological research. Why? Because the ontological autonomy of each individual is a condition of its becoming intersubjective. Intersubjectivity is something an ego enters into through its experience of others, and it only exists where a multiplicity of distinct egos *remain distinct* despite their coming into a complex – even harmonious – relation to each other. A solipsistic self must first exist as the 'founding stratum': 'that is to say: I obviously cannot have the "alien" or "other" as experience, and therefore cannot have the sense "Objective world" as an experiential sense, without having this stratum in actual experience; whereas the reverse is not the case'

(*CM* 96). The introduction of intersubjectivity, for its part, represents a new level of openness and intertwining of conscious life with the world beyond the simple forms of intentionality available to the solitary 'I'. But this is still only a more sophisticated form of the intentional being that we already enjoy as individual subjects. There is no sense then, for Husserl, in which intersubjectivity dissipates the individual consciousness or compromises its singularity. The transcendental ego, he says, is non-divisible. Ultimately, therefore, intersubjectivity can (and *must*, according to Husserl) be understood as a mode *of* subjectivity (*CES* §54; *FTL* §95).

On the other hand, Husserl would not want to claim that intersubjective experience is possible for the solitary ego alone, apart from any factical experience of the other.[8] The encounter with the other is the *sine qua non* of a subjectivity which is intersubjectively structured. Hence, Husserl aims to show that even the transcendental ego is only fully established as an intentional being thanks to a genuine encounter with the transcendent other. Husserl's claim, then, is that subjectivity becomes *fully constitutive* of transcendent objects (fully intentional, we might say) when it enters into an intersubjective context, and that selfhood in the full sense is likewise dependent upon intersubjectivity: 'Subjectivity is what it is – an ego functioning constitutively – only within intersubjectivity' (*CES* 172). We find in Husserl, therefore, a genuine embrace of intersubjectivity, but no compromise of the subjectivistic orientation of the phenomenological enterprise.

These tensions finds their explication in the *Cartesian Meditations* by means of the Leibnizian idea of the 'monad'.[9] Each subject is a 'monad': a self-contained 'substance' that nevertheless reflects the world of other monads within it. Transcendental intersubjectivity is then understood as 'the universe of monads, which effects its communion in various forms' (*CM* 156). The Objective world is established through the *harmony* of the representations among the monads. By bringing its representations into attunement, the community together constitutes the one identical world in which each individual monad places itself (*CM* 107). This harmony, however, is the product of various forms of communicative interaction within the domain of intersubjectivity, e.g. through common language, common practice and tradition, scientific discourse, and so forth (*CM* 108). In this way, despite the absolute separation of monads, we exist 'in intentional communion' with one another (*CM* 129). The unity or mutuality that exists, to the extent that it does, exists as an effect of the interrelation into which each ego in the community has entered. Intersubjectivity is thus not a trans-individual 'I'; it is precisely a 'we' (*CM* 107).

To summarize: Husserl's interest in the phenomenon of inter-subjectivity is occasioned primarily by its intimate interconnection with the phenomena of reality, transcendence and Objectivity.[10] The community of egos vouches for the reality of my experience, of my world. The fate of the entire project of transcendental phenomenology therefore rests on this transposition into the intersubjective register: for, if the phenomenon of transcendent reality can only be comprehended by a detour through intersubjectivity, then intentionality itself – i.e. the structure through which objects are supposed to be given *as transcendent* – can only be fully explained on intersubjective grounds. And, if the idea of 'intentionality' really is going to overcome the problem of knowledge (the characteristic question of post-Cartesian philosophy), then phenomenology must also include an account for the *mediation* of intentional experience through the intersubjective sphere.

THE PROBLEM OF METHODOLOGICAL SOLIPSISM AND THE EXPERIENCE OF THE OTHER

So far I have discussed the necessity of graduating from a solipsistic to an intersubjective conception of the transcendental domain. I have examined Husserl's arguments that this move is required to found a transcendental theory of the Objective world, and briefly explicated the idea of transcendental intersubjectivity. However, missing from the account so far is an explanation of the 'transposition' from subjectivity to intersubjectivity: if Objectivity cannot be properly constituted until intersubjectivity is established, how is intersubjective experience constituted? Indeed, is it even possible to give this transition a phenomenological description? That is, is it possible for phenomenology to trace the move to intersubjectivity, or does it reach its limit at the edge of the ego? Husserl himself explicitly raises these questions:

> When I, the meditating I, reduce myself to my absolute transcendental ego by phenomenological epoché do I not become *solus ipse*; and do I not remain that, as long as I carry on a consistent

self-explication under the name phenomenology? Should not a phenomenology that proposed to solve the problems of Objective being, and to present itself actually as philosophy, be branded as transcendental solipsism? (*CM* 89)

If phenomenology were unable to provide an account of this transposition, then we would at best be faced with two distinct forms of phenomenology – i.e. subjective and intersubjective – which we would have no right to regard as a single science. These, in turn, would have to look to some other form of philosophical enquiry to achieve their unification. But this, of course, would not do for Husserl. Phenomenology is to be first philosophy, which means (among other things) that it must be self-grounding, i.e. must account for its own grounds and possibility. In this vein, Husserl argues that not only must we employ the phenomenological method at the intersubjective level to investigate its constitutive possibilities, but we must also employ the phenomenological method properly to conceptualize intersubjectivity itself and its origins in subjective experience (*CM* §44; cf. *CES* 202). Transcendental phenomenology, then, is the method we must use to study the mysterious but all-important 'transposition' to intersubjectivity. In this way, Husserl maps out the challenge for his own phenomenological research: to provide a comprehensive and illuminating description of *the constitution of intersubjectivity for transcendentally reduced subjectivity* and thereby to investigate the origins of intersubjectivity. And this entails, more precisely, a study of the origins of the intentional components and layers out of which the *sense* arises that the world is 'experienceable by everyone'. (Putting it this way makes it clearer, it seems to me, how this remains a study of the sphere of transcendental consciousness. Husserl's discussion of intersubjectivity does not abandon the transcendental attitude [*CM* 148].)

Needless to say, the basic task and ground-level of this study must be the analysis of 'the constitutional level pertaining to the "other ego" or to any "other egos" whatever' (*CM* 107). But, again, the phenomenon of the 'other ego' presents phenomenology with unique difficulties. There seems to be a great gap to bridge between the 'reduced' sphere of my subjectivity and the ordinary experience of other people *as* independently existing beings like me, with their own conscious experience of the world. The complicating factor here, of course, is that other subjects are neither simple objects, nor even 'higher-level' objects (such as states of affairs), but are other *constituting egos* or *subjects*: 'I experience others as ... *"in" the world*. On the other hand, I experience them at the same time as *subjects for this world*, as experiencing it (this same world that I experience) and, in so doing, experiencing me too, even as I experience the world and others in it' (*CM* 91). Simple objects I am able to see through sensuous intuition, and states of affairs though categorial intuition, but I never 'see' the subjective experience that is the stuff of another consciousness. The other is essentially beyond me and inaccessible to me. So, how then do I intentionally relate myself to the other so as to encounter him or her as another subject? How can the other, who is essentially a foreign or transcendent consciousness, be made manifest to me through my experience? Is there a way for transcendental phenomenology to comprehend not only the appearing of *objects* but also the appearing of *subjects*?

Some have argued that it is not possible to do justice to the phenomenon of the other from the broadly Cartesian starting-point of Husserlian transcendental phenomenology. Emmanuel Levinas, for example, criticizes Husserlian phenomenology for its egological reduction of all otherness to 'the Same'.[11] As I have noted, however, Husserl himself does not regard the egological starting-point as problematic but as absolutely necessary. He thinks that the phenomenon of the other can be explicated phenomenologically: 'The only conceivable manner in which others can have for me the sense and status of existent others, thus and so determined, consists in their being constituted *in me* as others' (*CM* 128). But that is not to say the constitutional analysis required by the phenomenon of otherness is straightforward – Husserl's analyses are complex indeed.

THE APPRESENTATION OF THE OTHER

Husserl begins his account of the constitution of the other with the following general observations about the concrete experience of others:

> Experience is original consciousness; and in fact we generally say, in the case of experiencing a man: the other is himself there before us 'in person'. On the other hand, this being there in person does not keep us from admitting forthwith that, properly speaking, neither the other Ego himself, nor his subjective processes or his

appearances themselves, nor anything else belonging to his own essence, becomes given in our experience originally. (*CM* 108–9)

Whatever sense we might make of the mode of 'givenness' of the other, Husserl always insists that one can never experience the other as the other experiences him/herself. It is precisely the impossibility of this manner of experience that comprises the 'alterity' (i.e. otherness) of the other. The essential inaccessibility of the other is what makes him or her appear as 'not me'. The experienc*ed* subject is thus always given to me in a manner quite unlike my experienc*ing* subject. By the same token, for Husserl, not-being-given-directly is not peculiar to other egos. In fact, only a very narrow set of intentional objects are given directly. Every other set of objects has to be constituted in one way or another via founded acts. Likewise, the other person must be given through a unique sequence of founded acts. The trick is to determine what these are.

Circling in on the topic, then, Husserl observes (1) that even though the other is not 'presented', he or she is nevertheless actual and not 'merely presentified' (e.g. like an imagined or remembered object),[12] and (2) that the other is actually *experienced* rather than *inferred*. That is, there is no act of analogical *reasoning* behind the experience of the other (*CM* 111). We do not consciously reason that the object over there must be another person; whatever the act of constitution is that brings about the appearance of the other, it occurs 'passively'.

In light of these descriptive demarcations, Husserl suggests that the appropriate classification for the other's mode of givenness is 'appresentation'. The term 'appresentation' means that the other is given *along with something else*, something which *is* straightforwardly present. In this case, the 'something else' is the *body* of the other. The other is encountered in the presentation of his or her body as someone else's body. I 'see' the other person as 'co-present' with their body (*CM* 109, cf. 122). There are other forms of appresentation, but in this case what is appresented can never become directly presented. (This is not the case, for instance, with regard to the hidden parts of a physical object, which are appresented by the directly perceived parts and can also become presented in their own right.)

The mediating function of the body in the appresentation of the other requires some more detailed explication. However, before a body can be perceived as the body *of another*, Husserl argues, I must have first developed a sense of myself as embodied. My embodiment is just as much a condition for the possibility of the experience of the other as the embodiment of the other. Why so? Because, for the body of the other to be perceived as a living body, i.e. as the body *of another*, I must be able to observe in it something *analogous* to my own self. But the only analogy that could be grasped would be one relating my body to the body of the other: 'It is clear from the very beginning that only a similarity connecting, within my primordial sphere, that body over there with my body can serve as the motivational basis for the *"analogizing" apprehension* of that body as another animate organism' (*CM* 111).

First, therefore, I must be embodied and be conscious of myself as such. How I come to possess a grasp of myself as embodied is itself a complex matter. Suffice it to say here that I come to understand myself as an embodied subject through having *both* a consciousness of my body as my 'field of sensations' *and* an experience of myself as an object in the world (e.g. by touching or seeing myself, etc.). By bringing these two experiences into conjunction, I constitute myself as an embodied subject: as a being with a (bodily) presence in the world and for whom the world is present (*CM* 97). When I subsequently encounter another body that resembles my own body, it is possible then for me to 'analogizingly apprehend' that other body as animate like my own:

> Since, in this Nature and this world, my animate organism is the only body that is or can be constituted originally as an animate organism (a functioning organ), the body over there, which is nevertheless apprehended as an animate organism, must have derived this sense by an *apperceptive transfer from my animate organism.* (*CM* 110)

In the experience of the body of another, I discover a certain analogue to myself and my bodily experience. This is clearly not an analogy in the usual sense. Indeed, Husserl finds it necessary to qualify this expression with the counterbalancing metaphor of 'mirroring': 'the other is a "mirroring" of my own self and yet not a mirroring proper' (*CM* 94). But, again, even this idea is not entirely adequate. The other is not a mirror image of myself, but precisely someone *other* than me.

The rough ideas of 'analogy' and 'mirroring' are given more

precision in §51 of *Cartesian Meditations* by the concept of 'pairing' (*Paarung*). Pairing is defined as:

> a *primal form of that passive synthesis* which we designate as '*association*', in contrast to passive synthesis of 'identification'. In a *pairing association* the characteristic feature is that, in the most primitive case, two data are given intuitionally, and with prominence, in the unity of a consciousness and that, on this basis . . . as data appearing with mutual distinctness, they *found phenomenologically a unity of similarity* and thus are always constituted precisely as a pair. (*CM* 112)

What is being described here is that self-generating consciousness (i.e. 'passive synthesis') of a likeness between one object and another co-intended object which nevertheless does not go so far as to identify the two. It is the consciousness of a likeness between two things and a consciousness, therefore, that they are of the same kind. In the present case, the two objects are my body and the other body. This 'pairing association' forms the basis for a quite natural 'transfer' of sense, according to which the one is bestowed with the sense of the other. Thereby, a body which is similar to my own is 'paired', and the sense of being an 'animate organism' is transferred.

This apperceptive transference gives me reason to expect the patterns of behaviour of the other to follow a discernable 'law of motivation', even if they are not entirely predictable (*CM* 114). It leads me to interpret the other's acts as somehow motivated by the meaning-context in which they stand and the desires and convictions they hold. Hence, the analogizing apprehension allows me to set up a series of anticipations concerning the behaviour of the other, and to gauge the extent to which these anticipations find their fulfilment. Were my expectations disappointed again and again, I may begin to think I am not dealing with a conscious being after all.

Thus, I find myself attempting to apprehend the behaviour of the other according to the schema of 'motivated behaviour' on the basis of a transference from *my own* self-experience (i.e. as a motivated being). But because the 'law of motivation' is never determinative in the fashion of the laws of nature, I can never entirely predict and cognitively master the being of the other. My construal of the other as another personal ego thus simultaneously guarantees that he or she can never be completely comprehended and made an extension of my own sphere of knowledge. Likewise, my recognition of the other as another subject remains presumptive. It never graduates from being an *apperceptive* transference; it cannot hope ever to receive a definitive intuitive confirmation.

IMPLICATIONS OF THE RELATION TO OTHERS

We have now covered the basic components of Husserl's account of the discovery of the other who is another subject and absolutely transcendent in relation to my 'sphere of ownness'.[13] These constitutive achievements form the basis for the kinds of interaction that make community possible. Notice, however, that being in community with other egos has its sobering benefits. First, it is a short step to the realization that I am an 'other' myself:

> . . . I shall soon run into the fact that, just as his animate bodily organism lies in my field of perception, so my animate organism lies in his field of perception and that, in general, he experiences me forthwith as an Other for him, just as I experience him as *my* Other. Likewise I shall find that, in the case of a plurality of Others, they are experienced also by one another as Others, and consequently that I can experience any given Other not only as himself an Other but also as related in turn to *his* Others and perhaps – with a mediateness that may be conceived as reiterable – related at the same time to me. (*CM* 130)

Being one amongst others in this way negates any egotistical self-delusions and effects 'an *Objectivating equalization* of my existence with that of all others' (*CM* 129).

Concomitantly, the other, the world and every transcendent object that I constitute no longer appear to be an extension of myself, of my substance. Though I 'constitute' them, they are not-I. In this regard, the acquaintance with the other serves as something of a paradigm. The other is the first object whose radical ontological independence from me asserts itself, and it thus serves as a model for all subsequent encounters with transcendent objects: 'the otherness of "someone else" becomes extended to the whole world, as its "Objectivity", giving it this sense in the first place' (*CM* 147):

> 'In' myself I experience and know the Other; in me he becomes

constituted – appresentatively mirrored, not constituted as the original. Hence it can very well be said, in a *broadened* sense, that the ego acquires – that I, as the one who meditatingly explicates, acquire by 'self-explication' (explication of what I find in myself) every transcendency: as a transcendentally constituted transcendency and not as a transcendency accepted with naïve positivity. Thus the *illusion* vanishes: that *everything I*, qua transcendental ego, *know as existing in consequence of myself*, and explicate as *constituted in myself*, must *belong to me as part of my own essence*. (*CM* 149)

In short, then, the constitution of the other marks the overcoming of the illusion of metaphysical idealism, the very standpoint Husserl is sometime accused of holding. The lopsided impression one might get from Husserl's studies in *Ideas I* is thus readjusted.

From the perspective of the later Husserl, it seems amply evident that the transition to the intersubjective level is absolutely central to the phenomenon of intentionality, whose workings it is the central task of transcendental phenomenology to investigate. Thus, the idea of transcendental intersubjectivity, paradoxical as that expression may first seem, appears in hindsight to be one of the greatest achievements of Husserlian phenomenology. There are few who would claim that Husserl's own analyses definitively resolve the decisive questions. And from the hundreds of pages of notes and researches on the topic left behind by Husserl, we can discern that he himself never reached satisfaction with his position. Nevertheless, his investigations press deeply into a topic which is still very much at the centre of contemporary philosophical interests. And we have already begun to see a surge of interest in Husserl's investigations on intersubjectivity as his unpublished manuscripts have begun to see the light of day. The repercussions may well be far-reaching.

NOTES

1 In the collected edition of Husserl's works, three whole volumes are filled with reflections 'on the phenomenology of intersubjectivity' (*Husserliana*, Vol. 13 [1905–20], Vol. 14 [1921–28] and Vol. 15 [1928–35] [The Hague: Martinus Nijhoff, 1973]). Unfortunately, none of these editions has yet been translated into English, and so I have chosen to restrict my references where possible to translated works. There are certain points at which this is constrictive. But, on the whole, the arguments

found in the untranslated volumes are also present in translated works in one form or another, albeit often in summary form.

2 Reported by Alfred Schütz from a conversation with Husserl. See *Collected Papers*, Vol. I (The Hague: Martinus Nijhoff, 1962), p. 140.

3 In one passage of the *Cartesian Meditations*, Husserl likens this splitting of levels to the relation between Kant's 'transcendental aesthetics' and his 'transcendental analytics', although he is aware that the parallel is not entirely apposite (*CM* 146–7).

4 Paul Ricoeur, *Husserl: An Analysis of his Phenomenology*, trans. Edward G. Ballard and Lester E. Embree (Evanston, IL: Northwestern University Press, 1967), p. 11.

5 Admittedly, the idea that the appearance/reality distinction is something that must *itself* appear is also found in Hegel. But, at least according to received wisdom, Hegel's method for analysing the distinction shares little in common with Husserl's. This judgement of dissimilarity is based largely upon the grounds that Husserl never seriously studied Hegel's philosophy nor came under the influence of those who did. Moreover, Husserl seems to have shared the prevailing negative view of post-Kantian German Idealism (see *CES* §§56–57). However, leaving to one side these no doubt salient historical judgements, there still remains, to my mind, a substantive question concerning the *de facto* proximity between the two thinkers (especially in Husserl's later work). For a further discussion of the issues involved, a good starting-point is Merold Westphal, *Hegel, Freedom, and Modernity* (Albany, NY: State University of New York, 1992), Chapter 7 ('Hegel and Husserl: Transcendental phenomenology and the revolution yet awaited').

6 Edmund Husserl, *Psychological and Transcendental Phenomenology and the Confrontation with Heidegger (1927–1931)*, ed. and trans. Thomas Sheehan and Richard E. Palmer (Dordrecht: Kluwer, 1997), p. 249; cf. *CM* 130.

7 For example, Karl-Otto Apel, *Toward a Transformation of Philosophy*, trans. Glyn Adey and David Frisby (London: Routledge, 1980); Jürgen Habermas, *The Philosophical Discourse of Modernity*, trans. Frederick D. Lawrence (Cambridge, MA: MIT Press, 1987), esp. Lecture 11.

8 It should be clarified that once this 'primal institution' (*Urstiftung*) is accomplished, the horizon of intersubjectivity is established once for all (*CM* 111). The horizon of intersubjectivity does not collapse when I happen to be alone. Subsequent experiences of the other are immediately and passively situated within this pre-given horizon of meaning, i.e. *as* experiences of another (the meaning of which is now already understood).

9 The idea of the 'monad' is first introduced in *CM* §33, and is delineated in *CM* §47 as an 'original sphere' containing the entire transcendent world of objects as its intentional correlates (pp. 104–5). Husserl insists that despite his appropriation of this Leibnizian terminology, the content of the term is drawn 'purely from phenomenological explication of the transcendental experience laid open by transcendental reduction' (p. 150).

10 Hence, unlike some phenomenologists in the French tradition (but including also Martin Buber and, to some extent, Max Scheler), Husserl is primarily motivated neither by a desire to analyse the relation to 'the other' *in general*, nor to analyse the *ethical* relation to the other. The phenomenon of intersubjectivity may hold special interest for ethics, but Husserl's analyses are occupied with other, more theoretical, questions. This point is emphasized by Dan Zahavi who wants to prevent us from too quickly assessing Husserl's studies as though they were intended to give a general account of the I-Thou relation. He has in mind, of course, Levinas, amongst others (e.g. Ricoeur, Theunissen and Schütz), whose critique of Husserl turns on showing the inadequacy of Husserl's idea of the other as a basic concept for ethics. See Dan Zahavi, 'Intersubjective transformations of transcendental philosophy', in Donn Welton (ed.), *The New Husserl: A Critical Reader* (Bloomington and Indianapolis, IN: Indiana University Press, 2003), pp. 234–5.

11 Emmanuel Levinas, *Totality and Infinity*, trans. Alphonso Lingis (Pittsburgh, PA: Duquesne University Press, 1969), pp. 24–34. See also Alfred Schütz's objections in 'The problem of transcendental intersubjectivity', in *Collected Papers*, Vol. 3 (The Hague: Martinus Nijhoff, 1970), pp. 65–9 and 82–4.

12 To be precise, apperception *is* a form of 'presentification' (*Vergegenwärtigung*). But it 'presentifies' something real and not something that has been or might be (*CM* 115).

13 Husserl gives a more complex analysis of the act of 'transference', distinguishing those aspects of my being that I expect to be the same for the other and those I do not. For instance, he discusses the way in which I apperceive the other as experiencing the world as I would experience it were I viewing it from the same position (*CM* §§53–54).

CHAPTER 11

THE CRISIS OF THE SCIENCES AND THE IDEA OF THE 'LIFEWORLD'

The concepts developed in *The Crisis of European Sciences and Transcendental Phenomenology* (1936) concerning modern science and 'the lifeworld' are among the most influential in Husserl's entire body of work.[1] In what follows, I focus on a number of key ideas from this posthumously published book. They form clusters around the ideas of science, history and the lifeworld. However, these themes were only just beginning to coalesce into a new form of phenomenology for Husserl during these final years of his life and they are not well integrated in the manuscripts published as *The Crisis*. The editors have done their best to gather together the relevant materials for us. But, as always, we the readers of Husserl are asked to make sense of writings by a man whose thought refused to stand still. Even snapshots of it, like this book, come out blurred because of the pace of his intellectual development.

WHAT IS THE CRISIS OF THE EUROPEAN SCIENCES?

What is the 'crisis of the European sciences' announced in the book's title? When Husserl speaks of a 'crisis' in the European sciences, he is neither predicting their imminent collapse, nor diagnosing some systemic theoretical difficulty that the special sciences would have to overcome in order to progress. Husserl does not question the ability of the sciences to continue on their path of knowledge creation. Where then is the 'crisis'? The crisis of the natural sciences diagnosed by Husserl is a hidden crisis, but one that is nevertheless widely felt. It consists in the decoupling of the sciences from each other and from life *as such*. The crisis is that the sciences each follow their nose in interesting and productive directions, and yet remain oblivious to their purpose and meaning as social practices and as components in the universal search for truth.

The 'crisis' diagnosed by Husserl, then, is related to the crisis famously described by Max Weber as 'the disenchantment of nature'. As the sciences progress (and, importantly for Weber, the market economy becomes more pervasive), the 'rationalized' world that they construct looks increasingly dissimilar to the world as we know it apart from the sciences. The 'truths' of science lose their relation to the realities and meanings that make up the stuff of everyday existence. The one world bifurcates: from one perspective, it is the 'disenchanted' world of science; from the other perspective, it is the 'meaning-laden' world of everyday experience. And the two seem to be hurtling apart.

Now, we might hope that the sciences themselves would eventually account for this apparent rift. But, far from leading us closer to a resolution of the crisis, advances in science only seem to deepen the schism. The only resolution the scientist can offer is to say that the world as we are familiar with it is an *illusion* and that *the truth* is found in the scientific picture of the world. The variety of reductionism exhibited in this interpretation has been called 'scientism': the view that science *alone* has access to what is true and real, and that all other forms of expression are at best vague approximations to scientific knowledge, if they have any validity at all.[2]

On Husserl's analysis, the only reason we are tempted to embrace 'scientism' and to deify science in this way is because we are so impressed by its successes. From a philosophical point of view, however, dire consequences follow from this ill-advised move. We only do ourselves injury if we sign away the house to the natural sciences by allowing it to decide the meaning of 'reality'. If such philosophical questions are referred to science, then not only does philosophy suffer but ultimately the sciences do too. Why? Is this not just a case of a philosopher jealously guarding his academic territory? On the contrary, Husserl thinks there are good theoretical reasons for rejecting scientism and reinstating independent philosophical enquiry.

Useful as scientific knowledge may be, the *schism* between the world of science and the everyday world cannot be resolved by the scientist's mantra that what you are *really* observing is physical process x or chemical process y. This is because the sciences cannot address the question of their own philosophical, cultural or historical significance. They cannot explain the epistemological meaning of their own 'truths'. They cannot account for the meaning-laden character of the world as it presents itself to us everyday, the world in which we live. Nor can the sciences supply an answer to the question of *their* meaning *for human existence*:

> In our vital need – so we are told – [positive] science has nothing to say to us. It excludes in principle precisely the questions which man, given over in our unhappy times to the most portentous upheavals, finds the most burning: questions of the meaning or meaninglessness of the whole of this human existence. Do not these questions, universal and necessary for all men, demand universal reflections and answers based on rational insight? (*CES* 6)

Rather than addressing humanity's 'vital need', the scientistic attitude dismisses our lived experience of the world with both its richness and its crises. By simply insisting more loudly that the world of science is the 'true' world, its stance merely entrenches the alienation felt by the modern individual.

Only philosophy – and transcendental phenomenology, more specifically, Husserl claims – can bring some illumination to this issue, which is not just a theoretical puzzle but also one of the great cultural questions of the modern age. But this is finally to pinpoint where things, in Husserl's view, have come unstuck: 'Now if the new [i.e. renaissance] humanity, animated and blessed with such an exalted spirit, did not hold its own, it must have been because it lost the inspiring belief in its ideal of a universal philosophy and in the scope of the new method' (*CES* 10). On Husserl's analysis, the failure that led to the crisis in the European sciences was the failure to secure a philosophical foundation capable of holding together the Enlightenment project of universal science.[3] Descartes' philosophy was, for Husserl, the first grand attempt to provide such a philosophical foundation for the 'new rationalism' and a unifying principle for a universal science (*CES* §16). But, despite his brilliant and decisive insights, Descartes' philosophy was not radical enough to underwrite the Enlightenment project in its full immensity and scope (*CES* §§19–20). And, in fact, all the great metaphysical systems of the Enlightenment eventually collapsed even as the special sciences powered ahead. It is in this void that the reactive anti-philosophical philosophy of positivism (a form of scientism) found space to thrive.

But, as Husserl remarks, 'positivism, in a manner of speaking, decapitates philosophy' (*CES* 9); which is to say that it renounces the overarching project of philosophy to unify the sciences, and instead takes up a subsidiary and meek role as the handmaiden to the sciences (Locke).

What is at stake then in the crisis of the sciences is the very fate of European humanity and its grand vision. Europe stands, Husserl argues, at a point of existential crisis. Would it fragment into a series of irrational phenomena (and in the background here for Husserl is the portentous rise of fascism in Germany), or rediscover and rejuvenate the ideal of universal philosophy (*CES* 16)? Husserl's own stance is unequivocal: 'The faith in the possibility of philosophy as a task, that is, in the possibility of universal knowledge, is something we *cannot* let go. We *know* that we are *called* to this task as serious philosophers' (*CES* 17).

At the heart of Husserl's response to this situation is an analysis of the state of modern science itself – in fact, a tracing back of its fragmentation to the origins of modern science, especially in Galileo. But, before I proceed to explain the contents of Husserl's critique of modern science, it should be emphasized that his intention is to point out the *limits* of science, not to debunk science as such. Husserl is always positive about the achievements of the sciences, even in his most critical works. He makes his position clear in *The Crisis*:

> . . . we can never cease to admire [the sciences in general] as models of rigorous and highly successful scientific discipline . . . The scientific rigor of all these disciplines, the convincingness of their theoretical accomplishments, and their enduringly compelling success are unquestionable. (*CES* 3–4)

Where he finds reason to be critical, as I have already intimated, is the point at which the sciences dabble in epistemology or ontology, i.e. where they usurp the role of philosophy. So, for instance, scientism claims that reality is coextensive with what is scientifically (i.e. empirically) verifiable; but this claim is itself an ontological commitment, not an empirical result. Similarly, scientism holds that a proposition counts as true knowledge if and only if sufficient evidence has been adduced in support of it. But, again, this is a principle on which science is founded, not a conclusion from scientific research; that is, it is an epistemological claim, not a scientific one (in the narrower sense of the term). What Husserl disputes, then, is not the competence of the positive sciences to establish knowledge but their competence to ground themselves philosophically. Husserl therefore aims to provide an alternative account of what truth is, what reality is, and what scientific enquiry is, based on a rigorous philosophical method of enquiry – the very things the sciences are ill-equipped to do for themselves.

The philosophical portrait of science that Husserl paints must, therefore, account for the legitimacy of the sciences, but also for their one-sidedness. It must ground the sciences and show why they have a limited sphere of competence. These are themes we have touched on in previous chapters. However, in *The Crisis*, Husserl's conception of scientific enquiry undergoes a marked development. For the first time, scientific enquiry is conceptualized as an essentially social, historical and linguistically dependent practice. As we shall see, Husserl's new account of science places it in a context of lived experience which is broader than science but which incorporates science as one of its possibilities. This broader context is what Husserl calls everyday lived experience, and it is characterized by its being caught up in the 'lifeworld' (*Lebenswelt*). The final section of this chapter is devoted to a brief description of this concept of historical, purposeful life and the notion of the lifeworld.

THE ORIGINS OF THE CONTEMPORARY CRISIS IN THE MATHEMATIZATION OF NATURE

Husserl contends that the seed of the contemporary crisis of the sciences was sown by Galileo. It is due to Galileo that the distinctively modern *conception of nature* emerges: consisting of a spatio-temporal manifold that is describable mathematically, or rather geometrically. Recent evolutions in the modern scientific view of the world have merely extended the basic conceptual platform laid by Galileo. This idea of the natural world originates, according to Husserl, in a process of 'idealization', 'Objectification' or 'mathematization' (*CES* 348–9). Now, the act of 'idealization' had already been employed by the ancient geometers and logicians, but it was not until the modern era that it became universalized to the point where the ideal of *universal mathematical science* (*mathesis universalis*) could be taken up as the goal of all rational enquiry (*CES* §8). Galileo's innovation, which was firmly to establish the modern scientific conception of the world, was to move beyond 'idealizing' this or that phenomenon to seeing the world itself as an idealized, mathematical manifold of measurable time and space. But this, as we shall see, also has fateful ramifications. Allow me to unpack Husserl's analysis of these points in some detail. It requires, unfortunately, a rather roundabout avenue of approach.

Quite early on, in the course of thinking through the notion of 'essence', Husserl noticed that there are two kinds of 'essences', which he called 'morphological' and 'exact' (*Ideas I* §74). The term 'morphological' describes essences of which there are or could be *de facto* exemplars: e.g. cat, table, something bell-shaped, government, something fearsome, etc. The term 'exact', by contrast, designates essences that are 'ideas in the Kantian sense'. That is, they are ideals or 'limiting' concepts to which real beings can only ever approximate: e.g. straight line, something round, the perfectly just person, the average plumber. The key difference between the two is that exact essences are 'mathematical' and can be made the subject of mathematical calculations, whereas morphological essences are non-mathematical. The ideas in the Kantian sense, therefore, spawn 'mathematical' disciplines, whereas morphological ideas do not. So, for example, the idea 'triangle' gives rise to a whole subsystem of geometrical theorems; but the idea 'pear-shaped' does not. The former is a limiting concept, the latter is a morphological concept.

A central task of scientific thinking in the modern era has been to find ways of legitimately describing worldly phenomena in exact terms so that they might be made the subject of exact measurement, statistical analysis, or similar. This necessarily involves some leap from the morphological to the exact, and this is what Husserl calls 'idealization' (*CES* 24–8). But such a leap can never completely capture the phenomenon at hand, because real objects are *ipso facto* not exemplars of ideas in the Kantian sense. The world that we actually experience contains 'nothing of geometrical idealities, no geometrical space or mathematical time withal their shapes' (*CES* 50). Conversely, exact essences only ever describe pure possibilities and never actualities. Every act of mathematical description, therefore, entails a substitution of an ideality for a reality. For example, instead of measuring the area of this roughly rectangular floor, I compromise and work out the area of an idealized rectangle whose exact measurements approximate the actual floor. What I am measuring, therefore, is not the real floor *per se* but in fact the ideal rectangle that I superimpose on it by my mathematical thinking (cf. *CES* 313–14). This process is sometimes comically artificial. Think, for example, of a psychological test that asks you to convert your emotional response to some event into a number between 0 and 10. The translation from morphological concepts (e.g. 'I found it disturbing and repugnant') to calculable concepts (e.g. numbers on a scale) often sacrifices a great deal of detail and conceptual precision in order to have data in a manageable form. The sacrifice is essential, however, if the subject matter is to become the object of an 'exact' science.

For Husserl, the process of 'idealization', whereby scientific thinking manages to transcend the domain of morphological realities in favour of idealized descriptions, is at the heart of the modern scientific conception of the world, a conception which finds its origin in Galileo. For Galileo, it seemed that the truly objective aspect of every experience is its geometrical structure. Only this aspect of experience has universal validity, i.e. validity for anyone (*CES* 24). (This idea recurs, of course, in Descartes' conception of the world as *res extensa*.) Thus, Galileo abstracts from the individual's perspectival, sensuous experiences of the world that which is describable in subject-independent terms, namely, in terms of existence in objective space and time (*CES* 330).

The world of modern science is thus unlike the world of actual experience in precisely this sense: it consists in idealized forms of reality and disregards those aspects of reality that actually exhibit morphological essences. In phenomenological terms, this explains why it is correct to think of the 'world' of the sciences is an 'ideal object', i.e. something *not* given to perception, but given only to founded acts of categorial intuition. What the sciences offer, therefore, is not 'exact description' (as is sometimes claimed) but rather description using *exact terms*. Far from being an *exact* description, scientific description settles for an idealized description of the object which trades off its contingencies for the sake of possessing a description that admits of mathematical manipulation. It is this translation that makes scientific thinking useful. But the decisive role of this translation is almost universally overlooked.

But the mathematization of nature did not occur at one fell swoop. Some years after Galileo, in Locke and Boyle, for example, we see the tension between the mathematized world of nature and the world of experience played out in the distinction between those qualities that admit of precise, non-subjective description (the so-called 'primary qualities'; e.g. geometrical properties, solidity) and those that have an essential dependency upon subjectivity (the so-called 'secondary qualities; e.g. colour, sound, taste, smell). But, over time, techniques were developed to measure objectively the 'secondary' qualities as well, or at least to measure their material causes (sound-waves, chemical composition, etc.). Here too the Midas touch of mathematization could henceforth be applied. Consequently, the category of 'secondary qualities' came to seem more and more spurious. And, once this process of mathematization had been sufficiently extended, it seemed that almost *any* phenomenon could be better described in 'purely scientific' categories. The entire world of 'phenomenal qualia' (sense data) seemed at best a necessary means of indirect access to the world, and at worst an irrelevant surplus beyond the world of facts whose laws the sciences investigate. Slowly, 'irrationalities' standing opposed to the new rationalism – which here means every predication related to subjectivity – were being explained away or put out of play. The entire realm of first-person experience, therefore, came to be regarded as a mere veil of appearances behind which stands hidden the Objective world accessible only to science. Consequently, one comes to feel that the world as it is *'for me'* must be radically distinguished from the world as it is *'in itself'* (*CES* 164, 305–6).[4] The legacy of the ongoing mathematization of nature, then, is that the 'true world' that it offers appears increasingly foreign to the world of my experience (i.e. the 'apparent world').

THE LIMITS OF THE NATURAL-SCIENTIFIC ATTITUDE

The crisis of modern science, for Husserl, stems from science's *forgetfulness* of the relationship between its ever more abstract constructions and the real world in which we live. The origins of these constructions in some originary procedure of idealization from the lifeworld is forgotten. Husserl explains this 'forgetfulness' by reference to the *historical* mode in which scientific enquiry proceeds:

> [All sciences] have the mobility of sedimented traditions that are worked upon, again and again, by an activity of producing new structures of meaning and handing them down. Existing in this way, they extend enduringly truth time, since all new acquisitions are in turn sedimented and become working materials.

Everywhere the problems, the clarifying investigations, the insights of principle are *historical*. (*CES* 368–9)

The theoretical constructions 'sedimented' by the previous generation of researchers is simply taken up and worked on by the next. The origins of those theoretical constructions are not necessarily remembered, and indeed they do not need to be for scientific research to continue.[5] However, to proceed this way means that science is reduced to little more than a 'technique' for the production of new and ever more sophisticated theories. Its thinking, therefore, takes place simply on the 'pure' or 'symbolic' level and never returns to the realm from which its legitimacy sprang (*CES* 46). Its constructions remain active and meaningful at the level of 'sedimented (logical) sentence-meaning' but lose all contact with the 'actual meaning' or 'truth-meaning' that lies at the origin of the tradition. Thus, Husserl speaks of a 'forgotten meaning-fundament of natural science' (*CES* 48):

> The progress of deduction follows formal-logical self-evidence; but without the actually developed capacity for reactivating the original activities contained within its fundamental concepts, i.e., without the 'what' and the 'how' of its prescientific materials, geometry would be a tradition empty of meaning; and if we ourselves did not have this capacity, we could never even know whether geometry had or ever did have a genuine meaning, one that could really be 'cashed in'.
>
> Unfortunately, however, this is our situation, and that of the whole modern age. (*CES* 366)

In short, the sciences have no sense of the *relation* of their own activities to the world of everyday lived experience. The latter has long since been transcended and forgotten. But the result is a scientific practice devoid of any genuine understanding of *what* it is or does.

More perniciously, this forgetting of origins is followed by a spurious *substitution* of the world of science for the world of real objectivity, the sphere of origins:

> But now we must note something of the highest importance that occurred even as early as Galileo: the surreptitious substitution of the mathematically substructed world of idealities for the only

real world, the one that is actually given through perception, that is ever experienced and experienceable – our everyday life-world. (*CES* 48f.)

Having forgotten its grounds in the world of experience, the ideal world of the sciences is held up as 'the true world' *at the expense* of the real world of experience. The 'garb of ideas' that the sciences develop as tools for predicting the behaviour and character of natural phenomena come to be regarded as themselves the 'true being' (*CES* 51). It is this substitution that is the truly insidious error, for it means that the grounds of modern science are not only forgotten but rendered off-limits to any 'serious' scientific enquiry. Science cuts itself off from the remedy to its own crisis by refusing to recognize the lifeworld of experience as anything more than a surface world or veil of appearances (*CES* 383; *Ideas II* 374). Herein lies the source of the pervasive experience of alienation that characterized the Europe of Husserl's day.[6]

Husserl's critique, therefore, aims to make explicit the hidden debts owed by the sciences to the world of lived experience, i.e. the lifeworld. Husserl corrects the scientistic worldview by reminding it that (1) science is dependent on the lifeworld for its empirical evidence; (2) the objects of natural-scientific knowing do not exhaust all that is; (3) science is a phenomenon belonging to the lifeworld; and (4) science is a mode of transcendental subjectivity. Each of these points deserves some comment.

(1) The work of scientific research implicitly presupposes and relies upon the world of experience or 'lifeworld' as its field of direct observation and evidence (*CES* 127). Indeed, the scientist himself implicitly affirms the link between the world of science and the lifeworld by saying that the bearer of his scientific predicates is the very same object that is the bearer of experiential predicates, e.g. the stuff whose chemical description is H_2O is the same stuff you boil to make your coffee in the morning (*Ideas I* 134). This is a clue to the relation between science and the lifeworld: the sciences perform certain higher-level judgements or apperceptions regarding the *same* objects given straightforwardly to perception. But this is just to say that scientific thinking belongs alongside other modes of higher-level intentional acts grounded in perception. For example, consider a painting, say *Water Lilies* by Claude Monet. Straightforwardly, I may judge it to contain particular colours on the basis of my sensuous

intuition of the painting. In a higher-level form of categorial judgement, however, I may judge or apperceive it to be beautiful. But
equally, I may judge it to contain certain geometrical relationships or
perhaps judge it to be undergoing certain chemical reactions.
Judgements of the latter forms – i.e. 'scientific' judgements – are, for
Husserl, simply another class of complex *categorial judgements*.
Such 'scientific' judgements may possess a remarkable utility, as the
successes of modern science and technology attest; but, like all intentional acts from the simplest to the most sophisticated, they admit of
investigation and description by phenomenology. But ultimately, if
they have epistemic validity, they must relate back to the world that is
given prescientifically (*CES* 50f., 125–7).

(2) Contra scientism, therefore, *reality* is not coextensive with the
objects of natural science. There are other genuine realities: emo-
tions, social relations, social institutions, values, etc. And, to this
plenum of objectivity, various modes of description can be applied,
some of which boast a 'mathematical' level of exactitude, others of
which do not. But each of these modes of discourse has its standards
and norms of truth and falsehood. I can make a false claim about
the state of my friendship with someone (claiming we are on good
terms, for example, when in fact we are feuding) just as much as I can
make a false claim about the geometrical properties of a triangle. But
in each case we are dealing with different kinds of truth verified by
different means. It is entirely appropriate that we judge differently
according to the context and according to the purpose of our judging. Both scientific *and* non-scientific judgements ought to be
regarded as valid in their respective spheres of application. So, for
example, the art critic makes aesthetic judgements concerning the
work of art, whereas the art-dealer makes economic judgements
concerning the same object. The two kinds of judgement correlate to
different ontological 'levels' pertaining to the same real object. But
each has its mode of possible evidence and its own cultural sphere of
significance and validity (see *FTL* §106). (Husserl's removal of the
ontological restriction imposed by scientism simultaneously vali-
dates the human sciences, whose job it is to investigate the 'cultural
spheres of significance and validity'. The subject matters of these
sciences are precisely the spiritual communities and spiritual objects
that belong to the lifeworld as such and not to the world as it is
conceived by the natural sciences [*CES* 327ff.; see Chapters 9 and 10]).

(3) Science is itself one of the phenomena belonging to the *cultural*

world (as opposed to the *natural* world). This means simply that the idea of science is the idea of a specific *practical* project: it presents a *telos* by which one may order and direct one's actions and intellectual pursuits. Because science is itself a cultural and not a natural phenomenon, science could never be properly understood by the scientist who insists that the only true world is the natural world. In this connection Husserl observes:

> [All] the occasional (even 'philosophical') reflections which go from technical [scientific] work back to its true meaning always stop at idealized nature; they do not carry out the reflection radically, going back to the ultimate purpose which the new science, together with the geometry which is inseparable from it, growing out of prescientific life and its surrounding world, was from the beginning supposed to serve: a purpose which necessarily lay *in* this prescientific life and was related to its life-world. (*CES* 50)

For this reason, the work of scientific research can only be understood by studying it *as* a phenomenon belonging to the practical and cultural sphere, i.e. to the lifeworld (*CES* 382). But the more general lesson is that, just as the subject matter of science is intimately related to the lifeworld from which it is abstracted, so scientific practice itself is intimately related to the very lifeworld that it usually disregards.

(4) The final point Husserl makes regarding the forgotten origins of science concerns the relation of science to transcendental subjectivity: Even the scientific conception of the world is a *conception* of the world, and is therefore the correlate of an *intentional* relation (*CES* 382). Consequently, even though the objects of science are constituted *as* subject-independent, such objects remain objects constituted by transcendental subjectivity. Thus, there is no scientific theory that is radically subject-independent. Every object belonging to the scientific world bears in itself some relation to the world of 'subjective' experience which precedes science. Again, however, the dependency of science on transcendental subjectivity is completely overlooked by the sciences themselves. And, from the perspective of transcendental philosophy, we can see how this dismissal of the 'subjective' is a relinquishing of that ground from which alone science can be understood *qua* constitutive achievement: namely, the field of transcendental (inter)subjectivity. Admittedly, the 'lost ground' of

consciousness is belatedly re-engaged by modern science in the guise of 'psychology', but as Husserl argues here and elsewhere, psychology fails to bring consciousness into view *qua* transcendental consciousness. It remains a science of the natural attitude and shares the essential limitations of the other natural sciences (as discussed in Chapters 1 and 4).

THE PROJECT OF *THE CRISIS*

In order to reverse the obliviousness of modern science, what is needed is a form of enquiry that seeks to rediscover the origins or roots of the scientific disciplines from whence their legitimacy springs. The only way to remedy the crisis of the European sciences is to rediscover the rootedness of the sciences in the lifeworld. This project is undertaken, in part, in *The Crisis* (see *CES* 57–9). There Husserl attempts to trace the 'origins' of certain key scientific concepts. We have already seen some examples of these studies above.

However, Husserl is not attempting to do historical research *per se*. His aim is not necessarily to reconstruct the *actual* 'history of ideas' but to tease out what conceptual territory *must* have been traversed in order for these concepts to have been constituted. His project, therefore, is one of excavation or 'regressive enquiry' (*Rückfrage*) into the 'inner structures of meaning' that are present in concepts as we now possess them, and of analysing the essential interrelations between them as separate constitutive achievements until we return to primative lived experiences (*CES* 354, 371). In this connection, he speaks of certain decisive steps or 'primal institutions' (*Urstiftungen*), whose traces can be discerned in scientific theories or concepts as layers of sediment. At each stage in the process, presumably, these innovations must have achieved general recognition in order to have been 'instituted' and to have passed into the world-understanding of the intellectual community. These steps may have been so small or seemingly insignificant that their original founder may no longer be known. Who was the first person to identify the plane shape of the oval in distinction to the circle, for example? We don't know. But each of these conceptual innovations and distinctions *must* have been instituted at some point for the first time. Again, to say that these concepts have a history is not to deny the universal validity of such discovered truths, but to say that the discovery of universal truths is itself a contingent *yet largely rule-governed* historical process. The *eidetic* rules that govern these innovations are what Husserl seeks to uncover (*CES* 350–51).

Hence, although Husserl's method takes a 'historical turn', this does not amount to a rejection of his transcendental reduction in favour of mundane historical enquiry (*CES* 354).[7] What Husserl has in mind here can be thought of as an expansion of the notion of 'constitutive analysis' with which we have already become familiar. It adds a *diachronic* dimension to what we are already familiar with as *synchronic* constitutive analysis: the teasing out of a series of founded acts that are necessary for the constitution of some object. Husserl's own terms for these two forms of analysis are 'genetic' and 'static constitution'. Rather than simply considering a motivated series of intentional acts accomplished one upon the other by a single ego, we are now considering a series of constitutive acts that are accomplished individually and by historically separated individuals, but which nevertheless build upon one another over time. To reiterate, however; the important thing is not an analysis of the actual history but an analysis of the ideal or virtual history (if you will) implied by the concept or practice at hand. In one place, Husserl calls this 'the *a priori* of history' (*CES* 349).

What is ultimately uncovered in Husserl's 'regressive enquiry' is the hidden relationship between the 'subjective' world of experience or 'lifeworld' and the 'objective' world which is *founded* by it. Or, to put the same point differently, each higher-level ideality refers back through a chain of founding acts to a primal experience of truth which is the legitimating moment of the entire superstructure built upon it (*CES* 372). The enquiry moves in the opposite direction to the sciences themselves: rather than climbing up the ladder of ever more abstract idealizations, Husserl's 'regressive enquiry' climbs down the ladders set up by the sciences to unearth their grounds – to unearth, that is, the lifeworld itself.

The radical implication of Husserl's increasingly historical account of constitution is that it refuses to justify a privileged set of concepts as 'the' basic concepts of science. Unlike Kant's *Critique of Pure Reason*, which appears to wed itself to Newtonian physics, Husserl's studies do not pretend to 'deduce' scientific concepts. At best, the studies are able to display the origins of these concepts; but this does not rule out further legitimate modifications or reconfigurations. The basic concepts of the sciences do not fall from the sky ready-made, nor do we establish them once for all. We should not expect that they are our possession by right. At this point, the work of 'regional ontology' thus becomes historically self-aware (the necessity of which, it must be said, Hegel had already insisted upon over a century earlier).[8]

THE IDEA OF THE LIFEWORLD

In this final section, I would like to address more directly the concept of 'the lifeworld' (*Lebenswelt*), which has already been mentioned at various points. As the reader will have gathered, the lifeworld for Husserl is the world given to us most immediately: the world-horizon in which we live without making it thematic *as* a world (*CES* 379). Such at least is the basic sense of the concept. However, David Carr, the translator of *The Crisis*, has argued that Husserl has several conceptions of the lifeworld and that they are not necessarily compatible.[9] He may well be correct in this judgement. Nevertheless, we can pick out two main senses of the concept whose relation to one another is clear enough. I shall call these the 'thick' and the 'thin' concepts of lifeworld.

The 'thick' variant occurs when the term 'lifeworld' is used to denote the entire world given to us in immediate experience replete with cultural richness, manifold practical meanings and sensuous fullness. In this case, we are obviously dealing with a world that is itself the product of cultural histories and that is bound up with complex social, political and religious forms of intersubjectivity. Here we are faced with the overwhelming multiplicity of phenomena whose investigation is the task of the human sciences.

The 'thin' variant of the term 'lifeworld', on the other hand, is employed by Husserl to denote that narrower set of phenomena, also belonging to the world of experience, which are invariant from culture to culture. This thin sense of the lifeworld can therefore be called 'nature', or at least nature *as* it is subjectively experienced. It is at this level that we find the plenum of sensuous givenness out of which the idealizations of the natural sciences can legitimately arise (*CES* 375–7). Importantly, however, for Husserl this thin lifeworld is only ever an *abstract part* of the totality of lived experience. We always already find ourselves immersed in the cultural and practical world, and only subsequently do we come to isolate the world of natural experience within it.

Irrespective of whether we are speaking of the lifeworld in the thick or thin sense, for Husserl the lifeworld retains within it a reference to the embodiment of human subjectivity. The lifeworld is correlated to a functioning body: 'it is in this world that we ourselves live, in accord with our bodily [*leiblich*], personal way of being' (*CES* 50). This corporeality, with its needs, desires, traditions, habits, etc., structures our relation to the world, and to some extend remakes the world to its purposes. Similarly, the lifeworld is characterized by the feature of meaningfulness or purposiveness. Even the thin stratum of sensuous experience, the stratum of natural phenomena, have for us aesthetic, practical and even religious meanings. The meaningfulness of the objects of the lifeworld always contains an index to the purposes and needs *of human beings* (*CES* 379). As the correlate of our motivated goals and projects, the surrounding world (*Umwelt*) is first a 'practical' world (*CES* 376).[10] The lifeworld, then, is the world correlated to our 'personal' existence (cf. Chapter 9). The lifeworld is given laden with meaning for persons who live together in the world and who confer 'spiritual' meaning on it. Which is to say, once again, that the world is for us first a world of valuable and useful objects, not 'mere things'.

This notion of the lifeworld, as well as influencing critical theorists such as Habermas[11] has had an even greater impact on phenomenologists such as Maurice Merleau-Ponty, who came to think of the very task of phenomenology as a rediscovering of the layers of pre-theoretical life, i.e. of the lifeworld. The philosophical *desideratum*, therefore, is to develop *another* kind of scientific enquiry, one which aims not at simplicity, univocity and Objectivity, but which aims at uncovering the diversity, richness and contingencies of human life as it is culturally, historically and linguistically formed – as it is prior to our objectifying interpretations of it. And Merleau-Ponty broadly agrees with the fundamental thesis of Husserl's *The Crisis* that the mode of enquiry uniquely capable of unearthing this lifeworld is nothing other than phenomenology itself. The critique of scientific objectivism, then, is not only a path back to the lifeworld; it is also a path back to the transcendental problematic and is an argument for the primacy of transcendental phenomenological enquiry in philosophy. If *The Crisis* has an overarching argument, then, it is that only phenomenology is capable of revivifying the idea of philosophy as universal science and of overcoming the alienation of modern scientific consciousness from life. Indeed, the stated purpose of the book is: 'by way of a teleological-historical reflection upon the origins of our critical scientific and philosophical situation, to establish the unavoidable necessity of a transcendental-phenomenological reorientation of philosophy' (*CES* 3, n. 1).

NOTES

1　This is the date that two parts of the text we now know as *Die Krisis der europäischen Wissenschaften und die transzendentale Phänomenologie* were published in the journal *Philosophia* in Belgrade. But the text was much expanded by Husserl, although it was never completed during his lifetime for publication. For more details, see the 'Translator's introduction' in *CES*, xv–xxiii.

2　For a pithy discussion of the idea of 'scientism', see Simon Critchley, *Continental Philosophy: A Very Short Introduction* (Oxford: Oxford University Press, 2001), Chapter 7.

3　For Husserl, it is this project that gives Europe a unifying teleological understanding of itself. The European spirit is noble and precious precisely because it participates in this teleological self-conception, this Idea of European science and culture. By contrast, Husserl does not think of China or India as having a 'sense' but only as instances of 'empirical anthropological types' (*CES* §6, 15f.). Unlike Europe, these civilizations are not, in his view, galvanized by the shared sense of a cultural *purpose* or *project*.

4　Compare Husserl's more value-neutral analysis in *Ideas II* 89–95 and 217f.

5　Husserl locates the conditions for the possibility of this forgetfulness in the process of *writing*, by which results become sedimented and settled, thus taking on the appearance of unquestionable truth (*CES* 362). Here again there are strong similarities between Husserl's account of the 'seduction of language' and Heidegger's discussion of 'Idle talk' in *Being and Time*, trans. John Macquarrie and Edward Robinson (Oxford: Basil Blackwell, 1962), p. 35.

6　The present argument concerning the deleterious philosophical pretensions of science and its hapless obfuscating of the transcendental experience of the world is prefigured in *Ideas I*, §§18–26 ('Naturalistic misinterpretations'; see Chapter 4). The arguments are not quite identical, but they clearly belong to the same line of thought.

7　'This consideration is in certain measure kinetic or "genetic": a "genesis" that belongs to a totally different "transcendental" world than does the natural and natural-scientific genesis' (*Ideas Pertaining to a Pure Phenomenology and a Phenomenological Philosophy: Phenomenology and the Foundation of the Sciences* (Third Book), trans. Ted E. Klein and William E. Pohl (The Hague: Martinus Nijhoff, 1980), p. 117).

8　See Chapter 10, n. 5.

9 David Carr, 'Husserl's Problematic Concept of the Life-World', in Frederick Elliston and Peter McCormick (eds), *Husserl: Expositions and Appraisals* (Notre Dame, IN, and London: University of Notre Dame Press, 1977), pp. 202–17.

10 These dimensions of Husserl's account, it must be said, had already received a sophisticated treatment in Heidegger's *Being and Time* (1927). Husserl had initially been dismissive of Heidegger's efforts, but these late texts bear the mark of his influence.

11 See Jürgen Habermas, *The Theory of Communicative Action*, 2 vols, trans. T. McCarthy (Boston, MA: Beacon Press, 1984; 1987) and his classic study, *Knowledge and Human Interests*, trans. Jeremy Shapiro (Cambridge: Polity Press, 1987). Both works are heavily influenced by Husserl's critique of science and his notion of the lifeworld. Habermas draws a straight line between the post-Kantian philosophies of science and the logical positivism of the Vienna Circle, and charges them all with denying the possibility of *critical* reflection – 'critical' in the Kantian sense, that is (i.e. concerned with the nature and limits of knowledge itself). Husserl's notion of the lifeworld, for Habermas, provides a key vantage-point from which to envisage such a critique.

CONCLUSION AND FURTHER READING

Husserl envisaged generations of researchers labouring away at the new philosophical science he had established, undertaking concrete phenomenological analyses of the most diverse aspects of life. His phenomenological beginnings, however, never formed the basis of a unified and coordinated phenomenological research project. Even his most devoted students and closest colleagues took leave from his philosophical position in one way or another. Nevertheless, philosophy in the twentieth century has been profoundly influenced by Husserl's thought. Several of the most prominent philosophers of the second half of the last century were either students of Husserl or began their careers with intensive studies of his writings. Among them are such distinguished figures as Theodor Adorno, Jacques Derrida, Eugen Fink, Hans-Georg Gadamer, Jürgen Habermas, Martin Heidegger, Emmanuel Levinas, Maurice Merleau-Ponty, Paul Ricoeur, Alfred Schütz and Jean-Paul Sartre. Some, such as Fink, Heidegger, Merleau-Ponty and Sartre, would continue to identify themselves as phenomenologists. Others, such as Derrida, Gadamer, Levinas and Ricoeur, stand both inside and outside the phenomenological tradition. And still others, such as Adorno, found in Husserl a foil for their own philosophical agenda.

The present generation has continued to find in Husserl a seemingly endless source of philosophical possibilities. He remains a central reference-point for much so-called Continental philosophy. Therefore, as a 'movement' (loosely speaking), phenomenology remains a living and active force in contemporary philosophy. And, with the ongoing publication of Husserl's manuscripts and lectures, the scholarly study of his thought has never been more vigorous.

So much to suggest that many have found value not only in being familiar with Husserl's thought but also in dedicating substantial effort to mastering and exploring his writings. To that end, I have compiled the following list of suggestions for further reading. However, having read this book, the reader should have the basic tools to be able to tackle Husserl's writings themselves. There is nothing more worthwhile and satisfying than patiently working through one of Husserl's own publications and discovering the riches of the text for oneself.

GENERAL INTRODUCTIONS

Bell, D. *Husserl* (London: Routledge, 1990).

Bernet, R., Kern, I. and Marbach, E. *An Introduction to Husserlian Phenomenology* (Evanston, IL: Northwestern University Press, 1993).

Held, K. 'Husserl's phenomenological method' and 'Husserl's phenomenology of the life-world', in Donn Welton (ed.), *The New Husserl: A Critical Reader* (Bloomington and Indianapolis, IN: Indiana University Press, 2003), pp. 3–31 and 32–62.

Ströker, E. *Husserl's Transcendental Phenomenology*, trans. Lee Hardy (Stanford, CA: Stanford University Press, 1993).

Zahavi, D. *Husserl's Phenomenology* (Stanford, CA: Stanford University Press, 2003).

CLASSIC STUDIES ON HUSSERL'S PHENOMENOLOGY

Boer, Th. de. *The Development of Husserl's Thought*, trans. Theodore Plantinga (The Hague: Martinus Nijhoff, 1978).

Derrida, J. *Speech and Phenomena*, trans. David B. Allison (Evanston, IL: Northwestern University Press, 1973).

—— *Edmund Husserl's Origin of Geometry: An Introduction*, trans. John P. Leavey, Jr (Lincoln, NB, and London: University of Nebraska Press, 1989).

Fink, E. *Sixth Cartesian Meditation: The Idea of a Transcendental Theory of Method*, trans. Ronald Bruzina (Bloomington, IN: Indiana University Press, 1994).

Gurwitsch, A. *Studies in Phenomenology and Psychology* (Evanston, IL: Northwestern University Press, 1966).

Heidegger, M. *History of the Concept of Time: Prolegomena*, trans. Theodore Kisiel (Bloomington and Indianapolis, IN: Indiana University Press, 1985). ('Preliminary Part', pp. 13–131.)

Kolakowski, L. *Husserl and the Search for Certitude* (Chicago, IL: University of Chicago Press, 1987).

Levinas, E. *The Theory of Intuition in Husserl's Phenomenology*, trans. André Orianne (Evanston, IL: Northwestern University Press, 1995).

Mohanty, J.N. *Edmund Husserl's Theory of Meaning*, 2nd edn (The Hague: Martinus Nijhoff, 1969).
—— *The Concept of Intentionality* (St Louis, MO: Warren Green, 1972).
Ricoeur, P. *Husserl: An Analysis of his Phenomenology*, trans. Edward G. Ballard and Lester E. Embree (Evanston, IL: Northwestern University Press, 1967).
Sokolowski, R. *The Formation of Husserl's Concept of Constitution* (The Hague: Martinus Nijhoff, 1964).

USEFUL COLLECTIONS OF ESSAYS

Depraz, N. and Zahavi, D. (eds), *Alterity and Facticity: New Perspectives on Husserl* (Dordrecht: Kluwer, 1998).
Dreyfus, H.L. and Hall, H. (eds), *Husserl, Intentionality and Cognitive Science* (Cambridge, MA: MIT Press, 1982).
Drummond, J.J. (ed.), *The Phenomenology of the Noema* (Dordecht: Kluwer, 1992).
Elliston, F.A. and McCormick, P. (eds), *Husserl: Expositions and Appraisals* (Notre Dame, IL: University of Notre Dame Press, 1977).
Fisette, D. (ed.), *Husserl's Logical Investigations Reconsidered* (Dordrecht: Kluwer, 2003).
Hopkins, B.C. (ed.), *Husserl in Contemporary Context* (Dordrecht: Kluwer, 1997).
Mohanty, J.N. (ed.), *Readings on Edmund Husserl's Logical Investigations* (The Hague: Martinus Nijhoff, 1977).
Welton, D. (ed.), *The New Husserl: A Critical Reader* (Bloomington and Indianapolis, IN: Indiana University Press, 2003).

INDEX

Page numbers in bold indicate chapter topics.

Adorno, T. 198
Apel, K.-O. 168, 178n. 7
appresentation (of the other) 165,
   172–7
Aristotle 31, 53, 75n. 13, 103, 106–7,
   112nn. 9, 11, 136
Augustine 127, 141n. 1

Bell, D. 199
Berkeley, G. 50
Bernet, R. 199
body 144, 149–55, 159–60, 161n. 7,
   10, 173–5, 195
de Boer, Th. 199
van Breda, H. L. 4
Brentano, F. 2, 21n. 9, 67, 79–80,
   96nn. 3, 8, 131–2, 145
Bolzano, B. 10–11
Boyle, R. 186
Buber, M. 179n. 10

Cairns, D. 5n. 1
Carr, D. 160n. 5, 194, 197n. 9
categories 26, 31–3, 42–7, 61, 70, 117
Cohen, H. 11
cogito 52–5, 72–3, 140, 147–9
cognition, mystery of 17–20, 39–42,
   47, 85
consciousness 18, 35–6, 38n. 10,
   46–9, 60, 66–73, 79–82, 94–5,
   128, 131–41

absolute 53–4, 71–3, 75n. 12,
   125n. 5, 130, 137–41, 142n. 10,
   147–9, 157
acts of 40, 46–9, 54–5, 79, 82–4,
   86, 94–5
contents of 103, 116
intentional *see* intentionality
psychological vs. transcendental
   66–70, 72
science of 35–6, 47, 54, 63, 88,
   142n. 13, 171
see also time-consciousness
Conrad-Martinus, H. 89
constitution 48–52, 56n. 7, 74n. 5, 82,
   86, 90–1, 94–5, 113, 145, 148–50,
   157–8, 160n. 1, 162–77, 191–3
static vs. genetic 125, 193, 196n. 7
conviction 99, 148–50, 175
Critchley, S. 196n. 2
culture 154–6, 181–2, 190–1, 194–5,
   196n. 3

Depraz, N. 200
Derrida, J. 86, 96n. 10, 141, 143n.
   16, 198, 199
Descartes, R. 39, 50, 52–5, 57, 65,
   71–3, 73n. 3, 116, 129, 145, 148,
   160n. 2, 162, 165, 172, 182, 186
Dilthey, W. 154–5, 161n. 15
Dreyfus, H. L. 200
Drummond, J. J. 200

ego 48, 53–5, **144–61**, 162–5,
 167–70, 172, 177, 193
 alter *see* the other
 empirical 67, 145–6, 157–8
 personal *see* person
 phenomenological 145
 psychic *see* psyche
 transcendental or pure 44, 52, 55,
 67–8, 71–3, 142n. 14, 144–51,
 154, 157–9, 160nn. 1, 3, 168–70,
 177, *see also* intentionality
eidetic analysis *see* eidetic science,
 phenomenology as
eidetic reduction 57–8, 110
eidetic science **22–38**, 74n. 7, 121,
 123–4, 185–6
 material vs. formal 26, 30–3
 phenomenology as 34–6, 39,
 51–2, 57, 110–11
Elliston, F. A. 200
empiricism 9, 27–30, 62–3, 116, 144,
 148
epoché 57–8, 73n. 2, 110, 112n. 17
 phenomenological *see*
 transcendental reduction
 philosophical 57, 109–10
Erdmann, B. 10
essence 15, 22–5, 30–3, 37nn. 3, 4,
 94, 121–3, 125n. 5, 126n. 10,
 173, 177, 185–6
 science of *see* eidetic science
 seeing of 26, 29–30, 35, 39, 111,
 113, 120–6
evidence 54–5, 68, **98–112**, 124–5,
 165, 188–90
 adequate vs. inadequate 102–3,
 109–10, 124
 apodictic vs. assertoric 12, 41,
 103, 124
 principle of 29–30, 51, 101,
 107–11, 142n. 13
experience 22, 24–5, 43–6, 59–62,
 113, 145–8, 185–7
 intersubjective 163–5, 169–70
 lived 59–60, 70, 72, 79, 81–2, 103,
 147, 184, 188–9, *see also*
 intentionality
 of the other 170–6, 179n. 13

of truth 99, 105–7, 114, 193

Fink, E. 74n. 6, 198, 199
first philosophy 36, 41–2, 53–4, 57,
 171
Fisette, D. 200
forgetfulness of origins 70, 187–9,
 191–2, 196n. 5
forms *see* object, categorial
Frege, G. 10, 20n. 2, 85

Gadamer, H.-G. 198
Galileo 183–4, 186, 188
Geiger, M. 3
German Idealism 10, 178n. 5
Gorgias 40
Gurwitsch, A. 199

Habermas, J. 168, 178n. 7, 195,
 197n. 11, 198
habituality 19, 148–50, 158, 195
Hall, H. 200
Hegel, G. W. F. 178n. 5, 194
Heidegger, M. 3, 17, 20n. 6, 37n. 8,
 75n. 13, 96n. 4, 100, 106–7,
 110–12, 116, 125n. 4, 141, 143n.
 15, 156, 161n. 15, 196n. 5, 197n.
 10, 198–9
Held, K. 73n. 2, 199
history and historical sciences 149,
 152, 154–5, 159–60, 180–1, 184,
 187–8, 192–6
Hopkins, B. C. 200
horizon 60–1, 64, 71, 127–9, 132,
 134, 136, 155, 178n. 8, 194
Hume, D. 40, 50, 56n. 7, 57, 144–5
Husserl, E.
 Cartesian Meditations 3, 71, 73,
 127, 145, 147–8, 153, 159, 160n.
 4, **162–79**
 The Crisis of the European Sciences
 3, 50–1, 56, 126n. 8, 128, 141n.
 3, 158, 166, 168–9, 171, **180–96**
 Experience and Judgment 3, 25,
 37n. 3, 100, 123, 126
 Formal and Transcendental Logic
 3, 19, 56n. 7, 81, 138, 147, 169,
 190

The Idea of Phenomenology 40–2, 46, 48–9, 54–5, 68, 146
Ideas I 3, 16–7, 22–38, 49, 53, 57–72, 74–5, 82, 84–95, 96–7, 99, 102–4, 108–12, 120–6, 128–9, 137–8, 142n. 13, 146–7, 160n. 4, 167, 177, 185, 189, 196n. 6
Ideas II 3, 138, 140, **144–61**, 189, 196n. 4
Ideas III 3, 37n. 8, 161n. 12, 196n. 7
'Kant and the idea of transcendental philosophy' 44, 49–54, 91
life 2–4
Logical Investigations 3, 9–21, 34–5, 40–1, 52, 81–3, 85, 87, 93–4, 96–7, 98–109, 111–12, 113–20, 122, 125–6, 145
The Phenomenology of Internal Time-Consciousness 3, **127–41**
transcendental turn 19, 39–42, 50, 52–3, 56n. 1, 57, 145–6, 149

idealism 16–17, 39, 42, 56n. 2, 66, 86, 89–90, 142n. 11, 158, 177
idealization 88, 136, 184–7, 191, 193–4
ideation *see* essence, seeing of
Ingarden, R. 3, 89
intentionality 46–7, 58, 72–3, **79–97**, 98–9, 105, 111, 128–9, 134–7, 147, 151, 165, 169–70, 177, 191
transverse and longitudinal 134–6, 139, 142n. 11, 147
intersubjectivity 154, 160, **162–79**, 191, 194
transcendental 162, 167–70, 177, 191
intuition 29–30, 35–6, 45–6, 51, 91, 95, 96n. 5, **98–111**, 115–17, 128, 133, 135, 152, 172, 190
categorial 106–7, 111, **113–26**, 172, 186
fulfilling 93, 100–6, 109, 111n. 8, 112n. 12, 114–15, 119–20, 133

James, W. 132, 141n. 3, 145
judgement 11, 13–15, 99, 101, 106, 117, 148, 150, 166, 189–90
categorial 114–15, 119, 121, 125, 125n. 1, 190

Kant, I. 14–15, 17, 22, 32, 35, 39, 42–57, 65, 82, 89–92, 94–5, 96n. 5, 100, 109, 115–17, 142n. 11, 145–6, 148–9, 157, 160nn. 1, 5, 178n. 3, 185, 193, 197n. 11
Kern, I. 73n. 3, 199
Kisiel, T. 112n. 13
Klein, T. 161n. 12
knowledge 16, 22–9, 40, 42–4, 47, 54, 90, 95, 96n. 5, 101, 103–4, 114, 116, 148–9, 164–5, 183–4
a priori vs. *a posteriori* 23–5, 32, 43–4
Kockelmans, J. J. 56n. 1, 160n. 2
Kolakowski, L. 199
Koyré, A. 3
Kronecker, L. 2

language 1, 15–16, 33, 106, 111n. 7, 146, 169, 184, 195, 196n. 5
Landgrebe, L. 3
Lask, E. 112n. 13
laws
eidetic vs. empirical 24–7, 31–2, 36, 67, 122, 125n. 5
logical vs. psychological 9–15, 17, 42, 108, 152
moral vs. causal 154–5, 157
of motivation 175
Leibniz, G. W. 73, 116, 169, 178n. 9
Levinas, E. 37, 99, 111n. 4, 172, 179nn. 10, 11, 198, 199
lifeworld 113, 156, 180, 184, 187, 189–95, 197nn. 9, 10
Lipps, T. 10
living present 130, 132, 136–7, 139, 142n. 13, 145
Locke, J. 67, 116, 183, 186
logic 9–19, 24, 27–30, 32–4, 36, 37n. 7, 41–2, 53, 108
logical validity *see* validity
Lotze, H. 10, 14, 20n. 5

McCormick, P. 200
Marbach, E. 199
mathematization of nature 167,
 184–9
mathesis universalis 33, 184
meaning-intention 100–2, 104–6,
 114–15, 119
Melle, U. 161n. 8
memory 101–2, 112n. 8, 122, 132,
 135–6, 142n. 13, 152
Mensch, J. 161n. 6
Merleau-Ponty, M. 71, 75n. 9, 159,
 161nn. 13, 14, 195, 198
Mill, J. S. 10
Mohanty, J. N. 20, 200
monad 73, 144, 159, 169, 178n. 9
Moran, D. 125n. 2

Natorp, P. 11, 20n. 1, 142n. 14, 160n.
 2
natural attitude 22, 58–71, 88, 92,
 151, 155–6, 158, 166, 187, 192
naturalism 9, 17, 27–30, 40, 62–3,
 68, 88, 155–9
neo-Kantianism 11, 14, 90, 142n. 14,
 160n. 2
noesis 84, 86, 94–5, 165, *see also*
 consciousness, acts of
noema 84–9, 94–5, 114, 165, *see also*
 object, intentional

object 9–10, 15–19, 22–6, 28, 31–3,
 45, 55, 79–95, 163–5, 170–2,
 189–90
 categorial 115–22
 ideal vs. real 9–10, 15–18, 28, 121,
 125n. 5
 individual vs. universal 23
 inner vs. outer 67
 intentional 45–7, 79–89, 95, 96n.
 8, 173
 logical 10–11, 15–19, 115–16, 122
 natural vs. spiritual 155–6, 190
 noematic vs. actual 85–9
 phenomenal vs. noumenal 45–6,
 56n. 7
 temporal 129–35, 137–9
 transcendental 90–1, 94

objectivity 40, 43, 45, 47–8, 99, 107,
 117, 162–7, 176–7
ontology 16–17, 24, 28, 30–6, 58, 62,
 67, 70–2, 89–95, 107, 115–18,
 151, 168, 176, 183, 190, 194
 phenomenology and 34–6, 37n. 8,
 70–2, 74n. 5, 168
other, the 162, 164–5, 168, 171–7,
 179n. 10

Parmenides 75n. 13
perception 45, 48, 52, 60–1, 84–7,
 93–5, 97n. 16, 100, 102–6,
 113–20, 127–9, 131–5, 149, 163
person 68, 144, 146, 150–1, 153–60,
 173, 175, 195
personalism 161n. 15
personalistic attitude 154–6, 159
Pfänder, A. 3
Plato 17, 115, 125n. 3
positing 17, 26, 45–6, 51–2, 59–66,
 69, 72, 90–2, 94, 102, 114, 132,
 148, 165
positivism 27–30, 110, 182–3, 197n.
 11
primal impression 132–5, 137,
 140–1, 141n. 4
principle of phenomenology *see*
 evidence, principle of
Protagoras 40
protention and retention 132–7,
 139–41, 147, 149
psyche 10, 55, 67–9, 72, 79, 144,
 150–3, 155, 157–8, 160, 167
psychologism **9–21**, 27, 36, 41, 53,
 63, 99, 117
psychology 9–15, 18–20, 23, 27–8,
 36, 40–2, 55, 67–9, 74n. 8, 79,
 99, 151–5, 192
 descriptive 2, 19–20, 21n. 9, 40–1,
 67
 phenomenology and 36, 37n. 9,
 41–2, 66–72

rationalism 103, 116, 182, 187
reality 16–17, 23, 60–1, 69–70,
 85–95, 97n. 15, 135, 157, 162–6,
 181, 183–90

realism 80–1, 86, 89
recollection *see* memory
reflection 66, 103, 111n. 8, 137–41,
    142n. 13, 150, 158
regressive enquiry 192–3
Reinach, A. 3
relativism 15–17, 99
representationalism 80–2, 87
retention *see* protention and
    retention
Rickert, H. 2, 11
Ricoeur, P. 49, 56n. 4, 5, 71, 74n. 6,
    75n. 11, 85, 89–92, 95, 96–7,
    104, 112n. 10, 151, 161n. 9, 165,
    178n. 4, 179n. 10, 198, 200
Rodemeyer, L. 141n. 6

Sartre, J.-P. 94, 97n. 17, 160n. 3,
    198
scepticism 39–42, 53–5, 62, 64–6,
    144
Scheler, M. 3, 161n. 15, 179n. 10
Schütz, A. 74n. 5, 178n. 2, 179nn.
    10, 11, 198
scientism 157, 181–3, 187–92, 195–6,
    196n. 2
sedimentation 187–8, 192
self *see* ego
Sigwart, C. 10
Sokolowski, R. 200
solipsism 53–4, 72, 158, 162, 164,
    167–8, 170–1
soul *see* psyche
Spinoza, B. 116
Stapleton, T. 71, 75n. 10
Stein, E. 3
Strawson, P. F. 43
Ströker, E. 199
Stumpf, C. 2, 21n. 9, 67
synthetic acts 45, 47, 49, 82, 90–1,
    94, 104, 113, 117–22, 125, 126n.
    11, 134–6, 175

technology 17, 70, 187–8, 190–1
Theunissen, M. 179n. 10
thing 47–8, 71, 87–8, 92–5, 127–9,
    163, 167
thing of use 156, 195

thing-in-itself 45–6, 51, 56n. 3, 89–95
the things themselves 18, 51, 92, 100,
    104, 106, 109–10, 146
time, objective vs. subjective (phe-
    nomenological) 129–30, 135–8
time-consciousness 60, 112n. 8,
    127–42, 145, 147, 149, 160n. 5
transcendental apperception 51,
    146–7
transcendental philosophy 39, 42–5,
    50–1, 54–5, 56nn. 2, 7, 63, 158,
    191
    phenomenology as 20, 36, **44–55**,
    57, 71, 168
transcendental reduction 36, 45,
    49–50, 55, **57–75**, 88–9, 159,
    168, 170–2, 193
transcendentals 42
truth 12, 14–16, 22, 24–9, 98–9,
    104–9, 112n. 12, 113–16, 166–7,
    181–2, 196n. 5

validity 11–18, 20n. 5, 30, 35, 40, 55,
    65, 116, 163, 165–6, 168, 181,
    186, 190, 192

Weber, M. 181
Weierstrass, C. 2
Welton, D. 200
Westphal, M. 178n. 5
Willard, D. 20n. 7
Windelband, W. 11, 17
Wolff, C. 50
world 22–3, 45, 89, 128–30,
    187–91
    annihilation of 69–71, 159
    natural (scientific) 59–63, 82,
    166–8, 181–2, 184–7
    phenomenological (world for
    consciousness) 63, 86, *see also*
    lifeworld
    public vs. private 164–6
    surrounding, social or cultural
    155–7, 159, 190–1
Wundt, W. 10

Zahavi, D. 96n. 9, 139, 141–2, 161n.
    7, 179n. 10, 199, 200